GUPPY

James Kearns

ISBN-13: 9798866050284
ISBN-10: 1477123456

Cover design by: Jamie Hanson
Library of Congress Control Number: 2018675309
Printed in the United States of America

For Jamie Hanson

"The Guppy"

Whales have calves,
Cats have kittens,
Bears have cubs,
Bats have bittens,
Swans have cygnets,
Seals have puppies,
But guppies just have little guppies.

OGDEN NASH

GUPPY

PROLOGUE

When she told me, she made the same face she always made; it was the same face she made when she told me she didn't love me, she just didn't want to know.

I lose track of time, I said, what can I say? Well, lose track of this time, she called back, and threw an apple at my head. Don't worry, I said, it didn't hurt. Becoming serious, she replied: If I'd known the half of it, I'd have run a mile. I looked down at her feet, the stilettoes were as high as they were sharp: You wouldn't have got far in those, I said, straight to her face. The door slammed, and I followed her out of the flat. Loser, she said, loser. There was a strip of green wasteland before you got to the road, and watching her from behind, I wondered whether she'd sink into the earth. No such luck. It was hazy ahead and the streets were foul with detritus. The wind and the passing cars blew up great clouds of metallic silver. There was nothing round, nothing soft in it. But there's stuff to do, I called out to her back. She blanked me. It's breezy, I said, making chat. Blanked, for sure. It was so hot, it felt sinister; black winged ants struck you in the face, landing in your hair, in your mouth. She flicked her hand, swatting at the air. I can hardly breathe, I said. She said nothing, her eyes small against the glare of the sun. Come on, I said, or we'll miss the bus. That line made her laugh. Fair enough, she called back, let's go. The scene changes so quickly, and each one calls for an alternative adjustment. This one comes to the surface; sinking that one to the depths. Who said our lives grow rings, like a tree? Leaves fall, that's what happens. They fall. There are too many faces here, that's the problem, or not enough names. You must do something about your fear, she said, just as soon as you are afraid. Don't bottle it, whatever you do. That was the one single rule, but I didn't say it. Things were different then. This is now. One moment free: the next minute, this. The cubicles to each side of me are long and rectangular constructions, containing a single, occupied bed. Each night they're there, snoring and sighing, breathing or wheezing, screaming out to heaven knows who or, indeed, what. There they all are, perfectly harmless, forgettable. And now I feel it's about to begin. I'm in the middle, I want to say, I'm the partition … no, that's not it. Were we so easily forgotten? I say. Perfectly harmless words, forgettable. There is no time here, but I use the expression. Time, that's me: Murphy, thirty-four years old and now known to no one. Think of that, if you can. Here I sit, or lie, alone or nothing, it's hard to tell. And yet this nothing has something to say. This nothing still thinks. This nothing had a life, once upon a time. There are only days and then more days, and since I hardly recall one day to the next, one day from the next, I can safely say … well, whatever springs to mind. Unfortunately, we must stick to the facts; fortunately, Tuesday follows Monday, then comes Wednesday. As I say, there are no days here, but I am aware of the sequence. I'm no fool. Murphy's the moniker, and here I am, much better than nothing. The world, once and for all, will dispose of me, in time the breath fails, the end begins. But not yet. During those times when time did exist, the pain in my head increased, and the sounds I could hear were the groans issuing from my very own mouth. I could just make out someone calling me: Hey, nothing, it said, nothing. That must be how it goes. Just this once, she said. Or was that me? *Just this once.* These creatures are the ones to each side of me; the other names, in other words. Some such simple thing, a box, a piece of wood, a sink, a spool of thread, an insect entering from a nostril, perhaps another one settling there on an earlobe, waiting for the right time to strike silently at the bark of your brain. Fortunately, they never hang around for long; unfortunately, it is no use being forewarned. All nonsense, it must be, otherwise it would be hopeless. I am alone, that's true, only in the beginning were there the two of us. Then the trouble came. She could've said something, but she didn't. *Nice whores in Brixton*, the copper said, the other one laughed, then yanked my arm up my back. I didn't reply, not a word. Blanked. Alone now, nothing more to hear or say. When did all this happen? I ask.

There's no time here, she replied, for us; we're done. Then stops. There are a great number of faces here, but mine is not among them. Eye to eye, the signs of wear, face to face, the creases and the cracks, the contact. I have no face left to save. And even if the notion of time should dawn on this darkness, who could save me? Don't worry, she said, you won't die for some time yet. Why must I wait? I asked. I am just the messenger, she reminds me: You die the death you die; nothing more. We've … we've … we've, she said, then nothing. What more is there? I asked. When I looked back at her she was about to turn away. They have a fire behind them and see on the wall the shadows of themselves and other objects. One of them escapes, I said. Yes, she said, anything is possible. Those are the sounds I hear, I replied. You lose track of time, she said, what can I say?

CHAPTER ONE
MONDAY

I

Don't they sleep standing up? the good sister asked, shifting to the next point of departure: Well, anyone who's worth their salt reads exactly what they please, she said, changing the subject, again: The sturdy red-haired boy? Septimus, he's called. Really, she said, it's hard to believe. Didn't she like people who were ill? she said, silly mare. Horns and trumpets were ringing out, she said, you wouldn't believe the noise. What do you mean, his slippers? she said, they were just there – by which time we were all well and truly lost.

Skewbald or piebald, that's what she'd said, then Gypsy: Cobs, the exact word. Eyes closed softly, hardly alive, barely breathing, or so it seems. A twitch from one as though I'd struck a match. I sparked up, walking on through the first fits of fag smoke. The wet grass underfoot felt at once soft and hard and looked like pale green glass. The slightest crunch here and there from the thawing dew and the passage from shadow to light. I felt I was doing permanent damage to the land. The kerb works were there; it was true. Go down and look, she'd suggested, you'll soon see, she continued. And horses. Gypsy cobs, she said, or Irish. I walked on, slowly, as though out of bounds or wandering into a place unmarked on a map. It wasn't a ruse, after all; the good sister having a laugh. But, yes, it was all there, it was true. The kerb works, they'd called it. That was the main thing, the truth. The kerb works was the truth. There were trees with holes and grass like glass and fleabitten horses and barking dogs in the distance, but best of all, the kerb works was there. A cottage industry, you might say. Nobody ever said that; nobody ever called it that. Nobody. Murphy would have laughed: I get stuck in, he'd say, what else is there to do? And if you want to smoke, don't mind me. The men always arrived back dusty and dazed, that's how you could tell. I keep an eye on things, he'd say, by way of warning, light pouring down on him from the high window. Every day I live, I find myself agreeing, he said, the lines illuminated on his skin. All of a sudden, a horse will neigh, wide awake. There it is: or snorting. So much for sleeping. Only idiot games, this thinking back. Straining my ears to locate the farm dogs barking at the edge of my hearing, the horses neighing nearby. The universe battling and tumbling. The here and now. Perhaps it is something breaking, some two things colliding. Like my mother's laughter or my father's cough before he spoke. I was little more than a ghost sitting there, rather at sixes and sevens or was it twos and threes? These were the numbers my mother liked to recite. Twos and threes, talking, talking, sixes and sevens, chattering away, unaware of what was mine and what was hers or how to count them. I was soon overcome with the fear that I might lose a second of what she said. That's it, she'd say. Done, and dusted. Small as I was, a perfect form, she'd laugh, pinching my cheek. It was quite an effort to get me down from the chair. I'm flying, I called out. That view of things quickly changed. On firm ground, I took my bearings from the table legs. One in particular. There on the floor curled up by the leg was the yellow and black wasp my mother had just brushed off the table. It moved, I said, reaching out to save it. It's gone, she replied. Even dead, she warned me, it'll sting you, if you're not careful.

My candle was flickering, but that was a trick of the light; there were no candles, and I could not easily make out the expression on her face. Was she smiling or was it a grimace?

The good sister drags on her cigarette, taps the end into an aluminium ashtray, bits flake onto the desk: Within agreed boundaries, she says, continuing from where hardly matters. I watch as she brings the cigarette to her lips. She takes another drag. We have nothing in common, that much is true. I am listening. Her attention shifts to the window, looking out to the day ward, a sudden explosive laughter interrupts her flow. The moment passes, she resumes: We stand in the way of those who do harm, do you see? It was important to emphasise this, apparently. The *priority* of the men, she called it. That's all we can hope to do. She pauses again: We get in the way. These *boundaries*, which she'd mentioned earlier, must be taken with a pinch of salt, a phrase I have since added. I can see she wants to bring her speech back to agreed terms. The able men go out, she says again. I hang onto this important nurse's words for one reason: I am the new auxiliary, and I am showing up. Doing what? I say, a gathering fear of heights comes over me. I feel I might head the ceiling or struggle to get out of the door, if I'm not careful. The office has windows on two of the four walls. A glass cage. Making pre-caste stuff, she says, out of cement. There's a couple of auxiliaries down there, she explains, shortly. That's their job. Looking after the men, I mean. The able ones, she says again. Only men? I ask. She ignores the question. I look for something else. What kind of stuff do they make out of the cement? She seems unwilling to reply, but relents. They fix-up something for a local builders' merchants. Not kerbs, exactly, but smaller stuff. Edging stones. You know, that kind of thing. I didn't know *that kind of thing* at all. Edging, I say. Stones? She does something with her fingers, indicating the size of a small worm: Small kerbs, she says, pausing a second. Her finger gesture is disturbing to say the least, as though she were indicating something else. For garden paths and the like, she continued. You know, that kind of thing. The good sister's voice trails off and the wriggling worm is lost in the moment: You're new, she said, changing tack, making her judgement. You're young, she says. I'm nineteen, I say; she's twenty-seven, apparently. You'll get used to it. We all do, she said. What, being nineteen? I say. She ignores the query. It just takes a bit of time, she says, looking away, calling out, indicating something through the glass. Murphy, she says, are you ready? He laughs, pointing towards his feet for some reason. I hardly know it's me, Murphy says. The familiarity between them is fierce but set fair. Nothing to worry about, she replies, try wriggling your toes.

The door-bell rings, the day is still young.

There's an auxiliary standing there; another one, I mean, it's not me. Clearly there's no shortage of these individuals, for all they say. I notice immediately that he's staring through the toughened glass of the door. He looks like he's saluting me. His hand a karate chop above his eyes, protecting himself from the internal glare. He's as dusty as they are; a young man, as I remember, with a cow's lick tuft in the front like a ginger wave. An escort, and an auxiliary, like me. They say his name is Septimus, but who's called Septimus these days? As they filed in, I thought of the time I baked fairy-cakes with my mother. You're white as a sheet, she'd said, as dusty as a ghost. We weren't to believe in ghosts, I knew that much. Sometimes my mother hid; once she left me on a dark street. She was behind a wall when I screamed. I didn't hear her coming, her steps were silent. The cakes go up, I said. My mother laughed: We all rise, she said, we all stand up. If only the world would quake. I laughed, repeating the word *quake*. I said what she said, it made her laugh, and then she wouldn't leave me out in the dark, while she hid behind walls. The past is unfixed; it is imperfectly fetched. In other words, it would be a lie to say she didn't love us; she did. Light the candles, she said, a little later. Somebody jumped up and lit them, and I blew them out. My father, the one with the matches, the cough came later, joined in. You've some strong lungs on you, son, he said, which I took to mean the light that shone, which tells you everything. I was the son, you see, I was the light. And there was that yellow and black wasp, there on the table with what looked like a very pronounced waist. Like St. Michael's cloak, my mother said, and killed it with a spoon.

Well, that's just the thing, she said, everybody likes
Murphy. There's nobody who doesn't.

That would mean we had our work cut out for us. First, the door would be put back on its hinges. Second, that bit of scuffed linoleum would be cut out and replaced. Third, the sink would be returned to the wall.

Mr. Garnett's men were coming. And then, thought Molloy, what a morning, split between the closeness of a June day and the freshness following rain.

I am Murphy, but what is the point of saying that? Nothing, in the end, was ever agreed by us. I want to tell him, the shrink, but I prefer to keep my peace. I want to tell him – *I am Murphy* – but I am afraid to speak – there might be repercussions, do you see? Out he comes with it. Each and every time. I want to scream: That's not my name, fool; that's not it. I'm Murphy, that's who I am. What's with this Wilson? Who's he? Say nothing's best, I keep my peace. You can hardly forget your own name, now can you? That's the truth of it. That's not to say that there aren't times when I sit and say: *Who are you?* Your head is so full of scraps, boy; it is. That's what she used to say. My mother, see? I was her blessing, that's what she says. A kind of gift. I think about this when I stir, wondering how it was I ended up here. I'd walked over that bit of green, watching, I was, following close behind my girl. That's how it was. There they are, the memories, of course, fishing for me. I want to tell him that up is down, and down up, but where is the sense in that? What *is* up, or indeed *down* in the dead of night? *The inner landscape is in some sense shattered; do you see?* That's the consultant psychiatrist, the shrink, yet again, telling me the facts of the matter, telling me my name. Always telling; yes, that's him. He says so, I heard him: *To tell you the truth*, he says it (again and again), and a big fat lie is not far behind, waiting to pounce. Then this and then that; that voice of his – la-di-da. That's what mother used to say: That woman I clean for, her mouth hardly moves: *la-di -da*, that's what it is, *la-di-da*, she says, laughing, singing it. That shrink does the same: The privilege will be mine, he said, if you have something to add. But, no, I keep my peace. *The symptom is often viewed as an attempt to fill in a gap, the memory, of course, is shot.* The eminent man scans his listeners, explaining the world to them. At all times, he sits in judgement. *It is a type of compensation – that is to say, the reflection of whatever mnestic resources the patient has retained.* I watch him closely as he taps into my so-called resources. What nest-egg, I want to say; who's doing the compensating? But no, I keep the peace. You ought to be ashamed, my mother would've said – all of you. I listen intently, but his lips are still: up they go one by one, all lies, not a fair word in any of it, but the mouth is as stiff as ice. Such alterations are undoubtedly present in such instances. I think that was him again: This is obviously the only thing that can and should be saluted. These very alterations. Was that him? Do you see that? the shrink says – *Wilson's*. And again, he says it: It's *Wilson's … Wilson's*. But that's not me – I'm *Murphy – Murphy*, for God's sake, *Murphy*. We don't count for much; we hardly reach the value of numbers. We make up the *clinical picture*, but whatever the variety or regions or fragments of what it is, Wilson's not my name. These *features of the true affective state* is just someone sitting there, smiling across at him, like nothing. That's me. Nothing. At the shame, yes, we feel it. Shame, at least, has a name. You see some flicker of doubt. I mean, you listen: Sometimes you hear; sometimes you're deaf to it; gone is the day; gone is the night, make of it what you will. Simple as that. Let me tell you what it was that happened, let me tell you exactly what it was that went down on that hot and dusty summer's day. I mean, you'll listen: now begins to rise in me the words that have lain dormant, until now, that is.

It was a hot and dusty day, that's for sure and she's walking beside me in a high stiletto: vexed, very vexed.

We were just waiting for the bus; a request, it was, not a compulsory stop. I would have to stick out my hand, wave it down, something to remember to do. That was the start of it: walking or stopping, request or compulsory, thinking about my arm and when to raise it. People milling all over the place. One of those things. This woman was carrying on, might have been a passer-by, maybe a punter come out the pub across the street, said something to someone: *Drop dead*, I think she said, but this time not to me. I looked after them, but I let it go. Nobody knew who she was, or who I was, for that matter. How is it the people don't notice *you*? my girl says. I seemed to exist for no one, but her. The butcher man was raging. Came out of the blue, dried blood on his apron, that's what it looked like. But that's to come. Voices, I remember them well, but it was me saying it. Stop up these noises … These *voices*. I would have done anything for peace. What happened, came out of the blue, but it was not the first time it'd happened, let's just say that. I stacked in a factory then. *Replenishment*, that's what they called it. I loved that word: replenishment. It was a big word for a small job, but working at stacking was better than no working at all; you worked in those days, that is all there was; nothing else for it. Mother had need of money in the house too. I had scared him off, my father, that is; raising his hand to her face. One last time, slap, slap, slap. And me, a kid, stopping him in his tracks. Don't you forget this: I boxed with the Mackenzies, I know how to look after myself. Then what? He runs off with some bird, once and for all. That's what she says: Now look what you gone and done, son. You've done chased him back to that *bird*. That's sounding funny to my ears right now. It was no laughing matter then; no, lord, not at all. Then there was the darkness. That's what she says it is, *darkness*; wasn't the same as ours. Mother's was deep and deeper still. Darkness, son, that's what it is. Anyways, there was one thing worse than a job: no jobbing at all. True to tell, I might well be blinking through the cold dawn light of early morning, over and over and again, spending the day raising dust up into my eyes and ears, tickling then on my skin like creepy crawlies, but what was it they say: Work is worship; whatever, it was better than nothing at all. That's it. Well, that's what my mother says: With nothing to show? Nothing comes from nothing, you hear that? She pauses: Or you going to work like a man? It must not be forgotten, sometimes you forget, that it is all a matter of voices, listen, son, hear what they say: *Work is worship.* Did you hear that, son? And then she's off laughing again.

That light in the glass frightening me. You looking at me? It was *me.*

Yes, it was still there. Me, looking out, looking back. That brings me here, to them – request or compulsory – that's all it was. If only I could speak and yet say nothing. What can I say? But really, nothing? I say what I am told to say; I hear what I hear. That woman screaming and carrying on, You're evil, she says, look what you've gone and done. Evil ..., she says to me, you've ruined everything. Or to anyone else who will listen, calling me the devil. All we had to do was stick out our hand. The bus passed, that was the start of it. That was it, do you see? Safe to say, we missed the bus. Then me, suddenly, that reflection in the glass, until I kick it out. *Who you looking at*? That butcher man running out with a knife, something sharp in his hand. Shards of glass all over the place and me bleeding. He comes out after me. Police soon come; they take me away. What about *her* and *her* screaming? *Fucking nice whores in Brixton*, the policeman shouts back, just leave *her* out. That bit gets me. The thing looking back at me. That was me. The other policeman laughing, twisting my arm up my back. Who is she? they're calling out, passing words from one to another. My girlfriend, I shout back, who the hell d'ya think she is? That was the end of that, you could say. No bus, no bird, that was all it was. Criminal damage, a danger to the public, and all of this; all this talking which spews me out or swallows me up. I've heard it all before. Replenish became remand, banged up, in a way nobody can deny. I don't even want to think about it, do you get me? Yes, yes, I still have the taste in my mouth, of all of them, lording me, creeping across my skin, all of them. Each and every one. It must not be forgotten that being covered in dust and paper cuts from cardboard and the lines and piles of things you pull and yank was better than being here. *Replenishment.* Do you get me? Nothing's worse than being here. That's how the silence is, that's what it sounds like when the morning breaks and the horses neigh. All glass and shards. And the voices? Now all was silent. Alone now, nothing more to hear or say. When was this? I asked. Nothing sounds now but my own voice. There's no time here. *She's no whore*, I say, whispering into the darkness of the Black Maria: *She was my one and only brown eyed girl.*

II

"There is such a world," she says, "somewhere," the stillborn words are aimless. The voice is but a whisper, her breath, gathering at her breast, will sound the words just enough to be heard: "Yes, and there," she says, "it is immune to change."

Touch wood; touch earth, she makes it. In that corner of the world, it was raised on to the east wall where it was said to have taken indelibly the imprint of some three hundred years of customary behaviour. "So they laughed?" she says, "but hardly respected." There are no days here, she thinks, that's what it feels like, only time will tell. "Time," she says, "I am the foam," she says, her voice is getting louder, "sweeping, filling, all to the utmost rims of rocks, with whiteness and darkness … ." Her time will come, but first, the voices of the jovial men she cannot yet see or, for that matter, hear: "… besieged by spiritual temptations – *Turbulence*," he added with a certain visible eagerness of desire to be explicit. "Idle talk, nothing more," interrupted the younger man, cautioning his brother to lower his voice. They talk of a woman from the point of absolute knowing. They care not for such things as "from time to time" because that would dictate some sort of alteration to the proceedings. "The only solution is to burn it," the king reasons, "end these weird transmissions, once and for all." The young duke is unconvinced: "The queen's not mad, brother. Hold true to that." The king, however, is not a man weakly to accept defeat: "One can't indict the entire court for common jangling, brother." Transforming talk, indeed, or grotesque gossip? Call it what you will, the queen stands as the central pillar in all of this. "The burning of this tapestry," here the younger man points to the east wall, "will hardly do the trick." The king vehemently disagrees: "A diversion, brother; nothing more will be required. All eyes will then fall to other places." The young duke feels the queen is about to be mortified. The queen, in fact, is about to be unbending. Let us try and see where these considerations lead.

Here she is: "Consume me," she cries out, "am I not yet ready?" Headlong, she rushes into her chamber, smiling at the reflection she sees in a looking glass there on the wall. The expression seems rehearsed, the delivery, however, will be free, frank and, without doubt, fresh. "Burn it? *Burn it*? Are my ears deceiving me? Is that your decree, husband?" she said, making her inquiry distinct, "or your *will*?" She then casts her eyes sideways for her brother-in-law. "And you," she calls across to him, "you mean to do this behind my back? Is that it? Quaint," she said. "How quaint you *both* are." Neither man responds at once to the queen's encouragements, if that is what they are. The queen relishes the intervening silence: "There," she said, "then it's settled." The king turns his back on the tapestry, imagining he might eclipse it in some way. "It remains," he says, looking at the queen as directly as he could in a curious bout of shyness, "damnable though it is," he adds, equilibrium returning. The queen's implacable serenity – and formidable intellect – wielded as a weapon against the weakness of men, caused her to be regarded as the ultimate decision maker at court. The truth of such things is always little more complicated. She knows that he wants her to put her trust in him, but she won't. He knows that she wants him to make her a promise, but he can't.

The queen's chamber feels suddenly empty. A lady-in-waiting draws near, filling the gap. "O, there you are," says the queen. There was little face to salvage, that much she can see. The two men have steered fast to the liberating light at the door with but the simplest of bows in place of blows.

"The gentleness of the king was persuaded," the queen whispers to her lady-in-waiting, fanning her face, hiding her tears. "We are not gentle; and we are not persuaded by whims nor by the king's dreaming. Say nothing," she says, "nothing, do you hear? We must keep the tapestry safe."

"This grey, at once murky, then resolutely opaque, is luminous nonetheless," she explains. "One need only look" Just that morning, the queen had confessed to hearing echoes from the very same source.

"Look, just there, how perpetual it is." The king glances at the tapestry hanging on her eastern wall, but says nothing, waiting, instead, for his wife to proceed. "There is always some shadow there, do you follow me? But," she said, the slightest of pauses, "I am somehow able to see through the darkness. The murk is me." The king reaches out his hand. "Don't touch it," the queen calls out, alarmed: "it must *not* be touched." The queen raises her hand to the king's cheek by way of recompense – a part of her wishes to strike it. The weak early morning light provides the queen with a far from carnate complexion; watery, ghost-white and fragile, its present mark. "I've been so long finding it, do you see? Its depth." The king looks pensive. "My prime discovery so far," she continues. "Each part comes to daylight at the precise moment." The king is as silent as a grave. Not a little exasperated, the queen changes tack: "Is it justice you seek, my dear? For me, each day is dangerous, you do see that, don't you?" Patience is beginning to ebb away, for a moment she answered to nothing, and then she broke out: "You can see the repairs there, can't you? Look," she said, "to the wall. That much is surely visible to your eyes. Yes? Material things are so vulnerable to the humiliations of decay. Isn't that so?" The king takes a very keen interest in his wife's welfare, but he is quite unable to put his arms in imagination around her waist, to persuade her to hold true to him, and only to him. "Dearest," the king hardly knows how to begin: "You must put aside these childish visions. For pity's sake. Desist, I say." He feels as though he is struggling against all-conquering reason. "But can you trust me, at least?" he asks. The queen takes a deep inhalation of air: "How innocent he looks," she said, suddenly, diverting her husband's attention back to the tapestry. "Our own true child to come." She did not move. "I can see him," she said, "a son. Just there," she lifts her hand, pointing at some section of the tapestry: "Our own child." There is shuffling and distant voices without but she behaves as if nothing else is more real than this present danger. "Intolerable," he cries out, the king's voice rising, he begins to shake: "These dark arts must remain undisclosed. Intolerable, I say." The queen's interest remains fixed upon the images projected from the early morning light of a rising sun. The queen begins again, speaking her words free from her husband's interventions. "Nothing?" she said: "nothing will come from nothing. You do see that, husband?" Just before the door slams, he cries out, as though despairing: "You wallow without restraint in these obscene delights." She refuses to stir in the slightest. "They are like little animals, believe me, my darling husband. They sense the danger. Its instinct." When she looks to her side, she sees only empty space where once the king was standing: "My darling,' she whispers, "suddenly, I am lost. Yes, I will say it, of me alone in death." As she looks now deeper into the pastoral scene of the tapestry, we may catch a glimpse of what she presently sees.

Primrose and Convolvulus, poppy and furze, and
pears and apples, figs and gooseberries. "O, my,"
she says, "the colours. The colours. Look!"

She cries impatiently, but nobody else is present to see the purple-pinks of corncockles, silver-whites of angel wings, ablaze-yellows of fox-and-cubs, and the thorny-greens of Barberry. Amidst the countless atoms of soft blues and greys assembling, she sought to discern the dwellings of her most favoured creatures, great and small. "Just look, there," she whispers to her favourite butterflies, fluttering about the wall before her: Menelaus, Peacock, Hairstreaks, Swallowtail, and then the magnificent Clearwing moth appears, the colours of which were ineffable, fleeting, and still. "O, and look there," she chides the territorial snails as they slither along in the dark of night with spiral shells, sounding in brightest yellows and candy cane. "And here," she says, the red squirrels conceal their woodcraft, three blind mice turn and turn, and grey rabbits are bounding along, safe, and at home; and there, a brown hare, a pair of them, rake-fit, boxing and tumbling, and striking against the spring-tide downland. "O, who is this?" the queen whispers again into the silence of her own chamber. Afraid to step back, or to turn and run, she says:

> *"Whether there is substance and truth in it, I do*
> *not know; I saw but was not seen."*

The king's unkind words return to haunt him, not now, but soon enough they come: "Desist" and "Intolerable," and, last of all (and worst of all), "Dark arts!" Memories such as these will, in time, assail him, brimming up as slights, aggravating the moments of his utter desolation. He remembers her last words, *"Mother,"* holding the new blood-red babe in her arms, *"Mother,"* eyes fixed on the tapestry floating on the wall before her, *"Mother."* All grows black, or all glows bright, or all remains grey. Each one ends with *Mother.* "Childbed," Mistress Bridges was heard to say. The tears of all the gathering servants went on falling for days and weeks and months, stretching out until, quite suddenly, they ceased. "So young," she said, "and what's to become of the child?" The now redundant lady-in-waiting enters the kitchens: "The head gardener's wife's been called," she says, with strident efficiency, her lips curling in a smirk. The human voice at times has a disarming quality. "She has her own babe to nurse," Mistress Bridges calls back by way of return, making it appear to be for those immediately assembled. Heads remain bowed, but curious. These are not the usual exchanges. The lady-in-waiting retains her aristocratic airs; no, not airs, her being so. Mistress Bridges could usually be relied upon to utter amiable remarks. Today, the human voice circles the kitchen, indulging the speaker who no longer waits. "Well, now she's got two to nurse," reaching for the translucent pearl dangling from an earlobe: "One for each side, you might say, Mistress Bridges," the lady-in-waiting replies, saucily, walking on to the stone steps, then pausing for just a moment. "The king's brother," Mistress Bridges calls out, then winks, "has taken a liking to the lively lady-in-waiting. How could the good duke resist?" Almost out of sight, the lady-in-waiting trips on the first step before her, righting herself in time to save the fall. The words were like the first peal of a chime of bells.

We ourselves may never see the interlacing of that turquoise line with the stream of white water, hastening quicker to their ends: fresh water, salt water, with fast speed they meet, but there are rocks between them; they sever.

We may never know that there stands in each corner of the tapestry a single large vase and from these vessels grow garlands of branched leaves and fruits and flowers. Each of the four vases are filled with lavish and extravagant flora, nodding in great bunches. There were gatherings of bays and oak leaves, sheaves of peach-toned lilies and bulbous heads of Agapanthus blues and cream whites. Displayed too were the torched spikes of Acanthus, golden Coreopsis and gourds: bottle, bitter and snake. Here were the beige-yellow hazelnuts, black mulberries and wheat ears, and to the other side were beans of various kind: purple lima, red pinto, and neckargold, and, just there, the silver birch struck out among the rigid lines of pine tufts and the pyramids of spruce. By night the ancient material remained just as breath-taking. Even more so than by day. Indeed, so finely arrayed, so brightly fit was it, that if you were to draw it – and who on earth can draw in darkness? – you would need quite the palate of colours for your task. When he is silent, he thinks, his eyes intent on one spot.

Brew's up, I say, having never used that term before –
or since. (Do you know how to make tea, kid? the good
sister had asked: Wonders, she said, never cease.) I am
walking across to his bed in the large dorm-room.

Get to know them, she'd advised, if you can, she continued, but
with less confidence: Say no more, she said, tapping the side of
her nose. He is lying there, reading a book, mumbling the words
as his eyes scan the page. Murphy looks up, eyeing me, smiles
an easy smile. He doesn't recognise me, not at once. *I am content*
with weaknesses, he says, or something close. *My power is made*
perfect, he whispers, the bit I catch. Opportunity, I call out, but
he is back at his book, knocks. Thought-patterns percolate or
permeate: Weakness, he says, the ghost of any notion. There's no
need for unpleasantness, of course. Not at my age, his lips are
moving, he's murmuring: Not at any age. *How silly*, she says it,
and I know what she means. I cannot quite make out the words.
Call it weakness, he says again, his mind repeating the phrase,
weakness ... Grace is sufficient ... Grace ...

You'll forget me, she says to me ...

Drop upon drop ...

In time, yes you will ...

I saw it ... I saw it ... I cannot name it ...

Drop upon drop ...

I kept them in your name,

none of them ... is lost ... she replies ...

Drop upon drop ...

What a lot of needles there are, she says ...

Drip, drip ...

lying around everywhere ...

Drip ...

How easily they fall out, I reply ...

Dropped ...

He is enigmatic, or confused: That is all it is, he says, directing his words to me. Do you get me? he asked, pronouncing his question, stressing the four-fold word-for-word.

Do

You

Get

Me?

Yes, I do, I reply. (They'll get used to you, she said in her best bedside manner: Don't worry, she says, things'll work out, kid.) My better half, he says, do you get me? Connections hook fast in this place, he stops, I did my best. He stops. I wait a moment: We know that, I say, after a time (knowing no such thing), then casting my eyes around the little cubicle which separated him from the unnameables to either side, vacant at this hour, as if that's all that counts. On the bedside cabinet sits a St. James Bible. Leather bound, black; it was the one thing that remained. *By the great force of my disease is my garment changed*, he hums, lips shivering, *and I am become like dust and ashes*. He reads passages each day, lost in time, murmuring words which were only just about audible. *He grips me by the collar of my coat.* As I walked away, he calls after me, sitting up on the pillows on his bed, the tea shook. Eh, your moosh is looking good and red today, he said. Hot and pink. You've been out in the sunshine? I keep walking, and he called again: Hey you, out there ... Do you remember when you were small? You remember some of them olden days? I turn, and look towards him: Poured days? I call out, suddenly. *Poured out upon me*, he calls back.

Noises travel, coming back to our hearing, traversing walls, but may the same be said of appearing?

What part should I recall for Murphy today, which bits of the boy shall I combine with so many misgivings? One word is enough to lift those wide worlds. What about the time I was dunked in the sea at Bognor Regis and thought it would be as warm as a bath? The water touched the sky way above my head in a horizontal line. I saw another boy with a belt fastened by a silver snake. He was still, then shivered under the yellow sun, as his mum pushed one of his arms into a sleeve. A girl dropped the scoop out of its cone and cried as though her world would end right there and then. The sand wrapped her ice-cream in golden hundreds and thousands. I told you to hold it straight, her mother cried out, now, look what you've gone and done. I saw a man and a woman deep in conversation, passing with pitchers of lemonade. A school party, my mother said. Must be local kids. They're the teachers, so, she explained, out for the day. They're having an *affair*, she continued. The sand was as hot as it was bright. Affair? I said. Up close there was as much black as there was white amongst the tiny stones. My eyes are a microscope, searching minute worlds. Can I have a snake-belt, mum? I ask. Of course, you can, she said, this day is for you, she said. *Irish*? A woman with a younger one called across at us: *Irish*? she repeated, her voice rising. My mother smiled, and looked back to me. The sun felt soft upon my skin as the older woman grabbed up her things and moved away with the younger one. *They're having an affair, mummy*, I called out, and recall her roar of laughter. Now I spread my body on this frail towel which was damp from drying me. No-one told me that the silver sea ran all the way up to the blue summer sky. I am under the sea, I said, to my mother, and she said: It's like a looking-glass. That's what the sea looks like to me. Can you see yourself? she asked, but by then I'd lost the thread. She'd taken her glasses off; she wipes away a tear from her eye. In the sea, I say. In the sea, she recites by way of return. Yes, I remember when I was a boy. I remember the blue. I look back towards the cubicles. To Murphy. I do, I say, I remember … when I was a boy. Murphy lifts his hand and brandishes a thumb. That's good, he says, you keep on remembering them days. I think that's the end, but it isn't: Because soon enough, you forget. He waited, with me just standing there, looking back at him. And then he spoke again: *I have dreamed, I have dreamed, I have dreamed*, he said. Can you guess who it is? I have no idea: Who is it? I ask. He looks down as though to read the name: Jeremiah says it, he said: *My people to forget my name by their dreams*. Then, nothing; he takes his tea to his lips and drinks. The cup totally vanishes in his hand. He sips the tea, and, well, nothing spills. I walk away and then I hear his voice, calling out the line as though to the world: That's who it was, he says. *My people to forget my name by their dreams*. Jeremiah? I call back. You got it, his echo returns, Jeremiah. Silence, a bang reported behind a door: Hey, boy – why is your moosh so red today. You are a beginner in the circumstances of your own life. *Why*? I want to ask, but make do with this: I'm an absolute beginner, Murphy. *Why*? A good question, but there is no why.

The hard shimmer of the sun threw shadows onto the finest speck of dust and was now durable only as thought. The horses must be awake by now.

I see the dense black eye of the horse, fleetingly, wet and round and deep. Sleeping Cobs. Skewbald or Piebald, Gypsy or Irish. The sun is risen and I am pale. The grass is soft and saturated, fully green. The early summer frost is burning away. Who was it who said that without one's imagination life becomes unendurable, superstitious, and petty? Do Cobs dream? Only good can come of such an action. Was there a moment of imagining? Theirs. The harsh early summer made the world into a glitter ball, spinning, disorientating, and without a single sound. On the way back to the ward, I felt as though I were trudging along on the shiny surface of the moon, one short step at a time. Absolute beginner, I call back. That's the *Why*? of it, but what would it then *be*, would it even *be*? Voices are trailing away: Do you get me? he calls to me again, and laughed. Still smiling, he says something else or perhaps he's reading. A clock somewhere slices time into ticks and tocks and whatever lies between each of these tees, watching too my peas and queues. His voice is but a whisper: Are they not peaceful? Murmuring again, his ominous sounds, deep and resonant, shifting out of external things ... Never again, not now my name is lost, never again. I can see you, but I am beginning to misremember how it felt when you looked up at me that day. *There's nothing there*, she'd said to me. *There's no one there, don't you see?*

But wasn't *I* there; was it just me?

Alone, but hardly alive?

You must go on, she says.

Must you? I reply.

You must, she says, go on.

And now they have left me in peace for a while, will I look out at the trees? I am forgotten, but I can't, I mustn't, forget how it was, how *he shall be*, even now, *like a tree planted*. Or who, she said, it was. He is me, I say. When she looked up at me. Those eyes; *her* eyes. So sweet ... I wept before her; I could not help it. Leaving Murphy to his recitation, I walk on by. That's what it sounds like. The saint, he murmurs, watches over the sleeping city, he says, and wept. You must go on, an echo: I get you; I say it, repeating his line, walking back into the day ward. His voice trails off, reading words from the book he takes back up into his hands. Do you get me? How to look through to the other side. As though I'd drawn open the window to let the summer breeze break the immediate silence. It sounds from the stillness. There's no curtain to puff out as the invisible wind exhales. Rain or fine, is it? We always have something to say about weather. Well, changeable; if only the weather would make up its mind. I respond: Fine, but the morning was crisp. Indeed, I go on, if not in my character, then in my outlook on the world. There is no-one there but me, but the words are jostling for space. And at all events in my life, I say, and at the moment. I stop, take the next step, feeling the freshness as I walk out into the lighted room of the day ward. And yet this large white room is made suddenly spartan as the sun rises somewhere and forms yellow shapes and bars upon the walls. The ward feels warm, close, in fact. Shadows appear, just as quickly fade, passing away, forever. Now it was time to move. I am not paid to stand around, looking at shifting patterns on walls. I am finding it a little difficult, because it is all too new. The shape of things. Keeping my composure. The geometry of stuff is always a possibility. Are the shadows entirely silent? Do they make a sound when they move? The circumstances of such things hardly jarred the eyes, or ears, not to mention the other things I touch. Nothing could be further from the truth, the shrink explains: *The Wilson's*, he raises his voice: *Wilson's disease? Not simply a matter of psychic episodes. The Wilson's? Far more than that.* Instead, they make everything seem as ever it was. Same as it ever was. We heard tell of these observations, repeating them *ad infinitum*, regaining the territory of lost lives. The professional opinions, the pedagogic intensity. My curiosity was not yet satisfied. All at once it comes to an end. We could speak out without so much as a hint of sentimental feeling. Letting the days go by, as we do. Scraps of song ring out from the kitchen radio, the faded leaves torn and stuck together, the scent of verbena, the same shadow shows itself, the derelict railway tracks flung beneath the green fields, the skewbald Cobs, the odd piebald too, the size of a house, each one, standing alone, asleep; the crunching of early morning, early summer, frost melting there on the ground, saturating the world. We could assert the patience we need and the infinite care required. We could do this because we are enamoured by such things. A position to return to, permanently. So much for that. A new life, I say, full of meaning.

And you may find yourself in another part of the world.

He has been vaguely spoken of. One being someone near and not far off; not nothing. But for whatever reason, no one sees him. For a while, he is himself: Murphy. For a moment, he rests in peace. A woman stares at nothing or so it seems. Sister? I say, sister? I call out. (I was looking at the green light, she said, coming in through the windows: *The leaf shall not wither.*) There's a long interval. We wonder at the words and the occasion. The searching of faces. Green light? I want to say. We seek for further light on what these thoughts reveal: a flush of shame, a sweeping realisation of, well, not so very much. A long look into these large rooms, a day ward in white light, a shadowed dorm, and we may retain something of their human aspect. The sun turns, it takes a shift to do this. But it is not yet noon. The day is still young. Murphy's mind fills with crowding images; he watches the people passing. He calls to them, trying out jokes. Well, what happened that morning is about to be reclaimed. *And he shall be like a tree planted*, he whispers, softly.

IV

*"Can you hear that?" the little prince whispers to his nurse.
"Hear what, young Master?" Nurse Tink replies.*

"The leaves," he replies, "in the trees … and the birds are singing. Can't you hear?" She laughs: "Not a sound, Master; warp can't speak," she says. "Now come away, out of there." The young prince begins to feel a familiar attraction to this tapestry; to hold close and fast to the meaning it inspired in his mother. In her own love for it. This hanging, discoloured thing, stands-in for the sadness, the emptiness the young prince could not at once explain and yet, at the same time, it counts for nothing, but the power of eternity. He mourns for a woman who held him in her arms for but a matter of moments, streaking his pink skin with tears the colour of blood. He hasn't the words for it: invisible grief, perhaps. "Well," he says again, "you hear nothing?" His nurse looks concerned, fearful of her place: "Young Master, heaven forfend." The prince becomes impatient. "Nothing, nurse," he said, "nothing at all?" She turns from the fabric on the east wall, looking fondly upon the prince: "Really," she said, imploring him to come away: "you spend too much time with that dusty thing. The queen would not have approved." He turns his attention, sharply, in her direction: "My mother is dead," the young prince replied, rapidly, coldly, "she is no longer there." The young prince is drawn to the abandoned room, the queen's chamber. He hears it calling him, encouraging his presence, transmitting its meaning, and demanding his absolute attention. He listens at the door. One day, he stops still, hearing a man's voice, hailing from within: his father? "Tell me." He hears the voice again: "What is it you want?" Tattered and so old and so perfectly opaque and grey. "Anything, I'll do anything. Tell me again. Speak." The voice is certainly familiar and of his kin. "Father?" The young prince is perfectly sure he hears his father's voice, as he stands, as still as a statue, outside. "Father, is that you?" He looks in through a crack in the heavy oak door. He sees his mother's postered bed, a miniature from a doll's house nearby, it looks so small in the distant shadow, a replica of the Green Palace. The bed is presently covered in pure white cambric, blackened at the borders as day passes into night, life into death. "Father?" He calls out, his heart thumping. "It is me, dearest nephew, your uncle. Come in," the other responds. The young prince enters the queen's chamber. There is some scrutiny here: his uncle passes his hand across the material. The young prince winces, don't touch it, crosses his mind, don't, you fool. "Can you decipher it?" his uncle asks, neglecting to take his eyes from the east wall of the abandoned queen's chamber. "No, sir," he replies. "Decipher?" His uncle appears rapt by the tapestry's depictions. "It whispers so," his uncle steps in closer as though listening, "whispers so. One hears something, sees something in the light that enfolds these familiar, intimate things." The young prince feels awkward; this man should not talk of his tapestry in this way. "Whispers so, uncle: How so?" The duke smiles, his eyes crinkle a little: "Things are there ... hidden; sounding ... but silent. O, it's nothing. Your mother, you see. But it's so," he stops speaking, steps back: "Opaque." The boy would like to spit into his uncle's face or, better still, gouge out his eyes: "O Mother," he says, watching as his uncle departed the room, "dearest one, the only one who dealt with all that silence. Do not be afraid – it's only me."

> *Out in the Green Palace's parkland and terraces that*
> *once surrounded the great house, the young prince*
> *found little to enjoy. So often bored, despondent.*

In fact, he was often bored beyond belief. "Is there really nothing to do?" he would whine, "I'm so terribly bored." It was true that he was yet to venture out and beyond the confines of his relatively safe world. As far as he could tell, the gardeners were more than keen to kill anything which might do damage to their work. The slugs were salted, the toads tossed away, the rabbits horribly trapped. It was even rumoured that one of the younger gardeners had put a tube-like implement into a toad's back-passage and blew the creature up. "What kind of person would do a thing like that?" the little prince murmured under his breath. If true, that seemed a harsh sentence – particularly for the toad. But the little prince had not yet had the opportunity to witness such things, and, in many ways, but not all, he was glad; it seemed cruel, yet somehow intriguing. "It was a glass tube," Mistress Bridges said, angry that the young gardener had taken her tool for medicinal tinctures. "Tinctures, be damned," the young gardener called out, "it was a toddy dipper. For your whisky, Mistress Bridges." The older woman is not best pleased with this young gardener's boldness. "I'll be having words with the head gardener about this," she remonstrated. "About what?" the young gardener calls back, "the whisky or the toddy dipper?" Those gathered in the kitchens are now laughing. "Get off with you," she shouts, waving her arms at the young gardener, trying not to laugh herself. "He's my father," the young gardener, retreating, calls out, "the head gardener, as well you know." A man of some standing with the king. "That won't stop me," Mistress Bridges shouts back, fully laughing now. "Little imp." When the youngster's gone, Mistress Bridges turns back from her chores: "Best house on the estate," she says, "a favourite, indeed, is the king's head gardener." In any case, the young prince hardly believed the half of what he overheard: hoisting toads was the least of his problems. While mulling on his boredom in the gardens, "I'm so terribly bored" comes to mind on numerous occasions, he begins to feel a lightness of emotion, but why, you might ask. The young fellow who'd just come out from the kitchens, for one – the head gardener's son. "Have I seen him before?" The sun is in his eyes, but here is something which pricked the young prince's interest. "What is that?" the young prince called out: "All that wriggling about in the sack." The young gardener looks abashed. "It's a rabbit... ." The head gardener is passing. "Halt, you," the young prince calls out the older man, stopping him in his tracks. "Make him promise," he says, "that he will show me that rabbit in the sack." Uncle Penwith, hearing the commotion, walks towards his nephew: "What's all this?" Ignoring the question, the young prince wishes to add authority to the head gardener's promise. "You promise too, uncle," his nephew's voice is pleading: "Promise. Do." Finding the young prince tedious, Penwith, walking on, called back that he would make sure the head gardener kept his word. The duke stops, looks back: "That young gardener … who is he?" The head gardener is immediately fearful: "My son, you mean, my lord?" The duke smiles: "Indeed, your son; will he come with the creature?" he asked with a reassuring voice; imploring, but strict. The head gardener assented and Penwith was made to promise again. He duly did this: "Yes, dear nephew, I promise. You'll see the rabbit soon enough." There is *at last* a meeting of minds: "I promise too," the head gardener's son calls out, looking directly across at the prince, bowing deeply, a little mockingly perhaps. The young prince and the duke looked somewhat bemused, neglecting, of course, to provide the head gardener's son with a response. It was as if they were perfectly oblivious from whence had come that distant voice. "Never speak out of turn," the head gardener disciplines his son, following their departure. "Do you hear? Never. Our lives are secure here, let it remain so."

And now this noise again. Isn't this all becoming rather obscure? Torn out of its body, the carapace stood for nothing.

"Come, young Master; it's waiting for you." The young prince responded immediately to the alert, dashing off to the kitchens, hot and out of breath. How excited he was. Bursting with energy too. All this waiting must count for something, surely. Through the hum of voices, his own would sound distressed: "No, no, no, that's not the thing at all" – the creature had been stripped of its lovely soft fur and was tied up by its feet, all naked and pink. "That's not it," the young prince murmured. "That's not what I meant at all." The head gardener's son looked on. There seemed to be tears in his eyes. The rabbit had been removed from his hands and swiftly killed and skinned. "Damn you," the young prince shouts out to the head gardener's son. "Damn your eyes." His uncle, clearly enjoying the spectacle, came the rescue of the head gardener's son: "Come now, what way is that to speak to servants." His eyes were crinkled with hideous enjoyment. "He has hardly more rank than the hanging rabbit. Be kinder, nephew. Be kinder still." That was quite untrue: the head gardener was a trusted adviser to the king, everybody knew this. "The man's a marvel," the king would often say, "a true and natural philosopher. What would I do without him, I cannot say." The head gardener's son was not a labouring individual, but an apprentice to his own father. The family lived in one of the best houses on the estate, tied the house may have been, but the king's promise provided it for one life, and the next one. The young apprentice knew not then that one day he would ascend to the palace itself. Who could know this? "Now I measure, I preserve," replies the young prince, knowing nothing of what will be. "I am fenced in, planted here like one of my father's own trees." Uncle Penwith was as straight as a joust and quite as tall, handsome too, with his aquiline nose, those full lips, and that easy smile of his. The eyes were perhaps a little on the small side, but they had a glint as though they were made of glass and quite as reflective. He was the king's younger, and only, brother. A young-enough man; indeed, even when he was not. Penwith seemed always to keep his youth as if, somehow, and in some way, he was kept in aspic. The servants – out of his hearing, of course – would call him "Ever-Youthful." Behind the doffing and bowing, the scraping, the doing whatever it took to avoid the duke's legendary wrath, there lay the arms of insurrection. "Ah, dear nephew," Penwith said: "The dear creature's all skinned and ready for the pot" – not that the servants ever enjoyed such elite meats, of course – with the exception of one – "Mistress Bridges adores it, so I am told," he said, spitefully, his eyes looking about the kitchen for his target. Mistress Bridges, the head cook, seemed to shrink, and the serving girls, as silent as the grave, unused to the presence of such illustrious visitors, appeared terrified. When the young prince looked again, regretting the earlier misdirected outburst, the head gardener's son was conspicuous by his absence. The prince did not mean *his* eyes. Had he been dismissed? "Damn you," the prince wanted to say to his uncle, "damn *your* eyes," and this time he meant it. "Your eyes will fool you," crosses his mind, "your eyes," he says the words, whispering them, conjuring them from the tapestry which responds, weaving, shifting, swirling, sensing time in the warp and nature in the ultimate end of all things. The young prince said instead: "That's not it, uncle, that's not it at all." The young prince's voice rises to the singular word: "Uncle?" For a moment, there is some embarrassment. His uncle's eyes are as fixed as glass, disorienting his view of the hanging rabbit. "Uncle?" he said again. "That's not it. At all." The duke recovers, quickly, continuing where he left off: "Look, nephew," he begins, casting his gaze across the creature, the sightless black eyes, the coldness of the meat, the concealed bones. "Look, nephew," he continues again, "I kept my promise, did I not? Come on, young fellow. Can't you see the funny side?" The young prince made no reply, becoming bashful, hating his uncle with all his might. Hating him, hating him. Mind you, his uncle was quite in the habit of hating the young prince back: "One day," thought Penwith, "this young Nancy may end in the way of rabbits and hares, hooked and hanging!" The duke looked again upon the dead animal. He was smiling, his teeth bright and white, his eyes creasing with crystal mirth. He could so easily picture the young prince swinging on the hook, skinned-pink and dead. "That's not it. At all." Patience is losing ground: "Perchance, one day," Penwith continued, "the young gardener might trap another rabbit for us to play with. Won't that be of great joy, little one? I'm sure my dearest brother willn't mind us mucking with a bunny, if only for some sport. We'll cut it together, now how does that sound?" Hating him, the young prince revived: "I had hoped to see the dear rabbit alive, uncle," he said, primly, as

Penwith made his way out from the kitchen store, laughing wildly as he went. "Of course, you did," said his uncle, "of course, that is only to be expected. Things die, it's as well that you know this. Things die, do you hear? We all fail, I don't mind telling you. You light a lamp, and that sound is already you."

Life and death, a strange notion, not two and not one, and eminently open to suspicion. A riddle? Or what …

The young prince had wanted to stroke the fur, to keep the creature safe; an important lesson was learned that day. His uncle was to be watched, near-by as well as from afar; indeed, from the waft of the tapestry. Just there, an occasional presence, he would make out the "Ever-Youthful" Penwith. Yes, and yes again: he had looked and looked until one day he suddenly finds his uncle in the tapestry. "There he is," the young prince said, stepping back, all the better to see the duke. He watches his uncle, standing there amongst what looked like curling snakes, wrapping tightly around him. "He'll be trapped," the young prince whispered, remembering back to the hanging rabbit. "The glass cage," he reaches out his hand, "islands of light are swimming on the sea," he says, watching as the patterns alter, shimmer, saunter. "There he is," he says again, an old man seemingly frozen to the spot, the snakes circling him. His uncle's once handsome face fixed in pure fright and fear, holding a hand-glass up to his ancient, putrefying face: "Is he screaming," the young prince spoke the words aloud, "dying." The young prince marvelled as he watched the serpentine shapes change, then merge, then alter again. The snakes were of all sizes and colours, some appeared simply blue and green, others were entirely iridescent. Hating his uncle, the young prince smiled unkindly up at this tapestry as his uncle came into better view; hating his uncle, he wished him to suffer so dreadfully so; hating his uncle, he saw the whole panoply of this hideous man's self-love. "What's he doing there?" the young prince whispered up at the tapestry, "dying, I think," he whispers again, watching the swirling patterns of this passing world. "He looks so very, very old. Dying. Yes," he smiled, "yes – Damn *his* eyes." The gardeners were not yet in the tapestry, the grooms were absent too. "Ah, look," he called out, at the very moment the head gardener's son became threaded. "There's the one, he's there. The very one." He's holding a rabbit in his arms; his left hand awkwardly strokes the creature; she is curiously passive in his arms, not fearful, but still. What lustres his eyes, the young prince wonders, is it fortune, or is it fate? He will be mine, springs to mind: "It's only me – don't be frightened."

> *The young prince is overwhelmed at the sight of the*
> *hanging rabbit. His uncle's words fresh in his mind:*
> *"Death comes to all of us, remember that. Life and*
> *death, dear boy, the two are one, and the same."*

Out in the Green Palace's parkland the young prince runs and runs, out of breath, he runs all the harder, with all his strength to escape the memory of the stripped rabbit, he races too to get away from his uncle's account, and as he runs, he grows, he ages, and as he runs, time passes, and as he runs, the years fold away. Across the terraces that surround the great house, the young prince finds little to enjoy. So bored, really, so very, very bored. He stops, suddenly, and flops down beneath a giant aged oak tree, his hair falls into his eyes, a veil which hides the frustrated emotion. Knees up, his head in his arms, he weeps. These tears are short lived, he is soon enough relieved. A voice, a sound that seeks his attention. "Master? O, Master, please." The head gardener's son rushes towards him. "Sorry, Master," he cries, lowering his head. "For what?" the other replies. The prince dashes away whatever tears have fallen. "The rabbit's death." His heart is thumping hard, he feels a pulse in his neck. "That was hardly your fault; I should not have said what I … ." He stops, remembering his position: "… what *I said*," would have finished the sentence: "But was that not some time ago?" he asks, "the time has passed." The silence is soft, a gentle breeze sounds in the leaves, increasing, then falling back to rustling. He's bold, the young prince thinks. I should name him once, before I forget. The feeling of it brings solace, this naming. The head gardener's son holds out his hand. The young prince takes it, raising himself up to his feet. Face to face, the two see something familiar in the proclivity of the other. "His eyes," the prince thinks, "his eyes. Are amber."

Ah, there is a rich vein I must not lose sight of.

"What say I to him?" the prince ponders, "what words come near to this painful doubt? I could ask, well, something, but what? O, I am so exhausted by the strain, and the long, long time that I have held myself alone. Come … come, and then I'll say the name." He whispers the name, trying it out for size, saying it again and again, becoming as familiar with this name as with his own name. "Can we speak?" the young prince wonders. "Can you hear me?" he whispers into the breeze. He wanders through the fields, down to the ancient oak. He knows where to find me, thinks the young prince. "He knows where I am," he whispers into the warm breeze. You may stop, you may go, you are free, you are mine, you are never spoken of. He leans his head back against the bark of the tree, feeling the rigid shapes through his hair. He closes his eyes. The wind picks up, the tree sounds, a warm brisk breeze blows. Then a voice, familiar, deeper now. "Prince," it says. "Prince, my apologies." He knows where I am – you are free, you are mine, you are ever spoken of, ever thinking thought. He can hear me. "For what?" the young prince responds. "The rabbit," the gardener's son replies, "you remember?" He recalls the episode, but only because it was an earlier encounter between the two. "But that was ages ago," he replies. "The only thing at your back was your own haste."

The young prince, smiling now through the relief of what seems the passage of years and years. He recalls being so very moved by the contrite attitude of the head gardener's son.

"As if the years had passed by?" he asks. "Not like some curtain," the head gardener's son replies, "we might pull aside here or there, no." The mention of the blessed breast is aired, anticipating the juncture. The young prince begins to blush: "Your mother? She fed … ." The other notices, sensing his unease: "Yes, my lord. Wet, they call it." The word seemed strange in the context. "Wet?" The word seemed oddly placed. "That's what they call it." The word again: "Wet?" The prince seems taken with the word. "One each side," the young man replies, laughing heartily – "you … and me." The penny drops. "*O*," the prince exclaims, "*O*," not quite understanding the meaning of "each side," wondering at the split, "*O*." The head gardener's son, laughing still, looks abashed, wondering whether he would do what he was about to do. His hair blows across his dark-lashed eyes, he throws his head, revealing them to be amber. The young prince is silent and shaded too beneath the ancient oak tree, bringing himself down to the softness of the ground. "I'm doing it," in essence, crosses the other's mind. The head gardener's son follows suit, dropping to his knees, looking directly into the prince's eyes. With his open hand, he touches the taut white skin of the prince's body. For a moment, the young prince looks askance, even angry; the feeling of dismay fades fast. The other's name passes through his mind. The other's face falls away, for a time he is lost in another place, eyes closed. Another moment passes; another moment; another. The prince's face, so open, so honest, and true, grimaced as though in pain. Another moment, he comes. The head gardener's son would not stop short of a threshold, that was perfectly clear. "Swallow …?" What a question. "All," the head gardener's son replied, smiling. "You are beautiful," he says, wiping his mouth with the back of his hand, holding himself out for the prince to take. Perplexed by the pulsating vein, the prince reaches for his need, grips hard, then shifting his hand against the other's skin. "You are beautiful too," the young prince replies, the other now shudders, and this time it is the head gardener's son whose breath is short, then deep. Another threshold crossed; a thought flies through the mind of the young prince: there will be other parts to breach, in time. "Then we are one," the head gardener's son says, eagerly. "We are one," the young prince replies, "from now on." A moment passes. "One," he repeats, as though counting the word: "Yes … One."

V

Do you get me? He repeats the question: Do you get me?

The yard at the kerb works is lengthened by shadow, the darkness is deepened for a split second before being overwhelmed by a burning spot, its intensity no longer diffused, but fiercely hot. Now and then, between two traversing clouds, a bright yellow patch appears briefly; a moment later it was lost again, taking away its fractal lines. The sun is not yellow, it is purest white, and safety against burning must be sought on the dark side, cloud, or no cloud. The cosh, Septimus states with authority to his companion: That's what does it. He is referring to the side-effects of Largactil and Chlorpromazine which make the men's skin sensitive to sunlight. The cosh? the other man calls back, lighting a cigarette. You know, Septimus says, the cosh. Don't be a cur, you know what I'm talking about. The *liquid* cosh. The other drags on his roll up. Certain tasks are well known to the resident men, encouragement is nevertheless necessary. Concentration is rarely of the top rank, and their industry is not a matter of commerce or, it seems, much urgency. The workers are not there for the money, let's just say that. Recreation is a key factor. The day is still young. A fracas is on its way and that is why we are here, waiting to see what happens. Murphy kicks off – well here it is. A smoking pipe has been placed in an overall pocket at the front, chest high; fresh enough tobacco in the chamber pot is still glowing red. This has been done with haste; Murphy is intent on giving a warning to a comrade. Time and essence spring to mind. His caution is physical. Hey, man, watch yourself; all of them things – Look! They're crawling up on you. Quick … quick. That's what he says. Hey, you … He puts his hand out, slapping the other's arm. Duggan recoils, Perrott is knocked to one side, he drops to the ground like a beer barrel on a sack mat. He struggles to get back to his feet. A piercing, rasping fart cracks forth from Perrott's *effort*, also known as his arse. There's no time to laugh or to comment. Duggan bobs up and down, looking left and right, raising his hands, but he has no intention of striking Murphy. Duggan does not comprehend, but is silent; Perrott makes up for the lack by screaming to a pitch of shattering-glass-potential. He is still hauling himself up, shouting expletives. Murphy pursues his line, rather than holding it, following Duggan who's bobbing is ineffective: All of them, get them off. These things. They're crawling, I'm telling you … Get them off of you. Nobody remembers clearly what happened. Perrott is screaming. Duggan is weaving, and bobbing. Murphy's pocket is smouldering, it begins to burn the fabric; a little pocket fire ignites. It happened, that's all you need to know. The heat hardly helps. Murphy's pocket is beginning to burn – his pocket suddenly combusts. The sun itself seemed fixed above, now permanently so; its heat, however, was everywhere. It was the dust; the dust made you itch. There are no incriminating insects, no ants, no bluebottles, no wasps. Not that we know of. But the day is still young. Silver mote-bits from cracked open Blue Circle cement bags went off, mushrooming into personal space. Clouds of dust-driven heat, inanimate pests, pursuing the men, plastering their personal surface, intent on making statues of them. The cement mixes with the water in their eyes, fixing stares, or so it seems. Think of it. The same silver dust stiffens your tongue, your cheeks and jowls; skin stung and itched and along with this their tempers rose to fever pitch. And Murphy is about to go on fire. Feck you! he calls out to something, or someone, to Duggan, we think; swatting at him, lifting his hand to slap it away: There's nothing in this name, nothing for you to hear. Forget it, all of you. Feck off! A warning is called: *Murphy*, the auxiliary shouts, shaky authority in his voice. His hair is golden red, the swirling wave at the front of his head is truly shocking. His name is perhaps Smith – or Septimus. That's enough. Authority is not a given. The reply: There's nothing in this name, d'ya hear me? Murphy is not yet on fire. He's also not for being chastised, not in any way: There's nothing … The voice rises in pitch: Samuels, get the feck away from that hose. The other auxiliary shouts out, the one I struggle to recognise. His name might as well be Jones. He is gesturing, looking back to the sweet soul that is Samuels. (Will drink water, non-stop, the good sister says to me. Always watch out for him, he's a terror for water. I smiled: But why, I asked. She rolls her eyes, mocks my voice: *But why?* she whines, there was no why: You're on your own, kid, she says, calling me *Cur* under her breath.) The auxiliary's voice, louder now, rising, falling. But Murphy is on the cusp of kicking off, confusing his priorities: Samuels, I won't say it again. Put that fecking hose down. The unrecognisable auxiliary, Jones, is a potty mouthed cur; his hair covers his entire scalp as though a woolly, shaggy, hat, so dense it's dark but, in actual fact, it's fair. (At all times, Samuels must be watched, the good sister explains, keep him away from water. Taps and faucets. I don't ask *Why?* this time: There is no why.) Jones rushes around some badly stacked edging stones. Murphy must not be led astray by these muddied and ephemeral voices. Christ, mate, you're on fire, he shouts, suddenly: Feck me, son. He begins to slap at the other's breast pocket, sparks of red and burnt blue cotton fly off into the sunlight, falling to the ground. My chest, Murphy shouts, its burning, like feck. His call reaching the pitch of a howl. *Burning. Bitch! Feck this! Bitch.* Murphy is a potty mouth too. Perrott keeps on talking, no longer screaming, somehow unaware that Duggan does not understand a single word he says, at least that's what it seems like. Talking, talking, talking, as if everything could be talked out. All inanimate objects might be given a voice – to make the arguments put forward by wood or water – or, perhaps, a vote in favour of rainbows and concrete and wind – a say in things, you might say, an attempt at franchise, and all along with all this talk, there's more talk, rising to a pitch, accumulating, building, to a peak of total chaos. Something should be said. But no one gets the chance. We can never know, not now. How he shaped up in this tense and waiting world. How much time he had before the derailment of his mind made the bright sideshow of his life into a drag. Before the voices took over once and for all. The mood swings, the soul slips, the moon lights, the lips of silver'd sense, seizing him, mantling him and his world, all in the fullness of time.

The dissolution of his mind, that's the place he's headed – in time, according to the shrink. Ah, there it is. We have now regained some territory. All is dreamlike and dim to him.

Feck this – I'm on fire … this burden, Murphy cries, loud as hell – the heat … the heart … . The auxiliary's quick as you like: It's the fecking pipe, Murphy, old son … the pipe. The densely tufted, fair-haired auxiliary calls back, a call for action as he slaps the hell out of the pulsing flames: Yer pocket's on fire, feck all to do with your heart, son. The fire is contained; it's only a pocket, he's out in no time. Jones claps his hands to remove the black residue and then, as slick as can be, he lights what can only be described as an inappropriate cigarette, inhaling smoke and, along with it, the motes: Fag? he says. Murphy takes a cigarette, puts it in his mouth. Let's get you back, the auxiliary suggests, to the ward. Septimus, the one with the red wavy hair, comes into view: Don't worry, he says to Jones, I'll take him, leave it to me. To sum up, after that brief brush with the vanishing figures of dust and motes, what would clarify this sideshow? That they fell out of time, and forever, hardly holds. Their time was absolute; what of ours? That's worth bearing in mind. Murphy was put out, no longer on fire, his pocket charred, blackened cotton crumbling red to the earth. Was that the sum? We'd never leave this shrinking island, spending our lives in spirals and circles around the earth, reaching, each time, the same. The same as it ever was.

Death would be determined by the panic of this moment.

The entrance bell rang, earlier than usual, the tables were not yet set for their afternoon meal. The ward was washed in that clean silence that only early summer can arrange. Watt is standing at the cusp between day ward and dorm, aimlessly rolling up the sleeves of a tartan shirt. He hears the bell: What's that then? What the feck's that? Watt calls out by way of warning: *Somebody's coming*, he shouts. There's a strip of reinforced glass in the door, running on the right-side to the halfway point. One would usually make out a huddle of large young men on the other side, wearing navy-blue overalls and twill shirts. The relative confinement of the doorway can so often call for short spats and curse words. Usually, on days like these, they would look hampered by the heat. There was usually the same young man in tow: Septimus Smith. There should be two of them – not two Septimus's, two auxiliaries – but that's rare. He's a smallish man but pretty, his face looks like a doll with piercing glass eyes. Today this arrival time is earlier than expected. This is usually a bad sign. His hand is held above his brow, looking into the day ward from the other side of the glass. What's he looking for? I wonder. His hair has a lick like an orange wave rising from red horsetails, his eyes are vivid green, his cheeks are round spots of pink. The other man, presently out of sight, can be heard: If you were a tempest, that's the tale it tells, that's exactly what it says. What, man, you think I'm dreaming? Or some such. It says what it says: Pleasuring without issue, it says. Are you threatened by blood's loss? On any *other* given day, Murphy, without fail, walks across to you, and says a few words: Hello, man, he'd say, perhaps: Yes, dear, it's been a good day. He smiles warmly, shakes your hand while making small talk. But that's not what happens today. The bell's sharp tone is early and Murphy is alone, accompanied by one single auxiliary, Septimus Smith. This is the one with golden red hair, the cow's lick at the front comes as quite a shock, as though you're counting on a second wave to rise and fall. He's a fine faced kid and he is yet to speak. In the meantime, these are the first words Murphy speaks: The flames of a burning bush, that's all it is. Strange sounds, these noises. Voices. No need to ask me more. Just as that which falls as rain upon the red earth, the waters fail, swell and drop, swells again.

His voice rumbles on. At times like these, we look for the cause of the effect, the correspondence of one thing becoming the other, a bit-part, at least, that plays some role in the next appearance. At times like these, we think that if we can find the cause, the effect comes naturally. At times like these, we must accept that whatever is the cause, the effect is all there is. Fine night, he cries out, burns by day. The time is not for causes. No doubt, somewhere along the line, it is there; the difficulty, of course, is locating its flight. But what happens when this apparent transition to effect is so entirely removed from the cause? This is what happens: Live long day, mighty springs poured forth, unhearing, hastened by fires brought forth. Murphy intones, repeating: *Live long day,* as though chanting a hymn, calling out at something, swatting it, lifting his hand to strike it a blow – There's nothing in this name, he cries, nothing for you to hear. Do you get me? He hits the air. These were the moments of calm before the storm; a cliché maybe, it is apt, as you shall see. It had been a bright morning and there is that early summer silence. It was quiet, the day was still young. The clock could be heard to tick and tick again. There, suddenly, was Watt calling out, as though he was exasperated by the state of the world: Feck me, someone's at the door, he exclaims: Hah! He adored the slightest alteration to his day. I walk around the wooden partition which splits the large day room, orienting myself. I find only Watt with his broad smile, then a pose, as he looks down at his feet, at the burgundy loafers he is so proud to be wearing. They make an occasion, that's what he thinks. I hear the ringing. Watt has already seen somebody at the rectangular window. Murphy is now there, alone, slumped at the door. Watt calls out by way of warning: Somebody's coming, somebody's there.

Murphy, he shouts out, it's only fecking Murphy. Early as feck.

That's all you could make out through the toughened glass with the squared wire running through it. Murphy, alone. I have mentioned this before but that doesn't make it less true. I could add that the afternoon sun had a good while yet before it went out. Or that the glass is shimmering, liquefying somehow, that what it looks like. The pure white bars hold us in, that's what I could tell you. In short, the ward was washed in that clean silence that only early summer can put on. Watt is standing at the cusp between day ward and dorm, aimlessly rolling up the sleeves of a tartan shirt. He's heard the bell: What the feck's that then? That's what he said. But where will that get us? Is this unusual? the kitchen porter asks, just poking her head around the kitchen door. Something's up, she says, an inquiry of sorts. Jane Marple has arrived with a host of clues at her finger tips: Is this not unusual? she repeats, in a way, now channelling Tom Jones. (Well, she is called Olwyn, the good sister later comments. I look blank. Welsh, she explains, at least by name. I refuse to rise to the provocation.) The apparently Welsh kitchen porter is carrying out the elevenses of tea and biscuits on a tray for the residents who remain behind: For the time of year, she continues, expanding her meaning. She means the weather. The heat and the humidity. It feels like a storm is on its way. I put my hand behind my back for one reason: it holds a smoking cigarette which diminishes my effusive agreement. Boiling, I say by way of exaggeration: Storms, yes, I say, most definitely. What spot was the sun burning now? (I don't say that.) What bit of intensity withers before its attention? (Or that.) Heat is brought to bear in certain diffusion, pumping its intense warmth into soft chairs, the hard wood of tables, and the very fibre of our clothes. The white of the walls run in mercurial ways. Lined shadows seem weighted to stillness. The room feels tilted. We feel as if we are running on our sides. The knives and forks are set, suddenly put out by Williams, lengthened, becoming swollen and portentous, running off the tables, spilling down the sides, so light was the room, so close. Silver jewels dance on red-plastic tables. Large pitchers of water are rimmed with gold circles which remain everlasting to the eyes. Trails remain behind as you look elsewhere. Certain conditions have already been met in another place via unmet minds – causes, let's call them. An alteration was quickly sewn: an argument, an altercation, a shifting of positions. An aversion to people who prevent this from happening: an appearance, an application of pain; a pocket pyre, perhaps. How could we know that Murphy was about to be escorted back to us? Calm pictures change; of course, they do.

They change.

We were not to be lulled by this state of blissful ignorance. Things fall apart, what else can they do?

All hearts will open,

the centre will not hold.

They scatter feed as they walk,

pigeons and pilgrims:

But let them be,

let them ... *be* ....

We can fix whatever we like into all manner of words. But words and things bring very serious problems. What happened was not expected: Let the day perish wherein I was born, Murphy intones, but the darkness is yet to fall, the heat of the sun remains. One moment we're there, the next we are gone. But let them be.

VI

The head gardener's son is a great favourite of the young prince, they say: "A great preferred," Mistress Bridges explains, "inseparable, indeed. You can hardly tell one from the other," she says, "like twins," she says, then winks.

"The rabbit." The head gardener's son laughs, recalling with a tinge of sadness how distraught he'd been. "Everything changes," he recalls, "from that moment on." Emotion picks up as though caught by the breeze: "That's my fate," the young prince replies, striking his fair head against the bark of the oak tree. "I am about to meet – what?" He looks to the head gardener's son for some guidance, noticing at once the accessible mouth, the protrusive lower lip, the upper pressed in the shape of a pink heart. His black hair has deceptive streaks of red, presently lit by the dying rays of the early evening. "How light it still is," the young prince says, looking away, over to the setting sun, "falling dark in the west." The head gardener's mind is active, but he remains quiet, waiting for what comes; fighting to locate the words, he begins again: "We go on?" he says this; half bitter, half sweet, filled with lingering sensations. "I am destined soon to leave," the young prince replies. Impatiently, his friend begins to speak: "I am already at eighteen capable of such contempt for everyone here. But you? Nothing, but you. That is my triumph; I will not compromise. Not now; I will not live without you. And then you'll leave. You said so: I am not timid, you know that well, but I shall forever suffer the consequences." The other falls back onto pointless questions: "Why should it make you so melancholy?" the young prince asks. "I'll return, but first I must leave." It is met with some antipathy of feeling: "Leave then. Go now; I will not live without you. That was love, was it?" An element of confusion reigns: "Lo…?" The word catches in his chest. "Love," he tries to say it again, fighting for an acceptable phrase. He jumps onto the shoulders of the head garderner's son, wrestling with him, playfully, a momentary diversion from the sticky subject.

"Of course," becoming mindful, remaining silent, "he
is yet another to be loved." Here they all should be –
here but, thankfully, they remain uncaptured.

No footfall of the scullions and no sparks of the blacksmiths; the masons and the grooms are vague; not a king's messenger there, nor a falconer to be seen; the dog-handlers and the chamberlains and the laundresses are conspicuous by their absence; stoats are staked to a wall but the offending hands are nowhere near; no palms pressed in prayer at the chapel, no nuns nor monks, no priests, not a monsignor to shrive us. "Ah, here it is, yes, the moment of my little death. O, yes – yes." Swallows, the other says, looking up into the sky, they're back. Swallows and, yes, there's swifts.

The episode which brought about this simple
statement: "I am about to meet – what?"

The young prince had promised himself that he would keep rabbits when he grew into a man, but he told nobody of his plan. He laughs, remembering his childish self. He also vowed never again to eat a living creature, but made do by pushing all such matter to the outside of his plate. The innocence of it makes him smile. Well, he was the next in line to the throne, he could do as he pleased. "The meat makes me grim," he'd said to Nurse Tink. That was the end of the matter. "Grim, Master?" she'd replied. The boy smiled savagely at his dearest Nurse Tink; her face immediately clouded over. She hated him when he smiled like that. "Indeed, there is much else to eat," she'd said, stroking the little boy's cheek. "Much else, indeed, Master." Nurse is old and retired, but he thinks she still lives. Today, he will not sit at table for long when there are other matters which matter more. He begins to stride toward the great hall so that he might make his meeting in good time. One wants to say something, to feel something, suitably appropriate for the occasion. A bee drifts by, looking odd within the walls of the palace. The bee falls to the ground for but a moment, lifting again, humming round a bouquet of recently cut flowers. Transfixed, or deeply moved, he becomes anxious for the creature. He follows the bee so that he might bring it to safety. He paces behind, distracted, its causal flight seems measured, countable, deriding our immensity. He stops. The bee has settled outside his mother's chamber. The young prince is assailed with a bout of unmanly trembling before the oak door. He is but a boy again: "Do I, do I? Dare." He hears the voice of someone calling him, beckoning him in. "Could it be?" he says, "true. I'll find a way out of this; it won't be like the other times." He enters the room. The tapestry is lit as though on fire, washed red and orange by the western rays of the sun, striking at the east wall. It moves and it moves not, it is far and it is near, within me it burns bright, beyond all, without fire. The time has come and soon I shall be free again to venture back to the ancient oak and wait patiently for the time to pass. "There's much to enjoy; soon enough we'll be free again. He will pretend not to notice me, busying himself with some pretence at industry. But it is for this that I love the head gardener's son. I shall again leave him poems beneath the stone by the fountain, propose a time to meet, and I shall pass, incredible as it seems, into his life, as he will pass into mine. One, you see, I promised, but one, and only one." He shades his eyes with his hand and walks as bade towards the tapestry. "It *is* magnificent," he whispers, his eyes welling up, tears falling, "truly magnificent." The patterns swirled before his watering eyes as though he were stranded and curled up at the bottom of the sea. All else was obliterated; the outer world, the different sounds of daily life, the bustle of people passing by, and back again, the light and the darkness, both cold and cordial, could only be ascribed to their cause by a great effort of memory. "Yes," he says, his voice breaking, "yes, I hear you. Yes," he says, responding to the words he hears. "Which way am I to go?" the youth asks, extracting an immediate instruction from the tapestry:

"With the day in us, we know the day, and
with the night in us, the night."

"No, not at all," he calls out to the tapestry hanging on the wall. "The night is what?" he asks. The tapestry is still, silent as a grave. "Will you show me the way?" the young prince asks again – "And when?" Nothing. This time, nothing; not a whisper comes from the tapestry. Put simply, the tapestry was an everchanging map. While some parts of it were so familiar to the young prince, the trees and flowers were, the land hereabouts seemed common enough, at least the bits he knew, for he rarely ever ventured out to what the gardeners called *beyond*. Other parts seemed strange, uncanny perhaps, which is not a word he had come across, but eerie and perfectly queer. "Why is uncle Penwith in that room made of glass, holding a looking-glass up to his face," the young prince asked. "He's crying, I think," the young prince continued, but he could not think why. "Is he really dying?" He certainly hoped so, damn him, and his eyes. "Am I the night that put you into the light?" he calls up to his uncle's image, standing suddenly still within the tapestry. "Speak again," he shouts, stamping his foot, his trembling has passed. Silent as a grave, the tapestry is still. "He looks so very, very old. Is he dying? I certainly hope so." Although the present picture seemed so pure, more magical, and unreal, other sections appeared to be of other worlds and landscapes that might one day be explored. "Speak," he demands, "say what it is." Nothing. "What will you permit?" he whispers, his eyes ranging across what seems the time and space of the entire globe. "All," he says, "or nothing?" The tapestry responds:

"With the impossible in us, we know what's possible,
and with the possible in us, the impossible."

"No, not at all," he calls up to the tapestry hanging on the wall. "The possible is what?" he asks, "and the impossible?"

The tapestry's whist.

There, quite clearly, he could see a huge rock, black as a raven, rising-up from the sea. "A small island, it must be," he said, watching as the castle rose, coming into sight, dark and ever so forbidding. "Where is that place?" he asks, but no comment now issues, leaving only the impact of the alterations on the weave. Soon enough, he'd forgotten the words. The sea with ships and smaller sails and barques were familiar to the prince, his family had much knowledge of the near seas and the faraway oceans. There were stories of found treasure, of blood red rubies and opulent opals, of vivid green emeralds and jade from the East, and much talk of trade in rare and aromatic oils, spices far rarer than gold, and the persons held to service or labour who arrived, stark and stricken from the ships. Of these he had heard tell. Yet beyond the rocky island and the sea, beyond the slate roofs and the abundant gardens, there were the darkest woods and battalions of trees which were said to whisper truthful words to chosen people. Truths about beings beyond good and ill, and tales of all that was known and what unfounded, talk about concrete matters and evil spirits, and accounts of all the in-betweens of before and after and beyond. In the woods were deadly bracken where the larger fronds mimicked the smaller fronds and these the smaller – to all infinity. All the ferns were made of smaller ferns and then yet even smaller ferns, like mites upon a raven, and then the mites upon the mites themselves, forever made up, or indeed down, into evermore and ever-many-more mites. And there was clover and wild strawberries, and bluebells in spring, and white wild garlic too; and, in summer, would grow and climb, the purple Clematis Sugar, and there, in the shadowed light, pink and white and lilac Sweet-peas throw out their torrent scent which merges with that of giant pale-yellow Scabious. In the Wood was bramble and Traveller's Joy, and tea tree, bittersweet and honeysuckle, and healing white Valerian. Some of the climbers twist clockwise, some with twisting leaf-stalks, others by suckers they clamber over the trees. And then, roads and paths and rivers winding their way through valleys. In certain places it was hard for the young prince to tell where they went. The tapestry was well worn here and there; it had been patched and mended throughout the centuries with expert hands. That would be no hindrance. The young prince studies hard, seeks each single fissure; nothing deters him. He will make everything out in time. "That river there," he says, "suddenly it comes from nowhere. How so?" That's what it seems like; it's running and rhyming through an ancient market town into the estuary and out to the galloping waves. "Should I follow the water way?" His eyes range after that ribbon of white water, watching, marvelling, as it connects finally with the foamy seas. He studies first the bends and turns the river takes before reaching, wearing down, and severing rocks, on the way to the huge peaks and troughs of the ocean. He would re-examine the water way, again and again. He'd already seen the river passing under the bridge where the foot-soldiers in full armour took rest. How it shifted on and out towards the cliffs as it streaked a silver scar through the farmsteads, reducing to a brook and then to a summer trickle and out to the waving sea. He'd watched it keenly as it was passing the chapel into the valley haunted by the ghost-white owl's wisdom, hooting his mournful cries, echoing as you lie so still in sleep and dream. "O," he whispers into the tapestry's night, solemn and sad: "How I adore the barn owls." His confidence rising, he watched as the serpentine waters render and weave and warp the well to full abundance, and soon seen springing-up as a fountain in another place. "Water," he whispers, "water everywhere." He listens as it wends its way through the shaded wood, passing the cottages of woodcutters and woodscavengers, beyond the old sorceress's house – "Ylaine?" he says, her very name, Ylaine's in residence with her black marble eyes and her silver-wire hair, sitting there stroking Otto, her black marble cat, balking at strangers, hissing your retreat; the cat mews gently, purring there on her lap. "Who would ever dare to darken that indomitable lady's doorstep?" he says again. Yet the Woodman raises his hand across time's way to Ylaine, he knows she's safe, once and for all, when her wave's returned. "We are cast down." The voice seems clear, but who says the words? "Am I dreaming?' the young prince asks. Yes, through the sylvan wood the river journeys on and on until it reaches the sea and upon the sea sits a castle, sparkling a-top a mighty rock. "There it is, just there," in the left-hand corner nearest the bottom of the town, "the castle." The sun is shining. A golden beam strikes the very earth and is clear to see. A gale blows with bellow lips onto the right-hand corner, ever so close to the summit of the tapestry. The centre of the tapestry had suffered considerable damage across the years; mostly, it was thought, wrought by the fierce daily suns from the westerly windows. The once myriad colours were not so bright and vibrant as they were in some other parts. It was for this reason that the prince had spent so much time wandering and watching the tracks which passed over those borders – the faded flowers and plants were ancient threads stitched over in winter tide or during a single lifetime: the reds were muted, the yellows hardly to be seen, the purest whites were greys and the pale blues and lilacs almost entirely removed to the palest hues, streaked through like ribbons of crossing veins. The trees too were stood against the sky, like stakes, ominously struck, but magnificently so; stark and wintry sticks, leafless, blown, and desolate; once firm fruits blackened, softening at the base, rotting into deep and dark holes into the fabric. "The middle is the place to be," the young prince decides; yes, the centre held well and impressed him with their vague array of blue arteries lacking blood and pulsation. In other places, the fabric was washed in light browns and faded blues and mild variegated greys. These were the listing ghosts of millennia past, rising-up and out from their own ever-altering abyss. Histories and epochs were contained within this seemingly feeble material: "How much time," the young prince whispers, "how long …? What do these passing times foretell?"

"There," he said, a distinct deepening to his
voice, "at last. This fades to grey."

Just there, as though seen for the first time, he perceives the Woodman. Our lives boil and precipitate and change colour. "At last." A solitary human figure walking in the forest, his axe hangs at his waist, ready to hand as required to split fallen limbs for hearth and home. "O, Woodman," the prince calls out to the wall, "tell me a fable from past ages, please, tell me, do." It is well known that the Woodman held all the secrets of all ages and all paths passed, but it was true too that he often erred. The Woodman knew all, particularly when he knew less. "How long has it taken me to find you?" The young prince's voice seemed changed. "O, Woodman," he said, "dear friend in the darkness, awaiting my arrival." As it was for his mother, so it is for the young prince: … the sweepings of desolation from a chimney piece, the innumerable glittering of fallen ash, the glancing grey fragments, golden and sylveren too, the diurnal blue of the early flame rising, the green that falls upon the arid wastes of ages, the yellow pulsing the earth, once the smouldering punk is placed upon kindling, black match, slow match, tinder stick, lighting up the smooth gilt of those watching faces with fire, browns and blacks, frail pinks and stolid whites, kneeling, staring, believing, shading their eyes against the glare all the better to see circles of impenetrable lives, the river beds, the sea beds, the death beds, the flower beds, day after day, night to night, shaved wood slabs and logs lie, day breaks and light dies, before them, then after, singed with an explosion of what once was us is now only you … as it was for his mother, so it was for the young man. There could be no escape from the mighty decision. Perhaps it had been his age; a time before he'd locked eyes with the head gardener's son.

One day, slowly, slowly, a figure would be made out in the distance, only to disappear once again into the recesses of the tapestry weave. "There it is," the young prince cried at something coming into view. Not so much as one bit at a time, but as though it were forming and differentiating from out of a singular mist, progressively, diffusively. He had tried to fight it, to leave it behind. It calls him, leads him, demands his attention. There, for the first time, and there it would be for the last time too. And whatever it was would suddenly perish and be lost to view: "It's gone," he'd call out to the concealment, seeking now for its hiding place: "It's covered over," he whispers. He would marvel at the shapes upon the tapestry, shifting and obscuring. They seemed to move before his very eyes, changing and merging, moving him in his solitary silence. "Look there," he'd call out, suddenly breaking his quiet, "the colours are moving," he would say, "they are changing. O, look how they are moving." Nurse Tink would have attempted to hide her horror: "Master! Master?" Nurse Tink throws open the door, rushing into the queen's chamber: "Are you well, Master? Did you call for me?" The little prince would turn. He was looking shamed-faced. He was looking like he'd been caught in the act. He was looking somewhat sheepish. "Nothing, nurse," he'd said, "no, nothing at all." His presence once brought her great trepidation and fear; like he could hurt her: "Really," she said, imploring him to come away: "You spend too much time with that dusty thing," she'd said. "Your mother would not have approved," she continued. "My mother is dead," the young prince replied, slowly, coldly, "the queen's no longer there." But there's *is* a little monster in evidence, flits through his nurse's mind; what a horrid little child-cur. "Of course, Master," she says, alternatively; her head she bows: "May she rest in peace," the flighty little witch, she thinks but, perhaps wisely, neglects to add the thought.

VII

What, you think I can't see them, clear as day? You expect
me to walk by? Do nothing? You must think me a fool?
He's not referring to us but we watch his anger fly.

You must think I'm blind, Murphy says, his shoulders hunched.
Don't bring back them rushing stars, I'm telling you. Now! Only
then there broke out a bitter roar of laughter; it does not last, but
it leaves its trace. My heart is thumping against my chest. You
passed through them, he says, as anyone might. He wants to
explain something, opening his mouth, looking around at the
day ward, shielding his eyes from the light, seeking a safe
distance: You can't see them? he asks, are you blind, or what is it?
No longer laughing, but covering his eyes, somehow digging
deep for the history that brings such mirth to him. That burst of
laughter was chilling to me, on a physical level. He says: I must
change, I must … you can't keep me precise like this; possessing
me? No, I say. No, I will say it again, ask no one to speak of you.
Second by second, he becomes more perplexed, perpetually
listening, watching, waiting for something to come back to him.
The slightest sound would make him start and look about the
room, fearfully, fitfully. There are too many faces here, but mine
is not among them. Next minute, the kitchen porter appears on
the scene and almost as quickly she is moonwalking back from
whence she came. Tray in hand, her eyes fixed forward: Is this
unusual? she says, tea steaming, cups sitting beside biscuits for
elevenses on a side plate: Is this not unusual? she says it again,
and backs into the kitchen as though she has eyes in the back of
her head. I watch her with some disbelief. *How can she possibly*
see where she's going? Murphy is already alerted to this backward
walking, and then there was another howl of laughter, and one I
could relate to: That woman transfixes me, he calls out, thinking
up the words. The heat and humidity. It feels like a storm is on its
way. Murphy appreciates the kitchen porter's style: She's really
doing that? he asks, questioning her as much as me. That

woman transfix ... He can't land the words. Either he shall find them, or he shall not find them. That is all. *Transfix, yes*. It is true that he'd complained of a headache that morning. He was lying on his bed, the *big book* at his side. He behaved as though he'd woken from a long sleep, coming to, eventually, in a new world order. Me and this head, that's what I call it, he says. He murmurs, speaking to some invisible visitor: What do you mean? I can't even get myself out of here – they possess; all too precise. They can't even tell me my name, he continues (There's something about the eyes, the good sister had commented that morning: But I'm sure it's nothing. She looked away, swatting a fly, momentarily distracted by the smoke rising from her cigarette.) Was this misplaced confidence? Something else? The nature of the future insists that its opposite remains hidden. We live in hope, of course. I'm sure it's nothing, I replied, repeating her words back to her. (Really, I'm sure it's nothing, she'd said. Slippers. Haines, hand me that slipper. Haines! she calls out, suddenly alert to it. There you were, she said, turning her head, and you had to determine the note, mark it down, she said.) It sees me, he calls out, suddenly, an echo arrives: *It sees me. I only am escaped alone to tell thee*. World order or word order, this is an altogether different Murphy. Another one: quick as a flash. As soon as he awoke from overhearing dreams, he found his life transformed. They were his dreams. My people forget, he says. The second passes; he looks into the distance, but what he'd heard and what perceived is diffused into the blank spaces of grey matter: What is it? he looks me in the eyes. I would never kill – no one. Why am I here? It was broken glass, that is all. His voice begins that deep murmuring: I am in here for life. Simple. Simple. All the life there is. You could not wait for that. Who could? Let there then be light, but not so much of it, decrease it by half a degree ... I do not care to carry on. Even though I would do anything to have it. Just one more time. I never did see my girl, never again did I set eyes on her. Not once was she here – not once. Shame? Of me. Yes, that is it. It always comes down to that. None of your hoping here ... to come true in some way. And mother said the shame would kill her: Don't bring me shame, son. I'm telling you now. I won't mother. I must say it now. *I won't mother*, and that's a big promise. Should she hear me. I say it now. Has my mother passed? Would they know enough to tell me? They don't know a thing. Nothing. Why am I here? I ask. Not one straight answer. Not one. Is he singing, humming a tune? He goes on: I can't say how long. But it is a long time, the Lord knows. I walked long on the streets, and, boy, was it hot. But I walked them and walked them and walked them. And then some woman laughing, laughing. At what I cannot say. I smash up the glass and the shopman come out with a knife. A butcher man, he was. I put my foot through the glass and that was some end. All of it in tiny pieces. And wasn't there some woman. She was laughing, I tell you. Laughing, her laughing was too much to bear. She says to me: You're the devil, and I call her up: What you seeing there? Is it me? And then she's shouting and carrying on, all kinds of things. I wanted only to know why she was suddenly so mean. She was mean, that woman. Mean as hell. Mean. Mean. Mean. But she was not mean before, before all of that she loved me. It was this that put an end to us – that's the truth of it. Me, it was me, and that is that. Me, not she being mean at all. Me, it was; was it Murphy? But the thing is worth mentioning, let's say that.

He stops there (at the third consecutive mean) and I neglect to say a word for fear of the loss of the words he speaks. He looks at me.

It is not like being seen: it is as if he's grasping for what happened in this past precise moment. What was, he says, actual. The noise, he says: Outside or inside, I cannot tell. The temporariness of it seems to shock him, as well as the passage of actual time. There's no memory store there, but something recurring in his voice: And they come and take me away. That is all you need, they said. The police says to me, You're on your own, kid. He stops and smiles, looks to pick up his *big book*, keeping it light, but it is missing. The curtains are still pulled across the high windows in the dorm, but he cannot know this. The sunlight beyond is keen to come in, shimmering on the surface. A television set somewhere, floating on a bracket overhead, is heard and seen in black and white. Here is cool and calm. He looks at me. It's not like being seen. He sees through me. Murphy'd been complaining about bad dreams that morning: The horror seize me – And stops up my breath. (Nothing sees you; nothing, the good sister replied: Is it your head, Murphy? Your head?) He'd mentioned that he was in some discomfort. His voice trailed off, falling to not-quite a whisper. That's how the morning had started. We take what's there. We then ameliorate our being so, that being *there*, somehow softening its approach with ephemeral opinions. We loosen the line tied tightly round them. It is not a matter of commiseration, to be, for a second, like them. His words fell on hardened ears: Yes, it is, my dear. Like I am seeing things. Am I seeing at all, or is it they that do the seeing? It's hard, good sister; it's like I cannot see the world – and then I see it too much. You do see that, don't you? (Another one of those headaches? she'd asked: Your head, she said, head?) He looked dishevelled, having slept badly, dark rings are testifying beneath his eyes. There's a hoarseness to this voice. His book is open on his outstretched legs. He is reading, mumbling words, but when I first noticed him that morning, he looked fast asleep: If it wasn't for them things on my face, he says: They're, scratching, scratching, piercing me in the eyes. I can't see nothing. Nothing at all. It seize me, that's what it does. (Nothing sees you, Murphy, the good sister had said: Is it the head?) Next minute: Isn't it too hot for that? He's in his donkey jacket, standing at the door: I'll keep it on, warm myself up a bit, he'd replied: There's a chill on the morning. His face is now animated, he is clean, smiling, and ready to go.

But, well: Time Passes: the bell at the door to the ward. That's how it all begins.

58

Earlier than usual, it rings; and before I opened the door, I could see the cotton of blue-overall slouched-up against the security glass. The breast pocket of his overalls was mostly missing, partly charred and black. I was sure I could see his skin underneath. It's Murphy. He was leaning against the door. As I opened it, he pushed back, standing upright. Behind him was the red-haired fellow, the auxiliary from the kerb works. He was holding Murphy's donkey jacket as though he were about to put it on: There's been a bit of a barnie, he says. It's all blown over, but Murphy's not feeling well – a headache, isn't that right, Murphy? He speaks as though attempting to convince himself of Murphy's head. Or Murphy of his own. I look at him for something more, but that is it: he stops. I notice that he looks furtive but I am perfectly wrong. He looks afraid. He's not offish, he's nervous. I take the jacket. It feels heavy: Don't waste your time talking to me, Murphy says: Talking, talking, talking, that's all it is. Telling him a big ballad about nothing in particular. He pauses for a moment, and I begin to worry. The *him* refers to me: They have told me, explained to me, described me – that's not my name, Murphy continues: Telling *him* what it is, precisely. These are the things … no, not possessing me; not at all. He stops. Murphy passes into the ward, hunched, but paying little heed to his surroundings. He's murmuring about stars which are rushing about his eyes, blinding him, about a woman, escaping him: *My girl*, he says: Either I shall find her or I shall not find her. Murphy on a roll. I seem to have heard it all before; time is not past, not present, but is being made up from our future expectations. I feel immediately engaged, listening to Murphy: I am walking up there with the stars. Glittering and twinkling. He looks at me, but he cannot see me, that's how it seems. Self-organising is present, recognising others is absent. Only stars, he says: Them things, he says, in my brain, thumping, thumping, thumping in this head. *Thumping*, do you see? I tell her. I blow out the candles. She knew. *You did it*, she says, then she's gone. Mother. Then they go. Gone. And what about my girl? Gone too. The auxiliary is in a rush to get away. He steps back and then he smiles. Two front teeth are slightly crossed at the front, his skin is gently freckled with hazel spots, his hair is alive in the light, red and orange fibres, electric currents raying and criss-crossing to a huge wave at the front. (It's some cow's lick, the good sister says, shouldn't work, but he's such a pretty little thing, but sturdy. It defies gravity, she says, then laughs. And then that name, she says: Who's called Septimus these days?) What the feck, Septimus? I say, under my breath, holding the door ajar, liminal to the world outside and the one he can just glimpse within. What do you want from me, fella? he replies, but what he really wants to express is this: If you look outside then everything's a shock. All of it comes to a standstill – the world, the waves, the water, the words we have – everything, everything, blocking the way … or bound up somehow in *us*, in names … broken, multiple, and inconsistent … but where's the truth if it's caught up in bodies and in languages and in nothing else but that alone? But enough of this nonsense. What if I'm lying on a bed and feel it falling, what of the shade and the lamplight, the buckram shapes of the curtains, and the tweed hat of some dearly departed? What of my fingers, the cotton sheets, the softness of feathers, the down and the coming dusk? What is it that's in all of these, and others things, but worlds fresh-made as the hoar and silver frosted ice that passes away from the bright petalled flowers? I will kill myself … is that what you want me to say? There, it's said. He is smiling, lost for a moment. These thoughts are fleeting and framed instead as this: Well, his pocket burst in to flames, what more can I tell you? He speaks again: A row, you could say. Pauses for a moment. I say nothing. The auxiliary continues: Something kicked off between Murphy and Duggan. That was hard to imagine, I want to say, seeing as Duggan was hardly known for his conversation any more than he was for his fighting prowess. Duggan had never uttered a single word in his entire life. He's meek to the point of inheritance. Next minute, Septimus says, there's Perrott rolling around on the ground, then, quick as you like, screaming right into Murphy's face.

Something about a wheelbarrow. And then insects, non-stop talk of bugs and bluebottles. *Once you fall*, he kept on saying, something like that. On and on. *Once you fall*. Kept repeating the line about falling. Perrett was convinced that Murphy'd knocked the barrow over. You know how it goes. Cement everywhere! Dust all over the place. Chaos! And all this talk about insects and falling. Non-stop. And that was it. As a precautionary measure, he was brought back. Here he is: Murphy's pocket going on fire was the final straw, Septimus continues – Enough already! Nobody else injured. Just him. And falling.

Once you fall.

Murphy was, as I have stated, on perfectly good terms with all residents, as well as all the staff. I know that, Septimus replies – What do you want me to do with that? He doesn't mention that he's known Murphy far longer than I: There's only two of us. D'you know what I mean? He looks down at his feet and so do I. He's wearing dusty old black boots. Two is sufficient but not nearly enough. (Well, that's just the thing, the good sister said: Everybody adores Murphy. There's nobody who doesn't. That would mean we had our work cut out for us. What shall we do? we ask. Say nothing, she replies.) Good luck, Septimus shouts back at me. I miss him immediately, watching him as though he were about to walk through to another time, finding himself on the other side. I look again for Murphy. He seems stooped, not quite aloof, flicking his hand through the air. He'd struck the appearance of somebody who was being taunted by an aura invisible to all but himself. Regardless of gait, the auxiliary had still looked preciously small by comparison. The jerking hand movements must have been disconcerting to him. Good luck, the red-haired auxiliary called Septimus called back, turning quickly, and rushing off, calling. I shall miss you, I say, but he's passing into the uproar of another place. You mean not to return, I fear, but I did not know that then. He did not return; he fell onto railings from a hostel window. Drunk, they said. There's Murphy before me, stripping away superfluous garments, a shirt, boots, socks, a dark donkey jacket across my arm, as heavy as a body. I drop it on a chair nearby. I then lean my head on one side and ask Murphy how he's doing. I employ an imploring singsong voice. He mirrors me, leaning his own head to the other side, and singsongs back at me: And *what's* wrong with *you*, dearie? My heart goes, it is immediate annoyance – at myself (as well as him). He looks at me, looks away: My name, he says, forgotten already. My name, he repeats: Try that for size, you pink faced baby. There seems to be evidence of some distress in the frown, a certain distance to the eyes, a tightness about the mouth. I instantly forgive him. I touch my face, it feels hot. He continues where he left off: The big old city is all a dream to me these days, he says. All the city is uneasy, that's what it is, he says, none of it is real. It falls. He speaks as though he were answering an earlier enquiry. One day it might be that I wake up. Now that I am dead. And then he said: A big city must be like a dream, that's so true. A dream, he said again. He seems to be laughing: Dream, he said, once again. Tis all dreaming. He closes his eyes. I have dreamed, I have dreamed, I have dreamed, he says, trailing off. But we roar on: *My people to forget my name by their dreams*. I am drawn into things. Smashing the glass. Me. A good noise it makes. I smashed it. With this foot of mine. All attempts are made by staff to make his life as fulfilling as it can be, he seems unconcerned: The bowl is nice and red. Fires up really, really, well. I love a smoke. When he receives gifts, he takes them with gratitude. Each year, the same: pipes, tobacco, and slippers. His pipes bite the dust, red stars racing through the sky as fireworks. We know that much. But pipes are pipes and are easily broken. He throws them at the wall and they explode in petals of red light. There is a line for this, I recall it, but not who it is:

I burn and I shiver and as I do, I am released
from the shadows into this chaos.

What's happened here, I asked, pointing at the angry marking on his chest. He tried to look down, but his head jerked back as though aware of some inflammatory comment. I noticed that the skin remained intact, but the pocket had burned through. The donkey jacket had fallen to the ground, so out of place was it that I imagine it moving about or perhaps groaning. I feel it, he says, repeating words: In the morning. He always felt the cold in the morning. An early morning, early summer, chill. I feel it, he says, like falling into me. Deep, like. Murphy is standing there. His boots are kicked off, socks too; two bare feet look as though they've walked many miles: I shall then stand still, he says, we are weak, but you are who you are? The feet are swollen with time. Pilgrim's feet, he says. For a moment, he seems fixed to the ground as though something leaden had passed from head to foot. Next minute, he walks, swiftly, as though he's found himself on hot coals. Rapidly striding back to the exit. To the outside world, but there is no way out, at least, not for him. Then, abruptly, he stops before colliding with the door – it is locked, of course. It's locked, Murphy, I say. He calmed. I watched. He slowed. And then I think about the consequences. He stood there, looking up. He should've moved, but his two keen feet drew a negative. He'd found something of interest on the ceiling above his head: jerked back, looked up. The light of the day was bleaching. Sharp shadows cut into white. His feet swim on blue linoleum. His arms are fixed at his sides. He lifts one hand to his head. Aren't you going to do something, I ask. No, replies the auxiliary. What do you mean: No? But I am unable to hear my own voice enunciating the question. I think I am thinking it. It's me, speaking: What are you going to do? I no longer miss him, the red-haired auxiliary, I mean. No longer am I watching him as though he were about to walk through glass. I envy him; I am the auxiliary and I was thinking it. Or voicing my concerns, aloud: You're on your own, kid, I say, swift-like. Auxiliary, what are you going to do? It's me, a voice plays in my mind's ear; in my head and then issues into the external world. I am the auxiliary, making my reply: Wait and see, I say, but my mouth has stopped moving: Just wait and see. The words were silent, in thought alone, and left unsaid. Well, are you just going to stand there? Cur.

Still, my mouth was still.

The ecru trousers he's wearing are too short for him, and why? Because they are the trousers of another man, a shorter resident by far. He is wearing an aged off-white cotton vest. He smells of burning, of fire and smoke. The arm is triangulated in the holding of his head, accentuating the strength of the arm. The other arm just hangs there. He is speaking, speaking to himself, imploring peace:

Never was I a young father, he says;

I see, I saw, I was seen, he says,

reaching up to the ceiling;

O dear God, he says,

keep on walking the line, he says,

I saw what I saw, he says;

stuff like that, he keeps on and on, saying his chest is burning, itching, his eyes can see: I'm not blind, he says, do you want some, he says, then moving his arm, the one once hanging, he points up to where the sky might have been:

O Jesus, dear God, he calls out, his arm falls again.

I just can't be free.

Silence.

I saw what I saw, he says; nothing you can do about it.

Keep walking the line, he says …

Silence …

He's listening now, awaiting an intervention or a reply to his spoken words: What it looks like, what it's all for he says, one after the other. His voice resonates. The kitchen door is kept resolutely shut. The kitchen porter's behind it. Murphy's been back a while, but the ward is eerily quiet. Silence subsumes. He turns, looking for something terrestrial. He finds a seat at an unset table. Murphy's hand, the palm of it, his fingers too, are wrapped around his nose and mouth. A dark crab, suffocating him. He is crouched, and his back and shoulders appear forbidding. Only he is here. He is now seated, breathing life back into life. A Rodin figure, returning, coming back to life, cracking through the static. The quiet rumbling of his voice echoes on the ward. O Lord, just let me be free, he says; and then: It is just a little pink face, he's looking perplex: You're on your own, kid, I'm telling you … but the shadows; no, they are not the trees, but the horror of this light.

Persecute … possess … precise in every detail.

She is gone; that is all there is to it; she's gone; gone girl.

Swiftly, silently –

You're on your own, kid, don't let that slip.

What it all is, what it is all for?

It is what it is, and this above all:

One after the Other. And we all must follow

the night and the day, above all.

O dear girl, why can't you stop this scratching?

Above all.

He opens his eyes wide: he's staring. The eyes are bloodshot, as though he's been crying. His lifts his hand, the one that lay inert at his side. He places the palm and fingers around his head and for a moment I think he's going to crush his own skull with the power in his hand. But no, the hand becomes a crab.

*In thousands of connections, until I must have
begun to look as if I understood.*

There is some milling, a shadow moves in the background. Whoever it is shifts, swift as can be. A small number of the residents are out on a short walk in the grounds with the lantern jawed, auxiliary. The good sister is in the office, as quiet as a mouse. The others, the large men, are down at the kerb works still.

The silence is fearful.

Everybody knows what happens to the silence:

it is broken.

We break the silence into smithereens.

And then, to crown it all, there he is, just there, sitting silently, his face hidden with his hand. The fingers might bore themselves into the physical structure of his brain, grasping at grace, looking for favour. His handshakes, pressing fingers into bone, something sounds, cadences, hushed diminished notes from nowhere. Echoes, murmurs, the final words: Wait and see, that's what I am going to do. The existence of all that is terrible is in every particle of the air, shifting and nosing around. You breathe them in, these inquisitive parts, and, once within, it has you, hardening, acquiring shape, taking the form of your heart and lungs, right up to your throat where you are shouting, calling, perhaps you are screaming. Not a word of it is heard. It's Murphy – it's instinct. Moving in slow-motion. He has hauled himself to his bare feet. The quietness is eerie. Murphy has well and truly come to life. Right before my eyes, Murphy reaches his left hand over to the industrial sink. Right before my eyes, he simply, and without effort, tears the thing off the wall, and then – right before my eyes – as though he is surprised by the handling of the white porcelain, as though bowling a cricket ball overarm, as though what he has in one hand is of no consequence, he throws this hefty object and it flies through the air, covering an area of around twenty-feet in distance. It comes to a halt for one reason: it hits the door that leads into the dormitory, falling to the ground with an enormous crashing sound as loud as a bomb. It lands right beside the office windows which look out front and back onto both areas of day and dorm wards. It lands, yes, but it sounded more like an explosion.

I have waited and I have seen.

All I hear is Watt. He is screaming. I cannot see him. The noise is tremendous, primal; a sound for pity's sake. And, suddenly, silence. Not a whimper, not a sound. A split second? Yes, I heard screaming, screaming and know well who it is. I should run to find him, but I do not think to do this. The primordial howl judders to a halt; it simply and somewhat ostentatiously stops. Divisions in the making made then and there. All of it seems predetermined. Every bit was in place and willing it to split, as though a crystal cracked along these destined lines. We would never see each other again in the same way; an end was in sight, but it was not the one you might have expected. This sudden dislocation would inadvertently play a part in the death of one so tenuously connected to this sink made missile. I did not even hit any of the alarm buttons. These are placed in all pertinent areas. Instead, I follow him, striding in the direction of the glassy structure he's just thrown. I am walking, perhaps it's more like pacing. I follow him. I will walk right up to him, passing the wooden partition which splits the day ward between the eating and recreation areas. My hands are at my sides, palms facing out, this wasn't training, it was involuntary. It means: There is nothing for you to worry about. All is well. There was to be no offence against him. It's me; it was just me.

I can remember hearing the screaming, even
then; it was Watt. Just a memory.

Now there is the silence of a bomb-site. Not even that wonderful whimper. The door at the end was off its hinges. These were fire doors. I couldn't see the damage. He was now out of sight. The huge sink was intact and wedged between door and dormitory as though it had somehow been repelled. The sink weighed in at one hundredweight, that is, eight stones, over fifty kilogrammes, and it has just been tossed through the air as though it were a tennis ball. All I could recall was the incredible report and the glossy white rainbow it made as it crossed the space. The split-second silence. And then the screaming: a sound of doom and destruction, of flesh and blood, of boom and bust. Watt was nowhere to be seen. I looked back. Before Murphy begins to stalk; he talks too, but what does he say? Murmuring, deeply sounded, weaker and weaker, slower, faster:

Tis dreaming; dreaming, that is all it is.

That is all I have left.

What else is there?

Who pays for a name?

It slips fast, away,

as a dream, a solitude, inner moving – still …

Ah, there it is, again.

Solitude.

Who knows, who is … All …

above all?

Perhaps it was our fault …

all at once …

All …

I recall the good sister's voice, coming around to the other side, rushing from the office, torn between shock and confusion. Williams is now on his feet, but he did not move, his view is marred by the central partition. He was smiling. Utterly without concern. The good sister's voice, my voice too, the door-bell ringing. Quick, the sister calls to the tall, lantern-jawed, auxiliary, quick! A handful of the residents, returning with him, flushed from their outing. We made no reply, but needed all the help we could get. He walked back towards the office, on the same side as the sink; he knows the ropes. No water is escaping because the sink had been disconnected to halt Samuel's inexorable thirst. I follow him. The good sister suddenly opens the main door. The veteran auxiliary is now nearby, as quickly as he was gestured to be. The other residents are directed straight to the kitchen. A large area where a kitchen porter had been busying herself, putting cups out as well as engaging in the preparations for a meal. Amazingly, she'd heard nothing of the explosion. She'd already backed off, moon danced back to the kitchen. She now rushes to turn the radio down. Her long black hair streaked in silver strands bounced on her shoulders. The incoming residents' faces immediately begin to alter, eyes brightening, mouths widening. Come in, Olwyn says, the other is gesturing at her, letting her know. To the kitchen, she says, there's no time for fear. Her voice is soft; it soothes them. Tea, she said, turning the radio back up. Within the confines of the kitchen, she mentions tea again as though this word has suddenly become something of an obsession. The kitchen is cocooned within the external world, calm restores, bloodlust curdled. I was on the outside, following Murphy across the ward. There seemed only quiet, walking, stalking the huge man, following him. He kicked at the broken door. He reached down. The sink was again in his hand. He'd picked it up; he was just holding it. He saw me, coming now from the other side. I'd gone through the door to the right of the office. He was at the broken door to the left. He saw me. Standing in the shadow of the dormitory. I spoke and he is talking, saying something, but not, I am sure, to me. I explained everything was going to be fine, words like these: You are safe, Murphy; everything will be fine. Nothing was fine. I am lying. Nothing was fine. I am alone, but he knew me. The old Murphy knew me, but did this one?

This is what he says:

O God, so much is changing, so many things do change – and all this is work, and all this is labour. *Why*? Yes, why: still I am chased and not for the first time. I am not so safe and sound, not gathering at all, but that pink-faced boy, he means no harm, but skin and bone, he is, and hard as a knife. He wants to smile, I see it, but he can't; no, no, he cannot. Ah, and it is there, these things which are shifting and changing, occasionally fall. Falling, falling, fell. But it is quietly done. We're being spared: it will not arrive in time. Yes, all of this toil, this clamour. We may begin to believe. Only chains, it is; weakens and soon it becomes worthless, that picture on the surface of my eyes. Not *before* me but coming *out* of me. Hmmn, it slips among our amusements, a scrap of sadness, a burning sensation, standing in sun or rain. That fire burns, rising high, a raisin' in the sun. That fire is full-up in this brain. I hear tell that it may not be pierced in the end with a pin.

I am here, but invisible,

passing, changing, no more.

I am safe, yes, it's true,

a share in all these works.

Did I say? it spares me;

that shape spares and scraps me twice,

but that time has passed.

My time in childhood is lost.

Where was it now: a mother, she cries out, cries out, it is true; a father, fast and free, he's lost in time, slammed away. He boxed her face. He likes it. Wants it. I break him – I boxed with the Mackenzies, don't forget that. He runs. I broke him. *Husband*, she calls out. *Now look what you had done*? she says it to me. *Mother*, I say the word, but she's hurting. *Hurts*, she says it: *Hurts*. Nothing more.

This imprecise place is filled with noises, sometimes sweet, always strange. Ah, this air, this breeze. I feel it. Too hot the eye of heaven … shines. I feel it, and green and blue and yellow lights of life here which hurt me not at all. To trouble deaf heaven with these bootless cries, am I am safe; did he say it? This pink-faced kid. Spare me, forget me not in this dream. What is that – his foot-falling on the shiny squeaky floor. I hear it, yes, there's someone behind me. The kid. Again, he's there. The kid. Talking, talking. The observer. But I cannot hear him. His words spoil, not landing right, levelling elsewhere, a message maybe for him behind me – Too hot. The eye. Did I say it; I am safe. Take me out, if you still can, and keep me safe. That's what he tells me – there's nothing to worry about. Murphy stops, a frame stilled, animated only by the vitreous white sink swaying in his hand. Holding it there, just holding it. He is well aware of me: that much is clear. I can hear him, speaking, resonant, deep, but cannot make out the words. Only dreaming, passing, changing, and the word, *kid*. The sink? No real interest: he just tosses it out of his way. The simplicity of the action belying its crash landing. Its weight is plenty, the ground quakes. The door's hanging behind him at an odd angle, but it remained loosely connected. We do not raise the alarm. What is protocol, after all? We follow him into the silence. The shade of the dormitory startles your eyes – in reverse. Colours are muted. For a moment, surfaces reflect so much less. I could see our tall auxiliary, older than me, much older, but he's swift on his feet. He is now walking down toward the door, away from the kitchen. He will gesture to me through the window of the office, a reassuring indication. Of what? The good sister was coming too, but I could only hear her voice. Molloy, the auxiliary mouths at her, Molloy, then points. The next moment, the good sister was not yet behind me, the next moment, Murphy and I are alone. I could hear only one solitary voice and to this day I am unsure who was calling out. It was him, I think, a male voice. Can we come back to the point at which it started? Bring back something into being that has not been before? Watt's screaming had ceased. Yes, there's silence. We are talking mere moments here. Then silence. There wasn't a sound now in the early muted dormitory light. I could see only Murphy: *Overcome, subdue, anaesthetise*: are these the words I hear? There are no beginner's classes in life, kid. Know this: No beginning and no end. All I can know now for sure is this one voice, scored as it is into the present moment: *O God, Watt*? There was extreme panic in the older auxiliary's voice. All I could hear was that single drop, alone now, in a sea of complete and utter silence. Get to him, the voice demands, weakening with, *O God, where is he*?

Ah, this air, the breeze,

I feel it.

Too hot, the eye ...

I feel it, and green and blue and yellow lights of life here which hurt me not at all. I am safe; did he say it? The chaotic colour of a cloak would alter, the slab of black against a buttress wall would waver, the wearer of a pure white cambric shirt would cower – entwined, entranced, embraced in death, or by the work of a timeless theme.

VIII

One or the other would spin the thread of life, measuring out time in endless strands, until snipped short by some deadly unseen shears held in the hands of fate.

The light was strong, the tapestry looks to be on fire, caught short from the sharp rays entering the room from the western windows. The young prince could see things clearly now. "Have I not fought to flee these strange incongruities?" No matter, it comes without words of warning, a voice, silenced so; it comes again in myriad shapes, to sharpen his awareness, the taste on his tongue; it comes to combine old words with new, to satiate and saturate; it comes at the last moment, to expose an endless disgrace. "There's no perfect moment, is there?" he asks. Things before his eyes shift as though watching daybreak. A leader of light's soft movement, arising and perishing, a stilled stone, casting the long line of low shadow, the rosy crescent sun, whitening a dark line on the horizon, thick white bars moving, one and another, above the surface, pursuing, delineating, the transparency. "What else?" he says, "Please ... I want some more?" And clearer and clearer, taking a step back, a step nearer, then back again. Yes, he could make them out: among the magnificent oaks, the golden bronze of beeches, the flat-hand of sycamores, the obscure arms of the ash tree, all present and correct. And then one day, he saw these other things: unknown humans were making their appearance. All now seen so very clearly and so very distinctly. "A knight," the young prince whispers, "with his grey Barb mare. So, it is true!" The day is still young. Time passes. He is not alone; no, he was not. Time passed. Dismounted from his horse, the young knight is captured in the act of placing one arm round the waist of a beautiful young woman. "Look there," he said, quietly to himself, "her hair's as glossy and as black as pitch – a cloak, it seems like." In his other hand the knight is holding a sword, the blade curved, and ready to strike. "Well," he said, quieter still, not wishing for anyone else to hear, "well," he said again, "there he is, at last." For some reason, the knightly prince has thrown off his mighty armour, but why? His body is covered in pure white cambric, his hair is loose, falling at his shoulders, the helmet he once wore, thrown down, a plume of feathers pouring out onto the earth. "At last," the boy is murmuring, "yes. O, yes, he's here." The Barbary horse, as grey as ash, and the man, of course, were quite perfectly winning: the young knight with curls the colour of floss silk was extraordinarily handsome, and the woman, surely thinking likewise. "She's smiling," the boy said, "and she's looking up into the knight's face, her waist held firmly, safe and sound in his strong embrace. O yes, she's certainly smiling." He'd once heard his father say something strange: "There was an embrace in death," he'd said, but here there was one in life too. On her arms she wore long sleeves, and on her head a tiara of flowers from which her own jet tresses surely fell to the ground. "Damn," the boy was heard to say, an odd oath for one so young: "And damn again!" he topped it off. "I can see no further," he said, shifting his position. "Damned nuisance." The young prince wished solemnly to see her skirts, to see how she looked in her fullness. But he was impeded in this endeavour by a mighty chest of drawers. A great hulk of furniture held sway, standing firm against the wall, obscuring the very place he wanted now to see. As a little boy he had clambered onto this chest. Like this, he came closer to the altering patterns. Up so close, he would go cross-eyed, which made his father laugh: "Look, father, everything's doubled; everything's twice." But now, the cumbersome thing was a damned hindrance. The boy could not move the dark chest of drawers out of the way, it was far too large; indeed, the ebony wood was not just black, it was dense. His obsession grew. What lies beneath the pure white bodice of that beautiful woman?

He must see, once and for all, how she ends – he simply must.

One day, when the young prince was eleven or twelve years of age, it was decided that some of the furniture from his late mother's room would be removed. It was felt that the time was right to turn a new leaf. The ever-mournful king ordered that the posted bed be taken from his late wife's chamber, along with an array of other things. "Take that damned thing too," he said, referring to a nearby vase with the tiniest cracks that had gathered over the years, a jigsaw puzzle, it seemed, cracked in history. These offending items must be removed elsewhere. The tapestry, a dreary thing, his father thought, barely hanging there on the east wall, brought back such painful memories. All the old king could hear was his wife's voice, haunting him from the past: "O, my darling," she would say, when her husband happened upon her as she looked up at the wall, at the patterns which so captivated her: "Look, just there, how it changes. I can sometimes see us," she continued. "Yes, you, me," she pauses for a moment, "and there's a little boy." The queen took a deep inhalation of air, "how innocent he looks," she said, "our own true child is on his way." That we begin, and end, with groans, these memories were sounds assailing him. "But," he remembered her saying, her final words, "my darling, I am fading, can't you see? Fading away into the distance." That is now past: "Take that damned thing down." The tapestry would be removed with immediate effect. "Destroy it," the king called, "destroy it, once and for all." No longer would it hang there, a shadow pointing its finger at him, in pride of place, no longer, no longer. "Take it from the queen's chamber. Burn the damnable thing. Burn it … ." Murderous hate rushes towards the young prince's breast; he holds onto it, spreading his arms. "No, father," cried the youth, running back, appealing to his father's better nature: "Never! It is all I have of my own mother!" His father, the king, immediately relented: his pain must be the boy's succour. "It remains." The king could be heard, his rich voice made all the plainer for his son's benefit: "It remains." One last thing: "And the chest, father?" He seems surprised that his son lacks satisfaction: "The chest?" his father replies. "I should like it … ." His father accedes immediately: "As I say, clear it out of here," he said to the men who had gathered with him. "Leave the queen's tapestry. It remains." The boy wishes to dismiss the troop. "Father, I should like be alone with … ." He does not say his mother, the queen. "Get out of here!" the king calls to those gathered in the queen's chamber. "Leave the boy," he orders, "alone." Words come to him as though from the air:

"With the gentleness of the king persuaded, we know gentleness, and with persuasion, we know the king."

The tapestry whispers to the boy, standing there, a solitary figure, smiling up at the colliding patterns.

"We are not gentle; and we are not persuaded by whims nor by the king's dreaming."

How gently the words pierce his ears. "Mother? O Mother, Mother," replies the young prince – "All is safe." The warps and ways of the tapestry weaves these final words:

"With the day in us, we know the day, and with the night in us, the night."

It was not unknown for the widower king to be found looking fondly upon the tapestry. Disappointed that all he could see was mustiness and dust: "Moth-eaten thing," he said, a look of distinct resignation. This inability to see even the remotest sight of his wife disturbed him greatly. "Did she not say that she was beginning to thin? Did she not see her own demise?" He spoke these words to the swirling pictures that he was unable to see, to the shifting patterns that were not in the least perceptible to his eyes. "Speak," he said, loudly, "speak," he said again, pathetically.

Each day, each moment, he felt his heart weakening. "My darling, beautiful wife," he would call up at the tapestry, "you seem anywhere but here. Where are you, my dearest love? Where are you now?" The monarch well-being becomes a matter of concern at court. "The king must one day come back to us," the servants were heard to say; from the kitchen, Mistress Bridges, who'd known the king since he was but a young prince, called out, "O, gracious, the king can't go on like this; years it's been. And off and away from his duties for those long walks down at the lake. O, gracious, it can't go on." Mistress Bridges was not the only one with concerns. Penwith, also known as "Ever-Youthful," let his crystal-eye's gaze fall upon his brother's insufferable mourning. "Yes," passes his mind, "yes," this perfect affirmation: "Yes, one day, dear brother, you must swim for your life. Yes, swim deep, dearest brother, swim far." His laughter was sickening to hear. "Evil mirth," Mistress Bridges said, under her breath, of course, "that's what I call it: Evil mirth."

"I don't know what it all is," he said, "only me?" he
asked. There is only ever one seer of the tapestry.

The day arrives and there was much activity. A great deal of hauling and dusting; much shifting of furniture from the chamber. Standing back from the oak door, the sparkling motes made the youngster sneeze. He waited, and he waited. "Soon it will be clear," he whispers, looking into the room, "then I will see." The young prince is waiting patiently, but eagerly. He observes closely the assembled servants and fellows brought in from the tithed cottages. "Be careful," he calls out, "please, don't damage the tapestry. Move only that hideous black chest. Do you hear? Don't touch it, I say." At last, the boy enters the room. For the first time, he can see the tapestry in its entirety, and unencumbered. Behind the lacquered ebony chest, the colours are incredibly vivid. There is a shuffling at his back. A cough, a sniff. Outraged, he turns. "Get out of here," he shouted, raising his voice at one of the men. "How dare you remain – Be off with you. Get out! I say." There's no getting rid of them without naming them: "Harold, John, William, Guido, all of you – Be gone!" He listens, hears himself breathing, his heart thumps, inaudibly, but he feels the blood is hot. "I see it now," he says, speaking to the wall, "as if it were present," he says. Never nearer than now, never am I nearer now than touching, but he holds back his hand. "I see everything, everything. And it's thanks to you, I'll return to myself – at the end." Searching, he finds, once again, the handsome knight, dismounted from his grey Barb horse, the loose white garment about his shoulders, open in a triangle at the neck. "There he is," the boy said. One arm is wrapped about the waist of the goddess, one hand holding a crescent blade in readiness to strike: "Is he about to kiss her?" the boy asks, but the tapestry is silent. Her hair is of a pitch of structured black. "Like night," the boy smiled as he spoke, "more like a cloak," he corrected himself, "than hair." The boy might have recoiled had he not been riveted to the ground. What on good pleasant earth was that? "He looks as though he is asleep and awake," the boy said aloud, although unheard, "asleep *and* awake," he repeated – "at the same moment." Now he could see it all; he would see everything, as if for the first time. Colours more vivid than ever before: he saw the whole of her, from her jet hair down to what lay beneath the pure white bodice of the beautiful lady; he could see too that the knight's face was fixed on the reflection of the truly beautiful face of the other but, at the same time, the knight seemed unseeing, as though held by some unearthly enchantment. The little prince smiles, seeing each part of the whole for the very first time: "So," he says, "there it is." And what did lay beneath the pitch-black tresses? Well, there were no skirts there, no, there were not. Beneath the lily-white bodice there – could it be true? Indeed, it was fully seen: instead of a dress garment, the beautiful lady ended off in a big snake's tail, decorated with scales of a most vivid green and gold.

IX

I know what I have to do. Let's leave it at that.

The white bars are dancing, merging, as you pass, the blind-free glass enables sudden shadows to fall and to fail (That's dark light, the good sister says, so what do you know?). Sister Molloy sends the kitchen porter out to hold a white towel against Watt's fissured head; his mattress is dripped in blood so dark it looks like gravy splashed from its boat. We are aware of the heat and the rapture; Watt's face is not yet bandaged, not yet stitched, eighteen damned sutures it will take, and him wandering around, trying to show the wound to all and sundry, as proud as a kid. Mild concussion, but he's still going strong. O, what are we to do? (I must do something, Molloy murmurs, but what? I must go, crosses her mind, fleetingly: I must … she pauses: A ward sister must be prepared for anything, she says, encouraging herself. That's me – the good sister. *Me.* She barely expresses the words; a reverie, was it? People will hear me; they will, she whispers, a kind of exhortation. If the words would come there and then she would have to utter them: I must do something, she murmurs, squinting her eyes against the light from the high windows. Time for tea, she says, loudly. He's hardly what you'd call dangerous, let's just say that, she said, less loudly, and that was far worse than the silence: I'll do nothing, she says, that's what I'll do. Mallory will know what's best.) The eternal early summer remains intact for a while longer: sharp showers resonant of April pass, return, pattering at the windows, denying summer's lease. The dimming world of management, the leaders, were on their way. The working community would soon enough be divided from themselves. Solidarity was sold, and we all happily succumbed to the destruction of our ever-so-fragile union. That shadows were thrown by people and things. (My tear ducts are as dry as a bone, she says, then laughs, as usual. She walks to the kitchen, unaware of the friction of people brushing past her. She'll fix me with a stoical gaze: So, what's the story, kid? I look down at my shoes: Story? I say, there is no story.)

The structure is not spatial, it is temporal. (There's no now: they'll split the ward up, she explains, that's all there is to know, kid.)

The shadows need not denote our demise, or some sort of evil presence, or the denial of true existence – if that is what I mean. That was always the way; always will be. I shall never see this or that face again. Yet, I feel the moment has come for me to look back at you; not as proof of my susceptibility to atmosphere, but to simply walk in and turn on the light. The directional shift portends to our eventual termination and decay – perhaps I mean demise; we are no longer the bold and deleterious figures we once were. Impending doom, who says that? The ever-new possibility of what takes its place; arising and perishing, arising yet again, decaying. In other words, we have a choice, and we still have time. (Do nothing. Let's leave it at that. Molloy had an unsettling awareness of this eventual future. Play it down, she advised.) She was the last of a kind; cold and occasionally impersonal, perhaps I mean *imperial*. She seemed keen to press upon all of us that we weren't alone. Say it was an accident, that's all there is to it. I have to say, it was a nice feeling, but one I have now come to doubt. We assume that we knew what she was up to. No, we did not. O, yes, she said, and then those often-repeated words: We're one big happy family here, don't you forget it. That was always the way. Always. She stopped, smiled, as we fell for it. As she walked away, tending to someone or something, she was no longer laughing, neither quavery nor was it staccato. We are all integrated, but these are my words. As are these: In my case something remains floating, unattached. (All one, she said, you know what I mean, kid? No call for any of us to chase hares; if you get my meaning.) We suppose people know what is meant: No, they do not. Molloy sat opposite me. I am a new employee; she is the ward sister sounding me out. The ward-kitchen contained a large, central table. There were clean surfaces wherever you looked. The room was well-lit. Overhead strip lights were not oppressive, serving only to accentuate the white of the large gas oven. There was an equally large refrigerator. The presses on the walls, also in white, contained all manner of food for evening suppers and so on. There was an overwhelming feeling of white, but the eyes are still open to impressions. I can see nothing, but white, nothing but the moment when the world comes into its own, emerging from the negative image within, once and for all. Is that how memory works? I did not ask that question. Alternatively, what if what we see is accumulated? Isn't that it? Implausible, I would say, there's no time. No matter, it was exactly what you would expect to find in an asylum, if that is what I mean. *Asylum.* Something was scratching at the door, but it's nothing, really nothing. I can't recall any windows in this room, bearing in mind that the long, facing wall, geometrically speaking, ran along the same plane as the door into the ward. And so, on the other side of the wall, there was a long, long corridor which led on to the Hospital's industrial-sized laundry. Keep walking and you eventually arrive at the nurses' quarters. The corridor, when you walked it, seemed a never-ending travail. These were the walls which held back the cries of pain, of restrained humans, dragged away from whatever homestead they'd known, stripped off from the fastness of distant families. (Most of these people have never known home. But, really, she began, then paused: Grow the hell up, kid, she said to me, admonishing me, earlier in the day, raising her voice, but in jest. An American accented cry, as swift as can be.) She was holding out red roses when I entered the kitchen: For me? I said, and she laughed, sniffing the flowers in her hand. (Mothers, she says. Mothers? I reply. Mothers, she responds)

Yes. Mothers – occasionally one of them turns up.

The screams of their historical reluctance to be coerced

into stranger lands. Disparate snippets; receiving with perfect coldness whatever comes. What lives of oppression were predicated on these echoing walls. It was bad enough to hear it once, but twice was too much to bear. The walls were aware of this internal strife, the stretch of time, the faces seemed blasted and somehow captured in the plaster as patterns of compliance, or the reflections in the panes of glass which let in the light all along its endless, lugubrious way. Before me, she pressed a finger upon her eye brow. Her eyes are brown, continuously warm, but sharp. She moves the hand to the other side: Fecking hell, she says: Soft. Plucked off. Smooth and, what? Protuberant. She stops. Molloy was looking at me closely, she was smiling. I don't suppose you need to spend much time on your eyebrows, now do you? She is nibbling at leftover bacon, hard as can be, crunching when she bites. Up she gets: Say nothing, she says, that's my advice. She moves towards the door, but stops. Things might have been different. Should've kept him back. Do nothing, she says. Do? I say, what does she mean by *do*? Nothing, she replies. There's a pause. *Every breath you take*, she sings, walking to the door. The other voice rising from the transistor radio there on the side of us, positioned by the eight-slice toaster.

> *What have I got myself into? She thinks back to a time*
> *before the critical incident.* The Wilson's, *he'd said:*
> Something's off, *she'd heard him say it, clear as day.*

(Molloy is fearful that he's trying to say something. He *was* saying something, she says later: Under his breath, it was.) But Murphy thought the doctor could hear him. The Consultant Psychiatrist is, in fact, perplexed: *Something seems off*, he mutters to himself. Murphy's right arm is clearly shaking, an odd tremor takes place; his hand turning to and fro as though jangling change. That wasn't expected, not at all, the shrink thinks. His perplexity disturbs him. *Something seems distinctly off*, crosses his mind: This really is an immensely interesting case, he said, repeating himself, becoming more and more disturbed at what he finds. Murphy laughed, an action that seemed to go backwards, into his chest. And then, just leaning forwards, he puts his huge hand onto the doctor's old and grey head. He rested it just there, on the doctor's bonce. The eminent specialist's composure fell like a stone; the smallness of his smile was stilled: Your hair's like cotton wool, sir, Murphy said, laughing again. Cotton wool, sir. Your hair's like cotton wool. He laughed, looking across at Molloy, standing to the dorm side of the office, looking tall in the room. She winked, looking straight back at the shrink. Murphy closed his eyes, lifting his hand from the Consultant's head. And I am silent again, he says, perhaps only thinking these words, as pictures and flickers. He can see them: This, then, is where all of these people come to live and to die; yes, I have it as a place to die – there is no escaping this. The old shrink knows, I can feel it, as usual he is right.

This will be the sound I hear;

this will be where the stirring, the pressure of life,

becomes more urgent each day.

This is what puts the greatest fear into me.

Yeah, not the noise of it all:

More stones than there are stars in the sky,

And stones, and then some-

how the way lost,

but the silence of Lambeth

and the horror

of thy Croydon come ...

He wonders if he's said a word. His hand lands again, eyes close shut, he feels again the coarse hair of the other, suddenly seated, man. He might as easily have turned the wise and aged specialist's head as though he were removing a tight-fitting lid from a jam jar. There was some fear in the room; trepidation is the word. That is only natural in a house of mirth such as this one. He removed his hand, only ever gently placed. The eminent psychiatrist's calm worked to the extent that Murphy's actions produced little more than a snort of laughter. An image was before mine eyes, he says, murmuring, there was silence, and then I heard a voice. All of those around him are safe and sound – or so we thought. There was nothing in the least to worry about. Will the silence away, comes to Murphy's mind, will it away, leaving only this frightening noise. I fight it – these sounds, but the silent things enter deeply into this little head; I feel it. I break it, if I want to; make it bring these things out into the open. I am learning to see, but why it has taken so long, I cannot say. The consultant's heart is racing – he immediately panics, but holds his discomfiture well within the confines of his long white coat. We'll increase the dosage of … Do you agree … Poppy? But what did that mean? Abnormal attitudes, both manneristic and the more typically organic postures; that regression can be avoided with the application of newer medications; even manic hypermotility may be regressed. And we'll up his … He pauses, thinking, thinking: *Something seems distinctly off*, crosses his mind. I thought we'd cracked it, for a while. Now this. Regression occurs, continuity establishes itself, inner identity struggles and begins to diminish. His improvements have fallen off. That's what he wants to say, but makes do with generalisations. Progress: fallen off. After *so* much success – he knows not why – he says nothing about his concerns. Well, sir, Dr. Frankel begins, her opinion sought: We might try … He clears his throat, she stops, intolerable, she thinks, still smiling. No, he explains, no. Let's see how this comes out, he says. Come along, *Poppy*. *Something's off*. That's what crosses his mind: Something's off. Molloy leads them out of the office, she is dying for a fag. The once ebullient Consultant Psychiatrist walks on ahead, a temper rising, an outlet nearby. Dr. Frankel turned, looked straight at Sister Molloy, letting her know by her look that she has the angles and, what's more, the smarts. The good sister smiles, but it is only with her mouth.

(There was nothing in it, the ward sister said later: It was most certainly not a woman thing, she pauses, do you know what I mean?) Poppy walked on; her head held high, the strange shaping of her prop, the serpentine stethoscope, in situ. Molloy, about to close the door, is forced to pull herself backwards. Her eyes widen. Next time, the shrink says, make sure there's a fucking male orderly available. The Wilson's is suddenly unpredictable. Let's not take any chances – Clear? Keep me posted. She ignores him. He looks directly into her eyes. Clear, *nurse*? His voice rising, sharp grey watery eyes looking, seeking conformity. Clear, she responds, understood, she confirms. He turns fast, back brandished, a slab of pure white cotton, the garment ill-fitted at the thin shoulders. Molloy breathes, uneasily, locking the door again against the outside world.

> *(What have I got myself into? It's all too late for that:*
> *Mallory will play ball, that's what she thinks. On his*
> *way, she says. Watt's fine. I've seen far worse.)*

Who's going to put up with such levels of violence. She knows well how it goes. I can hear it now: *Would not, and most certainly cannot, be tolerated. Sister Molloy, are you paying attention*? Hypocrites, they know what goes on here. Logistical disturbance. Meaning what? Must, at all costs, be kept away. Fecking shrinks. Hasn't he done enough? The facts of the disturbance must be kept miles away from his in-tray. Wilson's, did you say? The Wilson's? He'd be sorry to lose his only case. *Proportion*, however, was, quite naturally, what counted: *Proportion*! Something Murphy had certainly not shown and, as a result, must be dealt with, even if this meant the death of our present resident's human nature. (Rampton will kill him, she'd rehearsed her line, again and again.) Yes, way. Proportion was what counted. He used this term a great deal, Proportion. (Molloy brings the house down, a little later: Now then, she says, the old shrink couldn't drag his eyes away from *Poppy*'s proportions, now, could he? Dirty old bastard! And at his age.) The Consultant Psychiatrist had hardly got onto the other side of the locked-again door. Proportions, indeed. It is hard to describe how much they laughed at this: *Poppy's proportions*. Who comes up with stuff like that? How nobody had thought of it before, and the fact that he was barely out of earshot. She looked across at Guppy. Murphy had gone to lie down; his hand was moving as though hitting an invisible tambourine against his thigh. Not Parkinson's, she would say. That was the thing – The Wilson's had perplexed him. Guppy appeared to be walking backwards. But he'd just clocked her dropping Murphy's pills into a breast pocket, just to the left of a dangling watch. (Too late: I know you saw me, she says, inaudible to all but her inner voice – Yes, you: Guppy. You crafty little shit.) She patted the pocket, and then, nearing the office, she made her joke.

Every hole's a gole, I guess. Dirty old bastard.

It was Molloy who pushed the door back, attempting to shore up the damage. It's not *too* bad, she'd said. The comment was greeted with stunned silence: not a sound, nobody uttered a single word. Well, sure, we understood her meaning: the door was hardy, purposive and strong. But we took it no further: *Is that what you mean?* was not said. It had stayed put, but it *was* made to withstand fires, wasn't that it? The Murphy-flung industrial sink had knocked the door off its upper hinges. The man-heaved thing had hit hard, slamming the door jamb into Watt's head. The actual mark to the wood presented itself as heavily gouged, a stiff scar-crossed mark. Watt's damage? A vertical fissure; his head appeared severed. The door had withstood the blow, but only just. Watt too had remained withstanding – a moment of sudden screaming, a run for cover, throwing himself under a bed, crawling to safety. The door is dusty and damaged, laminated wood is cracked in angles which jut and seem fragile; Watt's condition is one of shock and elation, but the dead straight line provides an effect of extreme severity. (It could be worse, the good sister said.) Things will get back to normal, you'll see. Hold still, Watt, Molloy calls. Just wait a sec. It is Molloy who, speaking quickly, said this: Can you two get the sink back? Then pointing up to the place from where it had been torn, then thrown. Leave it there, back where it was; then come straight back to the office. There was a not-quite understood urgency. Molloy was ahead of all of us, had already computed that Murphy would now be deemed a source of extreme danger. Minor incidents had peppered his past, but the Rubicon, this time, had been well and truly passed. Watt, we could see, was now sitting on his bed, it was no easy task getting him out of the office. Olwyn was speaking in murmuration: Hold your head back, Watt. Hold back. That's it. Pressing a pure white hand towel against the wound. The duty doctor is on his way, Dr. Mallory Jacobs ... he's on his way. Watt, although you can't see his face, is well pleased. Doctors are their celebrities, their brush with fame. Not the Consultant, someone cried out. No, not the fecking shrink, came the swift and sweet reply. The kitchen porter's face looked stern, as usual, her hair was flat against her back. She was no longer peering through the toughened pane of the kitchen door. No longer saying *Isn't this unusual*? We have moved beyond talk of summer heat. The residents who'd arrived back with the lantern-jawed auxiliary have drunk their tea; the others are yet to arrive back from the kerb works. A few residents, Haines and one other, had been dispatched to the dormitory to join a solemn and yet elated Watt. Williams was in situ, his usual place: he'd sat down again, quite calmly, after Murphy had thrown the sink. Really, only minutes have passed, but time is stretched and unforgiving. Williams's nonchalance suggests he'd seen worse, his smile suggests he'd been wrapped-up in similar flights himself. There were no witnesses; there never are. Only us – and Williams. And Watt – he's reasonably calm, placated. Murphy was now sitting on his bed, coshed with liquid, a grey blanket around his shoulders. You could hear him, that low sound: O, dear Lord on high, and: Help us, please, do this

once, for all. As well as the repetition of *Blessed are these things* –
a droning sound which reverberated gently but was meant to be
heard somewhere in another realm. The veteran said: Watt
could've been killed with that? They'll have to get him to
Casualty. Head x-rays at the very least, surely. It's a miracle that
Watt's still here. Really! I listened, then looked through the office
window, out to the dormitory. Watt was hidden by the kitchen
porter, but his ears were attuned to everything in the ward. To
the call of the alarm bells – if and when they came. To new
arrivals – if and when they came. To all dawn raids on shoes,
spats amongst residents, all the moments that led to the big
bang. Boundless inquisition, that was Watt's metier. He was
always to-ing and fro-ing through doors, staring through
windows, looking under beds, the linen store was a great
favourite for his investigations. As the lantern-jawed auxiliary
suggested, yes, it was providence (how else to put it?) that Watt
was alive or, certainly, not worse hit. On the day in question,
Watt's ears had been pricked at Murphy's early arrival. He'd held
back for a while, but not for long. A personal investigation was
called for, a synthesis of time and place, which must surely lead
directly to an official investigation. What else can we do? the
veteran auxiliary asks, jutting his jaw, his skin lined and as dusty
as parchment. The answer to this query? Do nothing – are you
deaf? He repeated this refrain, a good number of times, with
disdain, and I wanted to say that Watt was fine: So, shut up! Watt
was fine; entirely, and unusually. Watt's own proportion was,
and would remain, intact. Such subtlety is not easily explained,
his loyalty to his ward-mate, Murphy, was a given.

What if Watt'd been killed with that?

Dr. Mallory Jacobs is the duty doctor and he is whispering,
repeating the earlier passage of talk, neglecting to mention
diversion. He is responding to an earlier question: Who, tell me,
is not altogether a real being? Tell me. The more than obvious

question gets short shrift: Absolutely not. Are you out of your mind? He'd referred to Casualty. Not called – alarms were not raised, he stops. Enough with the negatives. The word arrives: Stitches – that's it, Molloy says. With hardly the words out of her mouth: Out of the question, out of. He halts, breathes. The good sister looks distraught, no doubt about it. There's no need for x-rays, he's fine. They'll strike me off, he replies: Are you asking me … I can't just. He stops. Do nothing, she wants to say, but that is not her meaning. Stitches is all that's …, she says it again. Stitches, man – stitches! Struck off or some other such talk is repeated and ignored. She says: Haven't we done enough? As though this brought some further clarity to Murphy's disorienting act. He ignores her question, imagining it to be merely rhetorical and seriously annoying. Sutures? he asks, as though this limited procedure was his idea. There were no positives here – haven't we done enough? Yes, she said: Stitches, she says, saying the word, *Stitches*, reverberating in his head, says the word to himself, but aloud: *Stitches*. Yes, he says, repeating her words: Stitches, but not aloud this time. Not aloud. Nothing was proved with this word: *Yes*. That will be it, Mallory. She calls him by his first name, she reaches out her hand. Mallory, their outside name: Mallory. They'll take him away, that will be it. Taken out of our hands. If we can't care for him here. Stitches? He responds again: His head is wide open, for god's … She stops him with a single hand, pressing it to his chest. Rampton, then. Rampton? You know full well. Rampton. That word, shared between them; that one particular word: Rampton. The name that no knowledge can circumscribe; it is, what? Don't force it, he wants to say. Rampton? This time he says the word as a question. This singular word hinders logic; the tales of horror are legion. Rampton, she says. Stitches then, he replies. Stitches it is.

X

Deep within the forest, the trees there hummed and whispered and rustled a song so harmonious that soon the knight was lulled into a state of indecision. "Come back," he calls out, his voice rising, imagining he sees lively unnamed creatures and other hiddenfolk darting beyond and between the columns of sturdy bronze trunks.

"Do not be afraid." Are these the words he hears? And then all at once he perceives the world beyond these ever-increasing, fleeting creatures. "May I" he asks, "pass?" An inner voice, perhaps, nothing more. Unsure and unsafe in its sounds, but with both eyes open, he saw, but not nearly as clearly as he'd like. "Is there something there?" he says, hearing himself whisper: "I am not afraid," he cries out, aware, and then unsure of his whereabouts. "I am not." He remains undisturbed by the patterns fashioned by the dappled light filtering through overlapping branches. "I see you," he says, "I do." But just as quickly would these swiftest of woodland creatures disappear from sight, suddenly halting, then glancing back. "You will aid me, is that it?" he asks: "Is that your purpose, little fellows? That I should take your lead?" He advances, flowing fast as one who is carried away by the sounds of rapturous music. "Is this a dream?" he asks. For the whole world seemed to have dissolved in this early morning light; figures loom large, emerging, disappearing – gone. "Is it possible that I have had a thousand years of seeking?" he whispers, watching a rent stitched back in time before his very eyes, a tear that somehow seems to flutter, yet fleeting and fierce, coating his mind with the traces of all the years that have passed and are passing. "How to see time," he says, "passing?" He has surely seen the moment whole, returning again and again, matters and deceits; these deceits matter a great deal. "Don't they all?" he replies. "Uncle? He is no uncle to me," he insists. He has seen them up close: the young man – the young man – the young man – is but a boy again, brought forward, or reversed, into these long-anticipated partings. A sharp blade at his side will rend the surface of indecision, he will strike at so many profound and intractable transformations; yes, despite all interventions, he will do it. "Has all of this been preserved, in my heart?" he calls out but, suddenly, there is no one there to hear him: "Am I the sky itself, drawn to it, or by it, together and unified? The blue of the sky, I say. Am I not set over and against it? This blue." Beyond the shadowed forest the sea is vast and deep; it is blue, speckled with white horses and sails. The ecru dune-fell sand arises as much as it perishes. Here. And there. Swept and sweeping by the spiky tufts of green then blue then golden grass: marram, bent and wild-rye. In this dreaming speed he eventually finds his way across the waters, over the shimmering sea as clear as glass, and onto the island, standing proud for all to see: "Black rock," he calls, breathless, "the castle atop." He is hot and he is tired, but soon enough respite must come. Through the metalled bronze of these indomitable trees – "These pillars" – holding back the dark, he begins to see white light. For the first time, he sees beyond the dense forest, for the first very time. At once, it seems unreal: the light is not white, but washed in a deep blue dye. His Barbary horse steps onto the hot yellow strand. "There it is." The young man blinks before the expanse of wide water. "But where is the huge black rock?" There is only the sea to see. "Whether there is substance and truth in it, I do not know; I saw but was not seen. And now …" The young man dismounts. Holds his hand up to his eyes, shielding them from the harsh glare. "The sea," he says, "remains; the sea." Behind him, before him, the shapes they make, some by argumentation, others by some other design, hard yet ephemeral, clear as glass. The sea, blue, deep, and streaked in white, but, O, at last, the dark stone, the promised rock, a spirit form clarifies out of the glassiness. "There," he shouts out, suddenly. "Yes, there really is something there," he calls into his horse's ear, "all of this is preserved in my heart." The grey Barb winnows, throws back its head, the slate grey mane itself a wintry wave; the sea's grey desert, is but a thought. "A huge dark mass; that rock." And then upon the top of the island, something true emerges: "There it is," he says. "At last, the huge black rock." Through the softest white sea-mist a castle is constructed before his very eyes, boulder by boulder. Or so it seems. Figured into towers and chapels and pawns and so move rook to square next to king and king to other side of rook: "That's the game," he says, "the chess board is ready," he whispers, "and I am here to seize the day." Black rooks circle at the summit, turning in acrobatic passage, a wheel of fortune, perhaps, and there are choughs, blacker than black, red sharp beaks, calling out to the young man: "One and all, one and all," they seem to say, and there too, the battalions of jackdaws, grey bibbed, heading *en masse* to land, only to swoop up again, and up once more, to puffs of white cloud dotted in blue skies.

"May I pass?" he asks, then waits: "Nothing. Then I presume the affirmative." An inner voice, perhaps, nothing more. Unsure and unsafe in its sounds, but with both eyes open he saw, but not as clearly as he'd like.

But there is yet some distance to go, he must go easy on his tiring steed. "Is that white light? True, at the time, I did not bespeak your name." The dream returns the sequence; one thing leads to another; he is surrounded again by the dark inducements of bronze metalled trees. The forest prevails a second time, and once again he fades. We must go on; the day is still young. From the forest roots which formed knotty stepping stones, he wanders out onto the warm yellow strand, his horse held this time by the reins. Now he's facing the sea as though for the first time. "It's still blue," he says, "it's nothing but blue. Yet I knew you better than the blue, better than I have known men." But where is the black rock? That question should have sprung to mind. Once it was ever true, but all that's left is preserved in one's heart. He comes to a standstill, sets his beloved horse free, and rests a while. From the enchanted forest, he could just make out the murmuration of soft sounds and delights, promising so much to his weary mind. "I was reared by the euphony of the rustling copse – when I was a boy." There, it was, in the distance, percolating, bubbling, waters. Now he must rest before he falls. In the diminishment of this celestial heat, the light was dimming from setting sun to make, in time, dark light. "Night is coming," he whispers, "but where is day?" He lies down on the soft sand; warmth enters his body. His eyes are closing, the lids becoming heavier and heavier and, before he could know, he succumbs to deeper and yet deeper sleep. Dune-fallen sand darkens to harder soil, blossom littered paths from past promises. The trees are canopy overhead, forming a measureless height. "Are these disquieting thoughts," he says, or hears: *Not you, his mother, nor his father, does he resemble*; not said, but thought, perhaps – or dreamt? The young man drops, inert for a moment, turns to his side. "Yes, it is possible, your joy," comes to mind, quietly, softly, one word connecting two places, and then another word: "These things are still within me, all embracing," The rooms, the towers, the well and the woman, all his wants, all his needs, his arrogance drives him far: Or a goddess, spirally sent, staircases that ascend to the castle keep. "The room by day," arising or perishing, "seems to me," no longer known nor looked out upon, the trees rustle in night breeze and bronze darkness, occluding pins of stars, darkness deepening on high – "Little to him, who wants more, the wild one."

Light fades from his eyes. All the corners never fully lit, drained of pictures; there only to provide nothing in return. Are you there? Nothing …

"May I pass?" he asks: "Well?" He waits. Nothing. "Then I presume the affirmative." An inner voice, perhaps, whispering less. Unsure and unsafe in its sounds, but with both eyes open he saw, but not as clearly as he should. For the third time he is returned to the forest and espies the unnamed creatures and other hiddenfolk: "I have seen you before," he says, "and before," his words are hardly audible. "You exist in another place," that he knows, "but when?" he asks, "and how?" He is once again astride his horse. He is yet again returned to the forest, exhausted, soon to fall heavily to sleep; he must dismount. He drops to the ground; soft, forgiving land. "I am here," he replies to the silent earth – at last, "I am here, in the untroubled light," he says, as though responding to a question. "Now the time of day has passed, the jewelled night's here." The soil was easy and plump and there were large silver stocks and crooked branches that had snapped and cracked and fallen from the trees hereabouts; from the horse chestnuts and the English yew, from the white and the black Lombardy poplars; from the common oak to the royal oak. These are the skeletons of trees, peopled only by woodland birds, presently still, appearing to us as humans might, resting after weary toil. Not in the least distressing, these wind-busted limbs are company for the young knight. He closes his blue eyes beneath the night-reddened space of sky; the sky's the canopy which must surely reach across the whole expanse of this sylvan wood. Bits of porous yellow pour through the overlapping branches, landing like sovereign change. There, as he lay, the ground seemed strewn with flat gold coins, but if you made any attempt to pluck one up would simply quiver and vanish and appear elsewhere. Suddenly, the last of the light was all about him, dimming, hiding, and hosting shadows. He runs his hand along the earth to test the mettle of his mind. "It's there," he said, "I can feel the soil in my hands." He is gripped by death, he sees it, and alone must fear it. A canopy overhead, as though blessed, forms a measureless height. Are these disquieting thoughts, this shifting space, lost and searched for – *time*; the young man drops, inert for a bit, leans to his side. "Is it possible? Yes," if only the world would quake, quietly, softly, one word connecting two scenes, and then another world: "These things are still; nothing shifts within me." And then another. These shaded rooms, the darkest towers, the well reflects two faces, one a prince, the other's no woman at all – "or a goddess gone from sight, to serpent," to spirally sent staircases that ascend to the castle keep: "The room by night," arising or perishing, "seems to me," no longer known nor looked out upon, the trees rustle in night breeze, occluding pins of stars, darkness is nigh, deepening on high, wrenching his heart.

"I'm here," she whispers in his ear. The fair lady is wearing a veil, her features can be just made out beneath the lustre of pearlescent silk.

He feels her warm breath and hears her soft voice. How he longs for this dream to commence, longing for the fair lady to come. "Here I am," she says, again, placing a hand so gently upon his cheek. "Do not be afraid," she says, "I am but a messenger." He sees the boy again, not the young man he now is, but small and weakly: "Am I but a boy?" he says, "am I?" He sits up. Has he heard this before? "Yes," the fair lady replies, referring to his concern, "you are but a boy. One day you will be the finest knight of all knights." She speaks of the man he would become: "The one who rides a grey Barbary mare." She smiles and her lips are precious pink and her teeth are ever so white, her face is lustrously silver. He is smiling and he is shy: "Concentrate," he tells himself, this injunction: to become fully aware of what she is saying. "Concentrate," he repeats his word. "You are the one who must travel to the unknown world. Say nothing," she insists. "You are chosen to bridge the great divisions – fissures," her voice deepens as though a man were voicing her concerns. "Humanity has developed differently there. Through thoughts of magic and multitudes of worldly spectres and not simply through the terrestrial power of the plough and the chariot, not simply through the shepherd's toil but through the machinations of the spectres and serpents. Do you comprehend, my dearest boy?" The truthful answer was an emphatic, "No." He struggled to hold on to a single thread of what she was saying. In short, he did not take at all well to the mysterious manner of this sullen woman. "These sudden details may come together within me? Is that it?" he asked himself, "and who are these spectres and serpents?" How can I, a mere boy, take issue with these great divisions? Two to one, you mean? But he says nothing, he dared not. He feels as though he cannot breathe. He feels as rigid as a board; deliciously soft he feels the hand upon his head. His eyes cannot move and his mouth is not quite smiling. If one of his eyes had been open, he might have used it to gaze across at her. How can he speak? How can he see? He is a faithful youth and he listens intently to what is being said. "There will be much for you to learn, my lord. In the fulness of time, you will venture from your own true land, through the forest you will fly, and then to the place where the pool-nymphs reside. Have you not seen so much in the queen's chamber?"

"Mother?" he inquires. "What of Mother? Mother?"

"The tapestry, child. You know well, do you not? Have you not made the moments merge? You're near and far, or up in arms, or hidden behind walls, everywhere, even in the facts of nowhere, do you see? Yet, with a tighter hold, she says: "You must do as you are bid?" Only then will she come to you in dream, dear one. All the characteristics of his mother's face are present in in his own. But the fair lady is not referring to his own mother; she means the young woman hidden behind the ebony chest.

That beautiful lady ended off in a snake's tail, pursued
in time by the gaze of a young knight.

"She," he says: "O, yes, she." So keen, he is, so easily losing focus. "O," the fair lady responds, reading his thoughts or words, her breath blows out the veil: "Yes, she is a beautiful young woman, as you well know. But what you do not know is that she sits and watches and waits by the holy well on an island far away; a maiden with night-dark hair to her waist, an obscure daze flows fast as a shimmering river from a halo of Convolvulus, delicate sapphire blue Linum blooms sprinkled with pink Cosmea. She waits." No, he could not move. He struggles to breathe, to hear, fighting to shift his head from side to side, to wake himself up, to return him to his inflammable heart. He feels as though he's awake; his heart races. He sees himself standing there. As he was, as a youth; he is his twelve-year-old self, or thirteen, walking solemnly in the grounds of his father's Green Palace. He is speaking, he is reciting the words, he is wandering in the plantation in the moments before the sun sets in the wonderful west. "And the stars were freedom," he announces. "All of this you did, in the end, just as it was required of you," but no sound issues from his words, as though he himself renounces them. His eyes open, he sees clearly and then, all at once, he can speak. "What's your name, fair lady?" he asks. This familiar yet unfamiliar face before him. "You must not ask me questions, my young knight," she responds in kind. Held in a halo of light, no present ground is given; she is a matter of pure place, and she is smiling out of the ambivalent mist. The lines at her eyes crinkle with such perfect kindness – "Are you still unsure? You seem unclear? You ask of me one simple question: 'What am I to do?' Isn't that it?" Was that the question? The young man shifts his position. He is leaning up, staring before him at the light that breaks through the darkening night – "So this is dark light?" he says. The bronzed trees circle about him; they are the sentries standing guard as the dew sparkles, falling as silver dust. "Or shall I go?" he says, "or where?" He is unused to such confessions which are not in keeping with his need for solitude. "Your destined meeting place? Your future life? Out of one's own-most possibility, dear heart, there must be unity." She pauses, smiles: Can he hear me? she wonders, can he? He is enamoured by what surrounds him, her silent mind is questioning. The fair lady smiles again before continuing: "There must be a meeting, first and foremost, as you well know – Oriane is waiting for you, my lord." A shocking scream echoes through the forest darkness. "O, what lies – what lies beneath it all?" he calls out. The young man's heart thumps fast. "What is it that howls so?" he asks. The lady, for just a moment, looks disorientated. Her calm drops, her voice falters: "I am called, my lord. Or, yes, or, perhaps … it is us, us … it is us; that urges us on, that insists upon the end to come. *We* are called. There is more, I must tell you. I have but little time." The young man turns to look: his horse is silent; in the dark, sleeping, all but invisible. But what is that whispering he can hear, the gentle fetters, whispering, whispering, incessantly. Then that roar, or screaming, through the blackness. "If only I could lie back," he says, "make this stop. There is an end," he says, "there must be."

> *The lady is lamp lit, but the halo is hardly made so*
> *simply, she is formed by pure light and, yet, in darkness*
> *she ever dwells. "Please, I wish you would go."*

He would sink back, and no longer speak this night, dwindle, and fall headlong from one moment to the next. Yes, fall back, again, and disappear into death; fall fast, again, onto the softness of the damp earth. But looking up, his eyes are not greeted by luminous stars but by the eyes of the fair lady bathed in yellowing light. So veiled is she that her features were lost entirely to his view. O, this lady is incessant with all her talk. "What rush is there," he thinks, her haste is not hampered with speed. "And you will find her beyond the forest of light and darkness." He's momentarily lost; who awaits me – who? She smiles, he notices the etiolation at the mouth, she fades: "Don't be afeared, young prince, for it is there you will see the island and the castle known as *Sparkling Waters*. Remember this: The causeway rises and leads across the sea. Hear me," her voice is raised. "*Hear me*, before it is too late. Here me," she calls. "Get up, listen." He leans back onto his elbows, showing certain attention. "The castle causeway rises out of the sea. Hear me," she calls, again. "If you are seen from some distance, you will appear as though upon the waves, you walk like a god. But you must wait for the perfect hour: the yellow and silver granite rocks of the causeway will rise high as the tide falls. As the tide falls, mind you. You hear? Then and only then may safe passage be yours. But beware not to cross it too soon or too late or the Sea Serpent will take you. Yes, have I not said? For you, dear boy, are its nemesis!" The scream, by reply, issues through the blackness, it rips and rents the housed darkness. "The Sea Serpent is waiting to devour you, to tear you asunder. The creature will take you deep beneath the treacherous waves; under and profound, going under, into the remnants of lost time: a hidden forest, blackened and calcified and reclaimed by the seas of centuries past. Beneath, and into the darkest depths, you'll decline. It is there that the erstwhile forest creatures lie in wait. Not for your devoured body, but to rip out all spirit; all spirit is lost along with your flesh. These creatures are no longer benign as once they were. Their wish is simple: they will take you into the Sea Serpent's dark waters and trap you in the hidden forest for all that remains of time. There you will suffer as though all thoughts and all memories have been erased from your mind. There you will dwell in memories of nothingness and nought known, forever and a day. "But, strong, young soldier," the fair lady continued, "if you cross safely, you will enter the castle known as *Sparkling Waters* and you will find there the woman of your curiosity: Oriane. You know of whom I speak?" He lies back again, the earth is calling his body, he cannot resist. "O, she is held, imprisoned, kept shut up against her will. Hear me, young one, hear me. Oriane awaits your arrival – only you can break this enchantment – only you. Do not be afeared, young one, you will see her only as a beautiful young woman." He rises upon his elbows, his lips move: "*Only* as a beautiful young woman? What can you mean, fair lady?" His attention is fixed, but the veiled lady is in a hurry, too preoccupied to respond. "Instead," she says, breathing deeply, her voice becoming hoarse, "you must swear to kiss whoever or whatever you find in the castle keep. Do you hear me?" she implores him. "Three times," she says "for it is only through the kiss that we shall bring peace to what was and is and ever shall be – each one a kiss: was, is, will be – entwined, unfolding, to be." There is a moment of silence. He breathes deeply, unaware of the long pause. "Three times?" he replies, eventually. Again, she continues: "Have no fear, the fair lady is not seriously ill," she says, referring to herself as though she observes her from afar. But perplexity only builds, hardly lessened by her own appearance. The fair lady's lips now seem drawn and blue, her cheeks sunken, colour begins to ebb to shadow. Her veil hides nought of time "Yes," she continues, breathing fast, "your soft pink mouth must touch the other's lips. That is the task: Will you swear it, my young lord?" The young man is now kneeling, he is raised up. He puts his hand on his heart and makes to speak, his lips trembled, and then he begins to say something. "Kiss her, you say?" The fair lady begins to fade, aging before his very eyes, impatient, she puts her finger to his lips: "Speak not now, but remember: before you kiss, the truth is within glass. You have seen its end." Overhead, but unseen, the suddenness of night becomes sprinkled with stars broken only occasionally by a string of silver cloud. Sky itself speaks of evening, one lit in the moment by the blooded hue of a crescent moon as it picked off the red light of Mars.

The young knight awakes and opens his eyes
upon the enchanted forest as before.

His eyes open and a new registration is forthcoming. All feeling of carefree dreaming is replaced with a hankering for home. "Our own oak," he says, putting his palms to his eyes. "I spent most of the day in the grounds," he says, but to whom? His words have no hearers, or none that he can see. What's worse, he is nowhere near the Green Palace. He recalls the distant past, his dwelling alone, no brother to roam with, not a sister to tease. All alone. He almost begins to cry: "Mother," he says, "died so young." The young man's horse comes near, snorting soft-felt steam from his nostrils. "Dear father, why did you do it? Why?" Little more than a decade after the anniversary of his mother's death, ten years plus one, that was it – perhaps he was twelve – or thirteen summers past. "O, father why?" The king could no longer be held up: "O, my father, to drown like that, in the cold depths of the lake." Pining, they called it, but after so much time. Perhaps it was the remorse of the survivor: "His majesty, alone like that, and so young. To lose her – *like that*," Mistress Bridges had said, the last part under her breath. These are the words he'd heard. "The queen bled to death," Mistress Bridges had said with some embellishment. The moment of his birth was a little tear that had rent the surface of that crimson pool. "The queen whispered something in the king's ear," Mistress Bridges explained to the kitchen maids. "I know not what. O, and then an awful cry." As she held her baby son in her hands, the queen's eyes were stark, fearful of what she saw pouring across the tapestry. The queen's eyes widened as she looked over the expanse of her chamber to the east wall ahead: "No," she shouts at the rest of eternity, at the patterns which thread one last picture. "Not that," she cries, "not my own true child." But there is more, holding her blooded babe in arms, slick with falling tears, her mouth moves, but the words are but whispers – if only she could dash the child against the wall unto its death. But she has not the strength to do so. Her breath weakens, her eyes begin to blacken. The king leans in, seeing the horror in her eyes, assuaging her, straining to hear her last words: "Death, dear … You, love, yes … water, dearest, the water," she pauses, her face rigid in fear or is it pain? And then, with the softest of whispers in his ear, she speaks her final words: "… *Murder … Murder … Murder*." Her last breath extols the virtue of herself and her child. That is what the king thinks: "I hear you; I hear you, love of mine." The king calls out to her cold dead eyes, shining and radiant still, staring wide across at the unmoving tapestry. "Her last words?" He demands attention from those who are gathered: "Her last words were." He pauses, he is aware of death's demand: "Hear me," he says, "hear me. Her last words were," and then he pauses, standing straight. "*Mother … Mother … Mother …*"

CHAPTER TWO
TIME PASSED

I

Click, goes the machine life: Click. Click, it goes – Click …

The door auto-locks. Clicks again, then again. The water rushes in with a disturbing whoosh. Malone places their hands upon the circular glass. The look of confusion hardly cuts it, trapped as Malone is within the confines of an industrial washing machine. They are not yet floating, and the drum is yet to turn. Their spectacles are damaged, one of the temple arms is missing; the face is bleeding from the blows received about the head. As they say, the dawn will not be always rosy, but the coming day is far from mind and matter at this moment in time. The head is held at an odd angle: it is an even odder shape seen through the concaved glass. We have to do something, Molloy says, but she was muttering to herself: We must. Do … she runs out of steam. Do, she tries again. The face looking out is as white as snow. A stubborn red stain trickles down from a gash in Malone's forehead; the hair is bleeding, that's what it looks like. The eyes look a little beady, steadying the gaze upon the outsiders. How will we …? Molloy says, halting as quickly as she had begun. (What? How will we what, exactly?) She neglects to finish what she was about to say. (*Explain* all this? Is that what Molloy means? Account for it?) Malone is just staring out of this enormous tin-can with their palms held fast and flat against the glass window: *Or if I am not yet*, must come to mind: *I shall be when I cease to be*. Some such expression. Guppy is now staring at the occupant with his two feet on *terra firma*, looking far from fragile. What have you done, little friend? Murphy says, his fingers stemming the flow of blood to his own face. An eye gouged. No emotion is shown, nothing; Guppy just stares, impassively. The still blue eyes look as though they've been skinned. He watches what might have been; he watches *as if* he'd lived another life, *as if* he'd been there, *as if* in another time and place. *Why doesn't it thunder at me? Why is it so quiet?* Perhaps these are the words, perhaps not. Whatever he thinks, he thinks.

Are we not capable of truth? The drum suddenly spins round, half-filled with water, unmarred by detergent, but not by blood which makes the water, well, a tad rosy. What was once the head is now legs, triangulated in a frog mode, and then the head returns to the top, looking wet, weird, and cross-eyed. It stops, a still life. An odd halting, the machine moans, sounding somewhat human, as if it is lifting a great weight. Malone's blooded face from the blows of the rolling pin is presently washed clean. The spectacles are now missing. They look odd without them, even odder in a washing machine. There is still a chance – of survival, I mean, but Molloy's merely muttering the words. The moment passes. (If only this, if only that – easy to say, Molloy. *But let me complete my ...* What, Molloy? Sentence?) The electricity was not shut off and neither was the glass broken with the rolling pin to hand – Molloy's hand. Nothing is said, or done. Meanest words, and needless, from the meanest of spirits. Malone is dying. End of.

The machine just carries on doing its job as
machines do: Click ... Click.

As they walked away, a muffled sound could be heard. A name, a silent name: *Mimim*, Malone says; muffled, yes, definitely: *Me me-am*, she says, as though it came from the drowned world. (It sounded like *me* and *am*, or something like it – who knows. It all happened so quickly, Molloy recalls, signalling something disturbing under her breath.) The lights are not shut off, they were dulled from the start in night-lights, an odd nocturnal shadowed place filled with vast machinery, whirring time away in clicks. How often does the strange become normalised? The person who walks beside you is merged with some external reality, leaving you to press on alone, conscious now of the darkness all around you, and the person who was once the light is now a thing separated from the mind, or the eye, now that they are as far away as can be, as though they floated up, up, up, into the night-sky. All nonsense, it must be, otherwise it would be hopeless. There is no time here, but I use the expression All this talk about what's light and what's dark. Our eyes and ears are fast sealed through numbness, or the pressure on them, that intangible stuff that blocks and blinds, or the unconscious realised almost with conscious effort, but only ever almost.

Me me Am. (Is that what Malone was saying? she asked,
Me ... Am? God, she said, I'm gasping for a fag.)

The light was dimming and the night nurse was yet to arrive. Camier had been at work in the dorm. When he came out into the day ward, Malone had disappeared. That was all there was to say. Gone, he said, who knew where? What could you see down the long corridor, he'd say. Nothing. Then doorbell rang, he'd explain, repeating the words: The doorbell rang. When he answered the door, a large man was standing there. Murphy! Camier called out, not a little hint of feigned surprise to his voice. What've you got there? he continued. Murphy was smiling, broadly, and in his arms, he carried a younger man, who seems to be but a kid. *Found me a little angel*, he says to me, laughing that deep and sonorous laugh of his. The skin by his left eye is torn, a long scratch too deep to bleed but, for now, Murphy is preoccupied with other matters. *Do you know, Camier?* he says to me, serious like: *This world works in mysterious ways? From going to and fro in the earth, and from walking up and down in it.* Camier let them in, that's what he'll say. Closing the door as they pass, he calls out: *And I only am escaped alone to tell thee.* Not another single word was spoken. Camier returns to the office. The night nurse soon enough turns up, flying into a kind of controlled panic. Following the intelligence of the lost, the *absconding* residents, but soon settles after a number of deep breaths. Malone was still nowhere to be seen. All their belongings are there in the office, a small holdall, a light rain coat, and the all-important bulky keys to the medicine cabinet.

The door was open, he said, *wide open*, Camier continued. *He'd closed it and waited for Malone to come back. And then Murphy, I thought he'd turned in; then Guppy. Yes, totally strange. No, no real explanation. Murphy can't recall; Guppy? Well, you know ...* What could he do? Camier waited. He's written some notes, he flicked at the pages in the log. It's here, he replied. Short staffed, as usual; Mercer was off. Phoned in sick, he'd explained. *What's next?* he said to the night nurse – *Search me; what do I know about procedure?* The night nurse has the phone receiver in his hand. Who would've thought to look in the laundry? Nobody was sure, but no stone was left unturned. (I was just coming back, Molloy explained. I'd been out for a couple of after-work drinks. Yes, Savage and me. She's flushed, not a little red. She continues: Well, I was sure I could hear something, Molloy said. As I passed; some strange noise from the other side of the laundry doors. She stops, puts her hand to her face. No, nobody else, just Malone – in that massive washing machine. How could such a thing happen? she said – a total mystery.) It will not be long before Watt – still bandaged in comical fashion – gets wind of things. The following morning, he knows immediately something is up. His attitude to the men in blue (there are, of course, women present, but not in this shade of blue) is exemplary (Feck's sake, he calls out. Been in the wars, one of the constabulary calls back, tentatively, but surprisingly confident. Fecking wars, policeman. Feck's sake, police. Right you are: Wars. Watt continues to repeat himself, overwhelmed by the excitement, making do with saluting them, lifting his hand to his bandaged head. And Haines heads for Guppy's vacant bed in search of shoes and solace.) Gorne, Watt says. Gorne. His words are misconstrued. Not for long, Murphy says, puffing on a pipe, an eye-patch over his left eye: Guppy will come back. I swear it, the other never catches hold, he says, I was never truly delivered from him. I lost, I am he who was so easily caught. Here I am. But Watt is not talking about Guppy, he means Malone – what will he do without his dear Malone? Williams knows well – he's been to sing and his song is so haunting – already he misses Malone too. Where is everybody? the kitchen porter calls out, carrying her tray of elevenses: Is this unusual, she says, halting her step for a moment, for the time of year? Savage calls out: Murphs, she says, you look like a pirate, she laughs, holding the buffer steady in strong sinewy arms: That's it, she says, a pirate. Murphy lets out smoke from his mouth before speaking: All at sea, he says, dear Savage, that is what it is. Savage likes the crack: You're missing your parrot, Murphy, she calls again. Fine words, he replies, and me ship. The ship is lost at sea. That's what they're telling me. Rocks and things, Savage.

II

*The trees hereabouts are weaving, but somehow silently so; the
strings of white cloud pass overhead, tying about the castle
keep; the sea, amorphous, is rippling away in grey lines; the
yellow strip above is burnished, gilded softly in solid gold;
the curtain's fallen, that's what it looks like, drawn almost
to its fullest extent; a spirit of promise still remains between
silver-blue seas and the viridescence of serpentine rock.*

"Here on this stone ground, have we not walked this path
before?" There is no response. "Hear me, snake? Here again? Are
you deaf?" Catching up to his guide, who leads the way, hissing
occasionally, as though by reply, then striking his snake-thin
tongue to left and right. "Here, again? Hail, snake. Answer me, I
say." The larger-than-life grass snake is, at times, hard to find.
"Surely, snake. We cannot walk this way again." The guide turns
its hissing head, looks at the young man, then shifts its
serpentine coils: "Come, pretty little prince," he hisses, forking
his snake-thin tongue, scenting, then winding along and away.
"We are very nearly there." Looks back by way of indication;
looks ahead, and away. The grass snake's locomotion is
beguiling. The prince looks up from the ancient pathway, and
feels he might faint. The granite was hewn from the cliffs
around the coastline, brought up on land-sleds pulled by mules,
aided by men famed for the sweat of their brows and the blood of
their lives. There is a drawbridge over the stream which seems to
be a folly. "Why, a man could so easily jump it," the prince calls,
remembering once there was laughter: "It could hardly keep out
a cat," his mirth rising, "or, for that matter, a hare." Pitiful chance
it would have, if there were a marauding force of men intent on
death and pillage, on decapitation. The snake guide slithering on
ahead, pays but little heed to the pretty prince's excitement. "The
grass snake's ahead," he says, "always leads – no respite: if only I
knew where to find her, I might strike out sooner at her pretty
head." Sometimes the snake guide's so far away; sometimes the

knight's near enough to step on its tail – suddenly hearing its hissing by way of censure, or warning. But then the young man falls back: "To go on squirming forever," he says, "at the end of time." Pauses for a moment, speaks yet again: "What a joy to know where one is," he shouts out, his voice echoes, a momentary return, and there it is, over again: "Without being there," he cries into the world – *without being there*. The snake guide seems unimpressed. They walk on through the steep gardens, perched high and mighty, terraced, and super-verdant. All variegated as though undefined: Here are yellow-greens and there are blue-greens, and then one sees greens with yellow lines running at the perimeters. These are like spears coming up from the very earth, and there is flax of greens and purples, and great spikes emanate to twice the height of a man, and the maritime pines, usually so scarce on the ground in this world, cling fast to the cliffs with shallow roots. They are not alone; we all cling to our roots, heedlessly. They are a pattern of plenty, a patch here, an interminable shadow there, the rising or setting of suns, freer, faster, jarring: "Better decipher what I shall now describe," he says to the softest of the breeze. One sees the ancient oaks, the sycamores' acer hands, and beech trees' ovate leaves; one sees those bars of silver-white trunks of birch, so at home with shade-loving hornbeams, with their brown-grey twigs; one sees over there the ash near a ribbon of stream and, well yes, there are countless others to be seen: it would take a mortal's life to pinpoint them all; one could do better than to sit in the canopy in a hammock high-up in the pale blue sky, and contemplate the abundance of life here. All changing, at all moments: the light the dark, the light again, as mating hares jump and ruck, and red squirrels dart along in any possible direction. "Look," he calls out, "there are rabbits hereabouts – and deer." As the sun skirts the earth, distinctly, turning, turning, round this celestial planet, in an arc of light, and shade – what? The flowers encroach, and seem intent on populating the paths upon which they walk. English bluebells in high necked green leaves, hyacinthine powder bunches, crocosmias' Satan red pitching for the very heavens, and their Montbretian cousins, the acid red-orange flowers lit from within, the pale green foliage striking high too. Then the spires of hollyhock and purple Agapanthus with bowls of Hydrangeas in purples and blues and creamy whites larger than a snowball. And there is the Gunnera with leaves as big as a child's six strides, and there in sheltered hollows, the young man sees reddish toothed stems that remind him of a ferocious rhubarb, and here and there sporadic violets and Anemones. "And … and, well, everything, and look," he says, "just across there, do you see there?" The young man is guided, silently, but the trees are not deaf; they have words of advice for the young stranger. "Beware, O knight," call out the trees, by whispers and murmurs: "Your life is in danger. O young one: Beware." They whisper, rustling their warnings of the path and the perils ahead. "Show yourself another way," they say, "beware. Just this once." But the young man cannot, or will not, listen; he looks across at the valley of shifting streams and moon leaves, and smoking pools and hot springs that emanate clouds of steam from the wet, white slip. "The day is still young," he says, as the sun skirts the earth, reaching the midway point of late afternoon and coming darkness: "Isn't it?" The thermal spring is too tempting. Without so much as a care in the world, he strips off his clothes such little ado and, naked as a new-born, he slowly steps into a bath of wonderfully welcoming water. Hot, he enters gingerly; he is half afraid of being boiled alive, but he needn't have worried. "O, snake," he calls out to his guide, "it is so very, very, warm." He splashes the snake, laughs again, then lets his head fall beneath the steam. "From where does such heat come?" he shouts, lifting his head up and out of the water. But the snake just coils up in a piece of shade. The young man closes his eyes and rests in the beautifully warm pool, fed first, most surely, from the centre of the earth. Surrounded by pinpricks of colour, he is, and the world is simply that – hues of every note and notion and nothing more. He closes his eyes. Birds flutter over and ahead and look down at the young man submerged in the water. "It is him," they whistle and sing across the expanse of sky: "Yes, it is – he will come." Eyes closing, resting within the water, a golden glow of a halo about his head, "he is coming." The curls of his hair floating on the water's surface are spectacular white swimming snakes: "He has come."

A lapping about his chest, and a breeze nags
at the trees; it's getting nippy.

How the hour glows, do you not feel it? The flame is dropping into the west, the pollens which drifted are at rest, there is only the silence as the sea soughs. The interlacing elements drown out the whispering trees, a conflagration of numbers and curves and blocks and triangles restore the prince's hearing: "Is that the sound of falling?" he calls out, "or quaking?" The leaves are falling, fanning out, and sun-dried, they suddenly rise again in a twisting sphere of fate as if devoid of all meaning or purpose. Instead of stillness, which might counteract the lip-service of the trees, the breeze fights its own battle. Is the day still young? The elements are under sway from the power of another. The trees fight shy of any such capitulation, for they have been silent long enough. No mortal has passed this way since some were sapling, forked, pliant and nearest, or catkin, harmless, loose and stiff. The duke was no such mortal; seduced and drenched in crystal glass, only death and decay await him. This young man, simple and true, is in mortal, serpentine danger; he is deaf to their entreaties: "Beware, O knight," call out the trees, by whispers and murmurs: "Your life is in danger, O young one: Beware." Breeze cools the young man in the pool, wakes him from his slumber as trees are stilled and silent. A slither, the boy hears, a hissing sound, from where? He opens his eyes. All around him the colours have altered and are now bathed in a golden red and orange wash. "The sun has not yet set, no," he says. Oriane is calling, but her voice is yet to reach him. The prince jumps from the still-steaming water and dresses quickly. Whether it was the abundance of his material which excited him is hard to say; it is even harder to look away. "Where am I now?" he asks, noticing for the first time a formidable oak door. His guide, the large grass snake, appears impatient, his snake-thin tongue strikes out and in, out again, over and over; he coils, lingers, slithers back, then forth in agitated fashion. The prince will soon enough pay heed. He turns and the snake guide is there, risen, staring into the young man's eyes. "Am I to follow?" Surely that is the creature's mission? To bring this to a head? "What hides beyond that door?" he asks, but the reply is a side-winding silence. He'll follow the snake guide along the path, passing by the flowers, some of which begin to close, content to put to sleep for the oncoming night. The smell of stock begins to emanate, night-scented and extreme upon its full arrival at dark-fall. He looks down from where he has come, down upon the sylvan wood, down to where they passed the whispering trees, loquacious, but unheard or, worse still, unheeded. They are silenced, drowned out by the breeze's susurration, blowing all around: "Sshhh, sshhh." His eyes are wide open, as though he sees what he sees for the first time. "How have I reached these rooms," he asks of the larger-than-life grass snake. The prince has passed through the formidable oak door as if in daze. "We have walked far? Is that it?" The snake simply passes on, not responding with words. "So, this is Sparkling Castle – we are here?" And the young man follows the guide snake through candle lit rooms, and these rooms are brought forth in candle light. "Spiral," he says, "and white; endlessly turning." The snake begins to ascend the whitest marble steps, one at a time. At the third turning of the transparent steps, the young knight looks down. He can see the twisting, turning spirals upon spirals and feels for a moment sea-sick. He is none the less on *terra firma*. He wonders how he will ever find his way back through the ever-unfolding locomotion – multiple and infinite. "Around and around, for ever," he calls out to the void. A slither, a hiss. He looks up. The grass snake has gone out of sight. The knight begins to climb in the grip of an unusual panic, as though something may remain unfound, or missing in action; that he will lose the life-blood necessary to save the goddess, Oriane. "I promised," he calls, running, panting, as he ascends the white marble stairs. "I swore on the hilt of this sword," he says, feeling the cold metal at his side, "but did I not drop my blade?" All is well, this instrument of war hangs inert at his side, making do with reflecting the passage of time. But his mind is rushing, he is deaf to ecstasy, hissing into the self: "I am called upon, to do this thing," he says, "for the goddess. Just this once; head-to-head," he calls to the walls, passing and panting, seeking his guide. "I am above the earth now; into the flame of the firmament." Suddenly, he can breathe, the thinner air brings headiness, "I sail on alone," he calls out to the passage of time, to the smallness of the world. He must hurry, the dead of night can come and bring veils, but he must not delay. "Did I swear my allegiance?" Or anything at all, crosses his mind: "We all rise, we all stand to attention. Rise," he says, the word running down the walls of his mind. Strength and resolve return. Now, he strides two steps at a time, catching the grass snake. "You're there," he calls "a dear friend," he calls out to the overgrown grass snake: "I must not sink; I must not fall." The guide is somewhat nonplussed, or so it would appear, and so continues around and around the everlasting spiral staircase of white marble. "This pretty prince is a queer fish," the grass snake is caught thinking. "A queer fish by half; more like a man of the land." The knight begins to feel dizzy. A strange feeling comes over him: memories of his boyhood flood his mind. "Unwanted," these fires from the past. The treachery of his solitude is returned. The time gathers, it heeps. Time ago, as once he was: roaming alone across the grounds of the Green Palace, hidden beneath the shade of the massive oak tree. His mother lost, never known, his father drowned, an orphan now, forever. Is this the life? His uncle Penwith broke his promise, the little rabbit was stripped and hanged: the tapestry would make him pay. "Kill him," had crossed the boy's mind: "Make him suffer so, an insect under glass." Being there, standing there within the frame of the tapestry: "Haul him out of these soft waters," the swirling patterns, threading to a clearer site and vision, "and onto the solid, green grass," altering all before his eyes: "Look," he says, "is that me?" He begins to emerge into an altered objective existence: "There … is … *Me*," he says, stepping back. "There I am – At last," he says. "I have been expecting you."

All of the pulses of the long-past, threading their way into this very present moment. Finer and yet still finer are these thoughts: from the thudding of logs falling down onto the shore to the workings of wood and water.

The solitude comes to an end; another's life takes precedence, a dedication to the one: "*It's not just me*," he had said, and the head gardener's son called him, touching his cheek: *You are so beautiful, my Prince.* Whose words were these? This sudden feeling brings him strength, to fight his dizziness, his tiredness, his lack of perspective, as he strides up and up, round and around, and as he closes his eyes, he halts, for but … a moment. His eyes open. "*Was that not me?*" He no longer circles the white marble steps. Was that not me up ahead. Another moment passes, he stands before a goddess: "It's Oriane," he whispers, "Oriane, I'm here. I said I would come." The lady is shadowed, silent for but a shift in time. "So, you did," springs to mind, "You did, so." This was a goddess … A goddess, no less. No human could ever hope to placate, or deny, her. Oriane will come and light him up. One must be sullen in such presence, whether storm-tinted or stripped to one's white cambric shirt, to one's breeches, a crescent sword worn at the hip; a young prince, never the less, presents himself to ceremony: "I shall be debased and hide-bound by the bestial and beautiful call of such overwhelming maternity." Who says what? Are these reported words, or heard, later to be set down? Or merely the multitudinous fragments which pass from one mind to the next in perfect silence? But there is more to come: "I shall rip the whoreson, soon enough, eat him like a stoneless fruit. Pretty little cur."

*This was, indeed, a goddess whom no one could
ever hope to placate – or deny.*

He is there – "At last!" – almost immediately a thought presents itself: "This *is* the tapestry," he whispers, halted still, if only for … a moment. "Watch carefully and you shall know what thou shalt do: Only watch." Are these the words he hears in his inner ear, or from afar: the present pattern seems static and still. He looks across the expanse to his goddess there: She waits for me, he thinks: "You will know everything," passes through his mind, but these are not his thoughts. The all-important passage: "You will at last *see* everything." The goddess seems hardly aware that he is there; in person, he stands. "You will be my own little prince," she whispers, "and we will have children and the palace will be filled with delightful noises and activity." The prince sees his own face reflected in a looking glass; he's much older, he thinks, but he looks like him. "And we will ride out on horses," the voice trails through his mind, a second inner voice, imploring him. Which voice to heed: "And there will be a world of people, and friends, and family, all smiling and, yes, at last, true, the very fullest happiness." And he sees this goddess and he hears her too. Of that, he is sure. She has her back to him. He advances, that's all that matters now, and he is greeted by invisible voices, and instruments he cannot see being played, and yet he hears well their sweet playing. This goddess is wearing white silken robes. "Watch while it's still: *See* it all. *Hear* too." The floor is strewn with pink and red rose petals, he slips slightly on the glassy ground. The petals are soft and moist to the touch of his toes. He slips, rights himself. He hears a squelch, but knows well that goddesses do not make such sounds. Meanwhile, out of earshot, but present nonetheless, the concussion of waves is breaking on the littoral. An owl hoots, impatiently awaiting the darkness of coming night. The young prince watches for a moment as the red fluid rises between his toes: "Like blood," he says, "but only red petals." Light fills the room, yellow and warm and silky; it shines upon them both. The sun has not quite set, and there are lit candles, fighting a faint black rim in the corners of the vast room – a lady's chamber, no less. This will be a goddess whom nobody can deny.

III

It never was funny. Funny? What's funny? – they're spreading shit all over the hospital. People are already talking. I had to laugh it off the other day – that auxiliary asked, How's Molloy, doctor? Cheeky little prick! An auxiliary? Talking to me – where's funny? Funny?

She immediately regretted saying the word – the reply was sharp. (The staff have *too* much to say, she'd said. That's the problem. It's no longer *funny*.) That's what she'd said. He'd said: The cheeky little prick. That auxiliary? Funny? Am I missing the funny side, Molloy? Immediately she wants the word to be forgotten. And Mary? she replies, *your wife*, as though this were a genuine question, and not some vain attempt to change the tenor of the talk. Her time was not her own. She can't bring herself to light another cigarette, her hands are shaking. She looks at the gold pack with the equal measure of dislike and yearning. She's supposed to be referring to the notes. Mentioning Murphy's general welfare. The Consultant Psychiatrist's been in – with Poppy Frankel. He's concerned. When isn't he? Worried about the change in the *presenting patient* – the Wilson's. That's what the shrink had said. Molloy is becoming nervous. She was glad to find herself walking the Consultant out; relieved is the word. Just as she began to close the door, he returned, shocking her: There's something off here, Sister, he'd said. And I intend to get to the bottom of it. Murphy, she'd said, by way of reply. Yes, Murphy, he cried out. *Something's most definitely off. Off*, he said again, emphasising the word, slightly spitting. Frankel had looked at Molloy, for the first time in a while, then almost immediately averted her eyes. She knows, Molloy thinks. She knows – but how does she know? As she made her way back to the office, heart racing, she almost laughed at Murphy, mussing the Consultant Psychiatrist's hair. (*Your hair's like cotton wool*, he said. Molloy could hardly believe her eyes. Molloy manhandling the old man's fluffy hair. Whatever next? Delicious, dears, perfectly quaint.) A little later,

Mallory repeats the proper noun: Mary? Molloy's heart leaps. *My wife*? Mallory says the name as though it's the first time he's ever heard it. *Mary*? Like that: *Mary*? She begins to explain: Has she said anything? Molloy attempts to clarify the situation. She doesn't care in the slightest about Mary.

She knows something's up, the doctor replies, states his lie thus: I said I was at a late evening consultation meeting. As if to check, Mary called the office.

The gist of it was this: Mallory's secretary was still there. She passed Mary's call to Poppy Frankel – it was all very convivial, apparently. Frankel was discreet, explaining that she wasn't entirely sure about the consultation or meeting – she made mention of the Consultant Psychiatrist's absence too. *Should I look in the diary*? she asked. Mary demurred, saying there was no need for that. Frankel explained that she'd been up to London at the Medical and Health Sciences Conference, but had returned early. Mary checked. There was indeed an International Conference running at the Tomlinson Centre, but Frankel wasn't named as a speaker. *I said she must've gone as a guest*, Mallory explained, *not as a speaker*. Mary was mollified – for the moment. This hardly explains things to Molloy's satisfaction: But, she pauses, resumes with: What about *you*? Where did you say *you* were? He aimed for the truth, but missed: I was caught out – I said that the meeting with the Consultant Psychiatrist had gone ahead; there was no reason for Frankel to be present, and Mary accepted that. That's it. But there's more to ask. But how did you know about the Conference? You were with me – Mary would've caught you on the hop. A momentary silence. The answer's swiftly put: Poppy prewarned me – she told me Mary'd called the office. When I got back, Mary was sitting in the dark. Well, she was reading by candle light. It was funny. She was smoking a cigarette when I returned to the house – all I could see was smoke and her in the shadows. She didn't look up from her book: she simply asked where I'd been. I said I was at a meeting with the boss. I said we'd stepped out of the office. When she mentioned Poppy – well, I was ready. She'd been up to London, I said. That's all I said – I didn't even mention the conference. And then I went to reset the switch; it'd tripped, that's it – the electricity came back on. Why, that was it. The awkward conversation ended. Molloy lets the confusion of this go; they'd been together that night – he'd been with *her*. Mary was meant to be staying over at her mother's; everything was set. There was a flat that Mallory kept in London for when he lectured – Mary and he both used it – and they'd been there – together: Molloy and Mallory. Molloy doesn't ask how *Poppy* was able to let Mallory know that Mary had called. The times clashed, surely. How could Frankel click with Mallory; let him know that Mary had called? The thought was unkindly recurring – shifting about in her mind as they talked in the office. Molloy immediately recalls the phone ringing in the apartment. The memory feels distant, but welcome. It seemed strange at the time The phone ringing. Why hadn't he let it ring off – it could have been Mary, she'd thought. Molloy now knows it was her – it was Poppy Frankel. She remembers his hushed tones, couldn't make out a word of it. *It's the wife*, Poppy'd said with a remarkably flat delivery. She always referred to Mary as *the wife*. He cups his mouth around the receiver. *And*? She tells him: *The wife's been on the phone*, she paused for a moment, *asking after your whereabouts*. A meeting, Frankel had said, covering for him. *With the Consultant Psychiatrist*, she'd said. Then switching to her own concerns: *Why are you at the flat*? Frankel asked – the hidden question in all of this. The faint surprise when Mallory had answered the phone. Or was it a confirmation of something that was weaving its way throughout all the wards and all the corridors in the hospital – Mallory and Molloy were having it off – the Mall-Moll affair. *Why are you at the flat*? Frankel had asked, suddenly, an even flatter delivery. He ignores her question in favour of his own more pressing one: *What did Mary want*? *Her mother* ... he'd began to say. The response: something about the electrics going out. Something simple: she became worried. Who should she phone – if anyone – an electrician perhaps. Mary had put off her mother. Something of no consequence. Frankel told her to find the fuse-box and flick the switch. *Mary laughed*, she said, Mary made comments about how practical Frankel must be. Frankel no longer likes saying *the wife*. She says instead: *But why are you at the flat, Mallory*? She pauses for a moment; he hears her dragging on a cigarette, he thinks he hears her gulping from a glass of wine. He likes the sound it makes. *I just knew you'd be there. I know* why *you're there. You're with that ward sister, aren't you*? She's no longer pausing for any sort of response. *You know what you are, Mallory*? Mallory refuses to answer – entirely aware of what he is, but what to do about it, that's the question. Frankel knows Molloy must be listening from the bedroom, that she's in the flat, no doubt lying naked in Mary's bed. *Mary*'s bed. Frankel's no fool. *A fucking cliché*, Frankel calls down the line, replying to her own question. A fucking something, but Mallory stops himself from laughing. It's nerves, he conjectures – and there's power hidden in the pleasure. (I'm going to fuck Frankel tomorrow, that's what he thinks, to make up for things – and she knows it, that's what he thinks.) It is time to set Mary aside; he wants Frankel's youth – he wants to make Poppy his wife. He holds back his rising mirth. He wants to reason with her – she is, after all, a highly intelligent operative; he wants to say this: *Come on, Pops, get real*. He'll explain that the ward sister's nothing but a bit on the side. He wants to say: *She makes me want you more*, but he says this instead: *A diversion, Pops, that's all it ever is*. Frankel has a little more to say, for the present: *Next time, Mallory, I'll let* Mary *know where you are – or where I suspect you to be. She's got your card marked*, Doctor *Jacobs*. He likes how she emphasised his title, freighting it with a hidden meaning. *Mary* – she's now officially on first name terms with his wife, he stops himself from laughing; *Mary*, she says, *knows what* you *are. She knows something's up*. He wants to laugh again, his hand is gesturing to the telephone, incongruously, as if the plastic might respond to his quiet imploring. Tomorrow? he whispers. She hears the poor control of his mirth: *Damn you*, she says. *Damn your eyes, Mallory*, she calls out before slamming down the receiver. Ah, there's his name, Mallory: That's the ticket: I'm Mallory, he murmurs into his own receiver with no one present at the other end. That's the ticket. Tomorrow, I'll propose, tell her divorce is on the cards. Anything to be with her – with Poppy. Anything, whatever it takes to be with Darling Pops.

She can no longer resist the gold pack just there on the desk before her.

You got the light's back on then? Molloy laughs. Throws her cigarette packet back onto to the desk, sparks it into life. Lights? he says, what lights? She pauses, about to take a deep drag: You said Mary was sitting in the dark – the power switch. The trip? She takes the drag she'd yearned for. Blowing smoke into the air before she speaks. Bad for you, he says, in a joshing manner, ignoring her question. So, they tell me, she replies, shortly, but firmly. Feeling cheap and stupid and insecure. Hating herself, she waits for him to speak, to reassure her, soothe her, which makes her hate herself all the more. She knows she is about to be sorely disappointed. She knows. And yet ... this knowing barely covers it. It all looks so, well ... *so* unprofessional. I'm a married man, he says, stating the fact that everyone in the hospital is fully   aware of. Yes, of course. I get it, she cuts in, I really do. She drags on the cigarette again; the end reddens to a point; she'd like to touch him, but they're in the office. Malone can be heard; they've just arrived. She can hear Malone's voice, calling out to Williams. Next minute, clocking the two through the glass into the office, Malone is silent. You don't want to stop, do you – *Mallory*? She hates herself, for saying these words, the emphasis, and in the workplace, of all places. She hates herself because she knows nothing can come of it. Even the sex seems worthless, perfunctory, at best, Molloy thinks; Clinical, Mary calls it, and Poppy? All that for some proximity, some way of alleviating the loneliness – is that what it is? What he is? She could almost laugh in his face, as Poppy seems to have done. She's noticed Frankel's frostiness upon the mention of a single word: Mallory. Her inability to chat as once they did; avoids all eye contact, at all costs it seems. (*We're the same age, aren't we?* Molloy remembers saying; Molloy turns out to be a year younger. Women in their twenties. *He's past it: creeping around with women in their prime.*)

If Molloy so much as mentions Mallory Jacobs, Poppy thinks, looking at the other as though she'd never heard of him – an affectation of complete disinterest, in the old-fashioned sense.

Now Molloy knows why. She hates herself for knowing. No, he pipes up: We'll have to neutralise Malone – put an end to all this talk. Malone's been gobbing off all round the wards, Mallory explains, convincing her. You know what Camier says? He's says Malone's spreading cur-talk all over the hospital. Malone? Would you believe it? Got to deal with Malone, there's nothing else for it. Divert attention. You reduced Murphy's medication, right? As I told you to. She looks out across the ward, listening for signs of life. Malone's voice, suddenly breaking into a laugh. In the office, Molloy hardly feels like laughing: Yes, of course, I followed your instructions, Mallory ... to the letter. He checks: Disposing ... She assuages: Flushed away. Nothing leads back, all the pills, she pauses, the evidence gone. Well, apart from ... She meant to leave this bit out. Apart from what? he asks. She flicks her fag into the aluminium ashtray on the desk. It's nothing. Guppy saw me, that's it. I was slipping the pills into my pocket. He raises his eyes. It's Murphy we're focussed on. Without the medication he'll blow. The Consultant's got it just about right – and the old fool knows it – the medication's as good as it can be, for now. Murphy's improvements had been noted – before the latest turn around; the recent deterioration in his behaviour. Soon enough this information will be cited in a case study. Now his growing agitation will throw a spanner in the works. Murphy's been building, you said – his head, he's complaining? The doctor waves his hand in front of his face, smoke swirls about him. Molloy sighs: Yes, she says, it's building. His mind is playing games – he's close to the edge. Keeps hearing things, seeing stuff, feeling it across his skin. It's weird to watch. Horrible. But if you think … He interrupts: It's too late to think, love. It'll only be a matter of time, Mallory says. Things will happen. He'll blow. We'll have to be ready. A diversion in the ward – that'll take all eyes off us. One last name: And Frankel? He knows exactly what she means. Poppy? he replies: What does she know? – is that what you mean? Even if she did, at this point in her career, she won't want to rock the boat. We just have to quieten the horses. A diversion always works; neutralise Malone. He follows her gaze out of the office window. He sees Malone, but says nothing. Molloy knows what he's doing: I didn't mean that, she says, I meant … she stops herself, changing tack: Diversion, you say. The awkwardness has passed. Let's stick to the plan, he says, taking up the slack: A diversion, Molls. Yes. That's all it will take. Nobody will get hurt. Forget Guppy. Murphy's the focus. A diversion will put an end to all this talk. Agreement is at last reached. The medication then? Forget Guppy. That's all – and wait. She laughed, mirthlessly, with too much effort, returning to something she'd mentioned earlier: I thought Murphy was going to screw the shrink's fecking head off. Neither of them laughs. The Consultant Psychiatrist has noticed the change in Murphy, that much they now know. Mallory's feeling queasy with all the smoke in the room. He waves his hand, Malone waves back from the ward side, thinking it's a gesture of good will. Mallory looks back at Molloy: O, yes, I heard about that; you told me. Well, he's an eminent man – his work is in Wilson's, you know that. But he'll wait. He knows something's wrong but, he hardly suspects you're holding back Murphy's medication. He wouldn't come to that conclusion – not in a million years. Nobody will get hurt, Molloy. A critical incident, that's all it will be. But it will take the heat off me – away from *us*, he corrects himself. He wants to laugh. We have to be careful … He stops:

Molloy? He calls her as though to wake her. *Molloy?* – you know what to do. *Molloy?* He's smirking. She recognises the flicker of his lips. He looks her straight into her eyes. She hates herself more than ever. Screw the ethics, she thinks. Then what more can I do, Mallory? She knows the refrain: Say nothing, he says – just remember what we agreed, Molls – Say … Nothing – a diversion. Nobody gets hurt, and that's a promise. *Trust me*, he says, with emphasis. Say nothing? she replies. That's it, that's all we have to do: Say nothing. Trust me, Molls, I'm a doctor.

IV

*"Do not be afraid," she says, her back to him, he voice barely
reaching his ears. He draws nearer, walking upon strong bare
feet; the image before him appears to be floating, or yet still.
After all this waiting; after all this time. Here, at last.*

"Soon enough, soon enough, the deed," she says, a look of infinite
irony, infinite joy, tinged with sorrow, flitted and faded from her
half-hidden face. To look into her eyes, he thinks, if only to see.
"Did you speak?" he calls out, his feet cold upon the petals strewn
at ground level. She had communicated, shared her words,
passed her poison; she would keep her peace for now. Once one's
drawn nearer; yes, near enough to see her as the one he's seen
before. The one reflected in the dark, abyssal pools of her eyes is
him, the little prince, looking back at him. There's an immediate
sense that he swims, sinking, lying at the bottom of the sea; to be
washed hither and thither, and driven about the roots of the
world. "All is glass," he says, "we are all glass." A shiver, a shake,
or something: "All glass," she replies: "Yes, glass," she says, "is
all." He might fall, but must refrain from doing so; he will look
upon her glossy lips, listen to the words of the goddess, for she
must be heeded, somehow placated. When forces clash, some
greater force must impose itself. *With the day in us, we know the
day, and with the night in us, the night.* He will watch them move,
this vermillion red and natural mouth will smile at him – in
time; her pearl-white teeth just glimpsed; she smiles, surely? He
will see her once, and for all – once, for all. Her jet hair absorbs all
colour and is presently drifting down her back from what seems
to be a halo about her head – her hair is somehow golden. "All
light," he says, "all," he says, "light." She is dressed in a long white
silken dress pulled in at the waist by a golden belt the clasp of
which was a jewelled serpent. "Am I to be derided all my life," she
says, at last speaking directly to the young prince, "afraid even to
say a solitary word?" Surely no goddess had ever looked nor
spoken like this: a creature of perpetual contradictions. "Let me

see you," he calls to the goddess. "I think I have only ever seen you from afar," he raises his voice, "hidden before in darkness, but now before me here, in coming light." The young man walks towards her, she does not stir, but remains inert, her back to him, her gown drapes to the floor. Yes, he knows how she ends, he knows well. This is the place of his destiny; he knows this well, but he is fearful of disturbing her. She's expecting me, she waits. "I know your ..." he whispers, "I know how it ends ... have I not seen it – Am I not sent?" Gaining closeness to this goddess, closer yet, clearer and clearer; nothing was quite so solid, nothing ever was so shifting. "I know how this ends." The voices, from afar: the patterns stilled in sudden stability. Why, he wishes to ask, but recall: "Say not why." Is that the voice, the whispering from the Green Palace? He hears again:

"With the possible in us, we know what's impossible,
and with the impossible in us, the possible."

He hears these words about his inner ear, it feels as though an insect is boring its way in, waiting for the right time to strike silently at the bark of his brain.

"With what's unseen in us, we know what's seen,
and with what's seen in us, the unseen"

"Yes, yes. Yes. Then what is seen is unseen?"

The tapestry's whisht.

The turn of the head is so rapid that it takes his breath away. "O, goddess," he says, anticipating her presence, his voice falters, he breathes deeply: "She binds us," he whispers, "holding us together." He steps nearer and nearer, walking so gently towards her, reaching her at last. "Here she is, at last; she's here." A breeze puffs out a curtain, giving the impression of an intruder hiding. "We are all glass," he says, but to whom it is unclear. He waits: "The sea smooths us away," she replies. The turn of the head is so rapid that he can hardly breathe with anticipation. There, in a silver looking glass on a facing wall, they are at last seen together, no longer one but two. "Ahh," he says, but not a sound of something found but something lost. "What," he calls out to the mirror, "is that?" Who, he wants to know is this other apparition? The human-sized snake beside him in the glass is smiling. The goddess's status drops; the goddess is surely lost. "This is no goddess at all," he cries. Any spectator would have wondered; anybody would have asked. "What on the good earth is this?" Did she lurch, rolling around, turning sharply, or leer at him? Well, her eyes hardly fell on his directly, but, still, he is stunned by what he perceives in the mirror: "There should be two of us." The shock is sharp. "Who is that?" he says – "that monstrous thing in the looking glass? That serpent, seen." The mirror's cracked, she wants to say. "Look," she says, "dearest prince, look to me. Only I," she says, "just me, in the flesh." Face to face, she is radiant, wreathed in smiles, ready for the hand of man. He looks back at the mirror: "The fierce snake," he says, "in the glass there. And me. Is that me?" He steps back, looking from mirror to monster. "As big as a human's head … and fierce." How should she convince him of this error? "You must be in dream, dear heart," Oriane says, "have no fear of that. You are quite safe." O, young prince, she thinks, think what *I* think – "It is not you and I; it is always already *we*."

> *He takes a step, Oriane is there, before him again. Face to face.*
> *He sees her, his goddess, waiting patiently. He steps nearer and*
> *nearer, walking so gently towards her, reaching her at last.*

She turns, he sees her; the goddess is resumed; the system of glass disturbs the pattern, he thinks: "Are there two of them: one in glass; one in life? Which one is which?" He looks back, from the goddess to the mirror. "What's that?" He sees again the thing most ominous, of vivid green, with a snake's head, and most hideously attired in a white silken gown. "Which one are you?" he asks. Which one indeed. "Do not be afraid," she says, speaking so gently, drawing a little closer to the young knight who stands upon his bare feet, wet with the personal juice of red and pink rose petals: "I am here," she says. "Just here." There is no place for the reflection of other things, the space now filled by the young man and his goddess. "It is not you and I" he says, repeating the words he's heard before, "it is always already *we*. Isn't that what it is?" How she is aching for her disenchantment. "Then kiss, young prince: Kiss. Keep the promise you made: Kiss was; Kiss is; Kiss ever shall be." He leans forward, eyes closed, to kiss, as bade – the lips are hardly puckered; the first kiss given. Placate, as he must. "Kiss, Kiss," she says, "yes, kiss again." The young man's mouth feels the touch of Oriane's hard lips, a second time. Deceptive to the touch, he feels no harm in it; "Kiss," she says, "yes, one last time." He kisses the third time. "So tough," he says, a most unexpected texture, he thinks, as the slither of a forked snake-thin tongue enters his mouth each time. He opens his eyes; he feels his breath taken. Shallow, his heart palpitates, stomach feels a piercing pain. He steps back, staggering, bringing his hand up to his throat. Candle light blurs his present reality, the fight against the faint black rim is lost; distant darkness comes ever closer. The looking glass is now opaque. The room seems to be darkening. "I am poisoned," he gasps, his eyes seem distanced, held in shock – or awe. Those fullest of lips of his, once pink and plump, begin to turn blue, thinning: "I am poisoned," he calls again, his throat constricting, his face he sees in the glass, but with all the clarity leached: "Is that me?" he cries out to the reflection – Is that me?

The young prince is becoming the colour of moon free oceans.

His lips are suddenly lapis, as cold as cobalt; his tongue turns to turquoise, stiff, frozen, pierced by the bifurcated dart; he falls, dropping like a block of ice, shattering blue onto the blood-red petals, scattered about on the cool marble ground. He no longer blooms but, like the light sliding down the looking glass, he drops; fallen, following the egregiously stolen kisses struck against his own mouth. The lips were harsh, his eyes closed, no longer trusting what he'd seen; saw instead only what he was meant to – an ethereal goddess replaced in an instant by the image of that human-sized snake. The third kiss was surely stolen; hadn't he seen for himself the image in the mirror, her snake-face, green and bilious? But, when she turned, he saw only the pure white vision of majesty. "O, goddess, I am here." He is frozen; he's so cold he feels burnt hot; a feverish fall, a cold-hot poisoning, striking at his heart. His guide nearby, the larger-than-life grass snake, looks on, little care, if any, is shown. Breaking cover now, the creature slithers across the cold crystal floor, making a circular passage through the red and pink rose petals: "The pretty prince is dead. Dead for all time," the guide hisses, seems almost to be smiling: "Soon to close the pretty prince's eyes; Oriane did turn, and Kiss … Kiss … Kiss … ."

Again, the tapestry's time returns, again and again, shifting and deleting; altering patterns and undoing egregious pasts; flesh turns to atoms which drive the forms, again, again, anew.

The breeze picks up, puffing out the curtain, a cone of swelling air caught in the light gauze. The candle flames bob in the gentle night wind. The clouds are sharp around a silver moon and only there, the wooded land beyond remain presently out of sight. Again, he takes his step, slipping slightly on the rose petals strewn hereabouts. "It looks like blood," he says, looking down upon his feet. He walks, slowly, towards her, Oriane, there, before him again – yes, yet again, he walks. "O, goddess, I am here." He sees only her back, his goddess, waiting patiently for her prince. He steps nearer and nearer, walking so gently towards her, reaching her at last. How he looked into her eyes, seeking compassion; he got instead a fractional and fragmented sight. He sees only himself as though captured and shrunk inside a black bottle. It is but a trick, only some part of him reflected in the dark pools of her eyes. "The well," he says, "darkness and light in the water. Light dark." He feels as though he might fall from exhaustion, or faint into indelible ink. But that he cannot do – not yet. He will not fall again into unconsciousness; he will die first. But, at once, he will glance at her lips, a moment only, before he closes his eyes: He's about to be kissed. And then she turns, *it* turns – for the creature is no human form – and stands almost erect. The white silk garment draping from its head like a scarf. "Did the prince put out his hand?" the guide hisses, remembering this fall from grace: "But it was not his goddess, it was no such thing. The pretty prince saw too late."

Yes, the robe was draped over its little serpent head, the beady eyes, as red as black, alert, and in its mouth the serpent holds a silver rose clasped between its fangs, so terrifying to the young prince.

The knight can hardly breathe, or see straight; he closes his eyes, but not only in fear, but only for a moment. The creature spits out the frozen, silver rose, and coils itself around the prince's arm, extending its frosty form towards his wrist and fingers. He strikes his breast, feeling the ice cold of something there. "The silver rose," he said. Twisting, turning, caressing, the human-sized snake rises towards the beautiful face of the young man. He looks down upon the rose of silver form about his petal red feet, spat out from the mouth of the serpent before him. He knows, and remembers his oath. "I recognise it; the pail, the well. And two of us." Yes, he knows how she ends; this is the place of his destiny; he knows well that she waits for him, she waits – be not afraid. "I know how she ends," he thinks, "have I not seen it?" Revolving herself around to the face of the young prince, turning, turning, the disturbing figure frames its head before the prince's face and then presses those harshest of lips against his mouth not once, not twice, but thrice; the snake-thin tongue is forked, poking out of its mouth, circled by a snakehead, and it sticks it right into his mouth. He will die, a squirt of poison in the kiss, mirth is building in the creature: "At last," it calls out to the Sparkling Castle, "I am free. I can hardly see in front of me. I am free."

The tapestry's heat and time comes forth, a smouldering at the corners, a smell of smoke emanates from the queen's chamber at the Green Palace.

Oriane becomes her true self; her truest self is Serpentina. "In true form, I am one," she calls out. A scream from the sea, a sound that splits the heart in two. The Woodman turns to his wife from the other side of the sea, from the dark wooded lands: "It has come," he says, "he has failed – again. It ends. Hear that scream?" The room is bathed in a silvery sheen from the moon outside, the sun has dropped into the sea like a stone. But it will return with fiercest heat to bathe the coldest blood of Serpentina: "How she grows," hisses the guide snake, "how soon she will join as one with the Serpent of the Sea – all-powerful, they will be." Yes, she has been kissed, yes, three times upon her snaky-lips. The whoreson has put his plump lips to hers – or hers to his, more accurately – and she is no longer the enchanted creature of the castle keep, captured within the sparkling glass of her chamber; she is soonest Serpentina. Sun set, the nightingale strikes a warning from the trees, it sings: "Yes, Oriane is not a she-snake, that hour has passed, the lips have been sealed. Yes, yes: Behold: the seas will boil. The world falls. Serpentina at last arises."

The patterns begin to turn, in spirals and shapes of some fresher scenes. The tapestry begins again to alter, smoking gently at the top as mist, cooling, wetting the fabric, putting out the smouldering material.

The time turns back, if time it was, impressing the patterns passed yet again *to be or not to be.* The young prince turns and the snake guide is there, coiling, sidewinding, then concertinaed. "Am I to follow?" Surely that is the creature's mission? To bring me forth? He follows the snake-guide through the flowers, some of which begin to close and put to sleep for the night, closing against the moist shards of falling dew. "Wait for me," he calls out to his guide, slithering up and along the white marble stairs. He looks down, "Infinity," he says, "turning, turning: Forever." He rushes to catch up to the larger-than-life grass snake. The guide snake's hardly surprised, or so it would appear, and continues around and around what seems like an everlasting staircase. "This pretty prince is the queerest fish of all," the grass snake thinks. "A queer fish by half." The knight begins to feel dizzy. "I loved this feeling as a child," he calls up to his guide. He has grown used to the silence. A strange feeling steals across him: sad and firm memories of his boyhood begin to swell in his mind: "Unwanted," these occasional tiles from the past. The exegesis means a solitude is resumed. This temporal groan gathers, it heeps; same as he ever was; there, sprinting like the wind over meadow, across greenest fields; alone, he crosses the grounds of the Green Palace, reaching soon his place of solitude; the light and shade of the ancient oak tree. "I did not know my mother," and "my father drowned," and then his "uncle broke his promise" – the tapestry would make him pay. The boy watched the patterns as if he made them with his very own mind: "Kill him," he said, "take him away and kill him. Bastard whoreson." Words were more than built in thought. "Make him pay," the young knight called out to the tapestry on the wall. And then, no longer shaded by the huge oak, but standing there, the swirling patterns of past and present, alter each moment before his eyes: "I am making this," he whispers, so softly, he is barely heard: "I am calling this forth, worshipping reality." There, he begins to see, there, he begins to seek his own life – "There it is," he says, stepping back. "Am I there? – At last: There I am."

V

Murphy leaves, the day still young, while one speaks another takes a peep. Murphy back, let him move, try and move, that's all we ask. The initial crack, that's Murphy again, and then the collision; then another Murphy. It was endless, that's how it felt.

It sounded like a bomb going off, I don't mind telling you. The elder auxiliary raised his hand to his chin, grasped it, letting it fall again to a cup of tea set on the corner of the office desk. You'll recall the crashing sink, flying with intent across the ward. It's hardly something you'd forget in a hurry. A mind of its own, Molloy, that's what it seemed like, the auxiliary went on. I was nodding at him, making him feel included in the moment. As ward sister it was the least I could do. He smiled, sipped his tea with a sound which, mercifully, meant his mouth was engaged in other matters. That so-called *bomb* was once the unknown and unthought of consequences of a diversionary tactic. Well, it kicked us off, that's for sure. As soon as I saw Mallory, I knew: knew well what I'd done. I look at the old auxiliary now, the repetition of what had just passed, but what did he really know? I wait for him to go back to his tea. What did he *really* know? So says the good nurse, Molloy, thinking, yes, thinking a criss-cross of lines, the making up of so many alternating patterns: I knew exactly what I'd let myself in for; knew where now I stood – my *standing* – let's call it that. The good sister, wasn't that what they used to call me? The one who could be counted on? It was obvious where it would end up. In *Mary's* bed, as he insists on calling it. Was that what it amounted to? I very nearly burst out laughing (burst my stitches, you might say) and in *Mary's* bed, legs wide open, awaiting his lordship with bated breath – I had to bite my cheek to stem my snickering. I'd seen more meat on a sparrow's knee cap, really! I'll say nothing more of Mallory Jacobs – for now … Well, I'll say one thing: the sutures did for him, did for both of us, but really did for him. An error, in retrospect. What was soon bandied around the hospital as, simply, *the cover up*. To say nothing about … What? I hardly know where to begin. We kept them all in the dark. Haunted, that's the word. A letter, of sorts; I wrote it all down at the time. Addressed to the authorities, but I never sent it: Who said all letters reach their destination? Especially the ones unsent. Everything gets there, in the end. I am *in situ*, forever, there's no escape; I never leave. How could I forget that look on her face – on Edwina's face – Edwina Malone, there, about to die. Wasn't she my friend? We did nothing to hold back the tide, the tumbling; we did nothing to crack the glass. The letter of the law? What standard of proof is set here: probability or doubt? A balance, everything is, of course, or beyond. Too far to comprehend, the doubt, I mean. What was there to know? After so long, it's a combination of both. I am not stone deaf, and I am not so gravel blind as to … the sounds somehow reach me; I see what I see, who doesn't? The trick is to follow your nose. But I try not to draw too much on memory, notably. I do not know if Malone heard it too. The words were stilled, eventually. The cry that issued that night. What kind of creature uttered it? Not a human one, in any case. And what little there was of humanity that night, will have to be lived with. No, there's no human creatures here or if there are, they've done with their crying.

"Is this unusual?" An hour or so before Murphy kicks off.

An uneventful morning, that's what would have been recorded in the notes. Watt had lost his shoes. That was about it. My feckin' shoes have been nicked … that's what's happened. He looked at me. He lisps; his upper and lower teeth have been removed. What to say? I say nothing. The philosophy was this: they bit. Should I render it as such? The whoosh in his delivery? To do so would be to patronise. To drop. To lie. To bite. When we all suffer no longer, or less, or can go no further, perhaps then we'll do it. We'll seize what's apparently real. He's a biter, was bandied about during my days of training. It made you afraid.

How physical this all is, I thought. How mental. A senior nurse, after all, should know better, at least by now. I see what I see. Mallory stopped talking to me, instituting silence, but you all know that by now, don't you? (The new auxiliary is all ears – he's fresh and eager to please: the curse of compassion. A biter? he says: Biter? I can't keep saying it, that's what I'm thinking: Yes, a biter, I say: Get a grip, kid. Watt bit. End of story.) Watt could tell that I wasn't wholly convinced that we should isolate the dorm as a crime scene, not for footwear. (They're just shoes, I said, mislaid, that's all.) I tried to walk away – Watt could tell I was finding the situation amusing. Thankfully, there was a lot of space on the day ward, as well as a lot of light. The others are out with the old auxiliary, leading no doubt with his chin; Watt remains behind with a few of the older men. (Shoes, he said again, nothing's fair.) I could hear him following me. I stop, look around and there he is. Watt, enunciating slowly, says: That's the feckin' truth. I try to look interested: What's that? I say, looking back. Nothing, he says. I pretend to look out of one of the windows. I run my eyes down the white glossy bars. He follows the line of my gaze. Whatever is out there is of no interest to him. The room is shielded in a chloral hue, crystal and so white it feels blue. Watt has a level of rudeness that was hard to forget. (No one left, I said, there's nothing to explain. The young auxiliary looks dumbstruck: If only I could make more of an effort, he says to me. You're on your own, kid, I replied, get a life.) It was intense and, at the same time, mundane; it was certainly funny and, at the same time, utterly pointless. At least it was to us. To Watt, his shoes, and the lack of these, was all that the universe had to offer, or to refuse. He is made to feel that way. What else would *you* do within the closed system of ward and dorm? That's all you've got – each day. Today he too is out of humour. There is something in the air. It's shit. Lose. Find. Lose. Find – Nicked. he continues, by way of confirmation: Lose again. Feck! Nobody paid too much heed to the apparent theft of a pair of shoes. There were other things to think about. Shoe-things happen, of course they do, but these occurrences are, to say the least, not unusual. If Watt had his way, he'd lose something each and every day. If for no other reason than this: it might provide him with the golden opportunity to swear the feck out of his unbelievable boredom. (Are we to blame? the new auxiliary asked, batting those long black eyelashes, looking as though he'd cry, flicking back his blonde overlong fringe out of his eyes. I looked at him with disbelief. Get a grip, kid, I says to him.) That's the fecking truth. It's hard to explain, but Watt's complete lack of space, or too much space, or people who were there for his welfare, or who were not there, or who would, or would not, pass the time, made him behave, routinely, like a bit of an old clout – hardly a ward sister's words, but you get my drift. Why, then, was he so popular? As he himself would say: Feck knows? As I say, he's no fool. (The new auxiliary flicks his fringe like a tick, the eyes are moist: Endangered eyes, I say. Endangered? he replies, innocently, let's say. Green, I say, like you.) Watt is adamant. He says that his shoes have been taken by some mysterious stranger – a fecking old clout, he says (of course) – in the night, apparently. The mystery eventually unravels without the services of any particular Ruth Rendell level of deduction. Haines will be later found with strips of leather from one of the shoes. The other is hidden under his bed. (Where the rest of the damned thing went; who can tell, I said. The young auxiliary's face was a picture. Did Haines eat the rest? he asks. Get a life, kid, I replied. Who else ate them?) In the present moment, there is no need to send out a search party. And why: because an alternative pair is easily localised in the linenstore. That part of the morning passes off without further ado. Watt ends up wearing his best shoes, and he has these on when Murphy arrives back: Sunday fecking best, nothing less, he calls out, keeping it up with a singing delivery. At one point, he does try to sing his pleasure: *Find, lose, find. Lose, find, lose – Found again: Feck. Feck again, found – lose, find, lose. Find, lose – Found again: Feck.* A tongue twister, of sorts – in some ways a thought experiment on what was the situation at hand. Watt is decidedly pleased with himself, the limitations of word signs in the song do not mar his pleasure, not one tiny bit. He presents a crafty smile when he catches your eye. Every now and then, you'll hear an overwhelming sigh. I caught him – actually, he caught me in the act of spying on him. He was bending down to check on the tassels, brushing invisible dust from his burgundy loafers. Best shoes … Lose. Lost. Find. Found. Feck! These were the moments of calm before the storm – a cliché maybe; it is apt, as you shall see. It had been a bright morning. It was quiet. The clock could be heard to tick and tick again. There, suddenly, was Watt calling out, as though he was exasperated by the state of the world: Feck me, someone's at the door, he exclaims: Hah! He adored the slightest alteration to his day. Who wouldn't? I walk around the wooden partition which splits the large day room, orienting myself. I find only Watt with his broad smile, then a pose, as he looks down, yet again, upon his newly-clod feet. I hear the ringing, but head back to the office: the phone is ringing and the new auxiliary came into view. Watt has already seen somebody at the rectangular window. Murphy is there, alone, slumped at the door.

Murphy's here, he shouts out, it's Murphy. Feck. Found.

My heart raced; of course, it did. Who would be held responsible? Impossible to say. I slipped his medication into a breast pocket on a daily basis. (It won't take long, Mallory said.) We'd name it: Mallory's strategy – *diversion*, that's the word we're looking for. I'm certainly at its circumference, there's no denying it. Spinning like a top. There's no escape. In the end, it comes down one thing: survival of the fittest. To that alone. It was a measure, the balance, the maximal and the minimal, as far as discerning its limits is concerned. A complete count. Guppy saw – he didn't miss a trick: I watched him, slinking away. Guppy was all eyes: he saw. Did he register some alteration in Murphy's well-being? Did Guppy read the situation? Murphy's eyes, may be? He should never have been there. What possessed him to push Malone's legs into the machine like that? I still say nothing, I've no objection. And so, nothing came of it. I am there forever. All depends on the nature of the change. Questions kept unfolding – the Constabulary were one thing – the wooden tops – but once the brass arrived ... Well, we were in knots in no time. All the strands and how to unravel it? All of these Murphys, Molloys and Malones, the dread of the Mallories and then there was the Mary – who remained dignified and singular throughout. Mary was no Madame Bovary, let me tell you; not one bit. I was not surprised – after so long a silence, the hue and cry would be called upon. Mallory suggested that the Consultant Psychiatrist was negligent in some way. The shrink looked shocked. He suspected everything, quite naturally. The time of it came. They have all made me waste my time, suffer for nothing, speak of them when, in order to stop speaking, I should have spoken of me, and of me alone. This has been my confession, or a summing up, if you will. Yes, better a sum. *Ergo sum.* Mine and mine alone. *Therefore I am.* This is Molloy lives – not dies. No, here all change would be fatal, and I was destined to live, once and for all. There and then. What would I say? All – or nothing? Perhaps it was, as I say, nothing more than something breaking, some two things colliding. The Consultant Psychiatrist, of course, took Murphy's blood; Frankel evaporated after her quite unnecessary corroboration. Not conclusive, but enough: there was something irregular in what showed up. Hushed up, more like – isn't that what they say: Hush is not silence, you see. If only we weren't obliged to manifest. Be there, in a manner of speaking. You hear me now? What kind of creature uttered it? Not a human one in any case, there are no human creatures here, or if there are they have done with their bleating.

Javelin, doctor, she replied; old clout spreads to mind,
she smiled at the Consultant Psychiatrist.

I heard Molloy say it, replying to some comment made by the

Consultant Psychiatrist. I've got a mean right hook, she said, laughing in that way that makes her point. Your shoulders *are* broad, the shrink had just commented, as though noticing something for the first time. (How dare he? Little old clout. The words had crossed her mind, the very cheek of it.) Broad shoulders, sharp tongue, she replied, that's all you need. He begins to laugh, exacerbating the falseness, marvelling at the lack of an obsequious manner. He likes people low; she can't stand the smell of him. Shall I show you out? she asks. Yes, he says, pausing for a short breath: I'll need to arrange to see the Wilson's again, he said. I'll ring, would that suit? Humming vaguely, a sharp-witted man. He knows his name, she thinks: Murphy? she responds. Yes, that's the very one, she says: *Murphy*, indeed. Skimming widely, throwing caution to the weeds: Then why don't you say it? she says, showing the shrink the door – His name is Murphy, she says.

Recall the dusty cement, making slow-moving statues, day after day my lips are tight pressed; the bird flies, butterflies flutter, the flower dances, but all around the sea is silenced.

Upon his return, Murphy would usually takes some chill – but the exception to this would prove the rule: that something was amiss; his meds had been messed with. Normally it would run like this: I'll smoke a little pipe, he would say, taking it out from a breast pocket, filling it, burning the tobacco. From his puffing, it looked as though the entire day ward would fill with smoke. They have a short shelf-life. By January, after each Christmas, another gifted pipe was bust, biting the dust as it flew, sparking red heat against the wall, splitting in two. The Wilson's disease, Molloy would explain, the outbursts. Not temper, she looks for the words: No, not temper. There's something there, you see. To him, and then he reacts, fighting it, repelling it. Reassurance works, but it's escalating, she pauses, a knowing enigmatic smile curls about her mouth: I just don't know how much longer …

She neglects to tell of further time. (How much longer, I say, for what? The good sister smiles: You're on your own, kid; there's no place for the faint of heart here, remember that. His life? Who knows, we go when we go, swift-like.) But I seem to have retained something by way of description, despite myself. (How much longer, she repeated herself, but not as a question – before he bursts? How much longer? – a pocket full of antidote, a pocket full of poison, never the less. The kid's got a point.) You call this bit the chamber, Murphy might have said, packing the pipe with fresh tobacco. The chamber, that's what it is. Then there's the draught hole. Savage is yet to stop her work: Draught hole, Murphy? I'll give you a bit of draught hole, she calls out, have no fear. She does a dance with her hips, inappropriate, of course, but you have to laugh: You're like the St. Bruno man, Murphs, that's what you're like. Savage is calling out over the humming din of the lino-buffer. All the birds'll be after yer, Murphy; they'll chase you down the road so that they can get their hands on yer pipe, her laughter insists she stops her work and repeats herself: If it's a bit of draught hole you're after, Murphs, look no further. I'm yer girl. He blows out some smoke, mouth and nostrils simultaneously, enjoying the fruity nature of her talk, in unison with the swivelling of hips: That's big old talk, Savs, he said. Murphy is puffing his pipe, filling the ward with a copious white. The aroma lifts the room in a far from unpleasant way. That's what they tell me, Savs, he says: Those were the days, he's smiling now, of birds and flowers, calling across to Savage, long ago – lord knows, a grip of me pipe, as you say. He begins to laugh, his pipe raised in admiration of Savage's fine words and her work on holes and hips. Every hole is a goal, she shouts out, still roving her hips. Savage's machine soon enough whirrs back to life, and she quickly disappears into smoke and mirrors. Murphy's still speaking: What do I want with this pipe? he says, but his voice is for himself. Look at this smoke, he continues his thread, white and fluffy is all, and the smell of it; the smell makes me nervous, makes these things cling on to me.

They come out of it,

pillows and people,

faces and fists, and me changing a little more each time.

A lull, a glaring from within the shadows,

and my name,

the one they foisted on me,

again and again,

they say it, and, yes,

from the shadows, as I said:

I remain unnameable.

VI

*Eyes wide open. He no longer circles the white marble
steps. He is standing before a goddess, "It's Oriane," he
whispers, "Oriane, I'm here. I said I would come."*

He is here – "At last!" – to the very letter, the place he saw as
a boy: the same light, the shapes and the patterns, the shading
too. O, and the colours – "This is the tapestry," he whispers,
brought up so suddenly – this is surely it, if only for the moment.
"Watch carefully and you shall know what thou shalt do: Only
watch," are the words he hears in his inner ear, or from afar, or
is it near? The present pattern seems suddenly static and still.
He sees across the way to his goddess there: She waits for me,
he thinks: "You will know everything," passes through his mind,
but these are not his thoughts. The all-important words: "You
will at last *see* everything." The goddess seems hardly aware that
he is present; in person, she stands so very still. A breeze puffs
out a curtain, giving the impression of a person hiding. "We are
all glass," he says, but to whom it is unclear. "The sea smooths us
away," she says, by way of reply. That sound again: he hears the
hiss once more and, when he turns back, the goddess is looking
out toward the open window. He moves, nearing her, the curtain
blows out, softly, then returns to flat form. "There is time,"
he says, "time again," he continues: "The dream returns." The
young man walks towards her, she does not stir, but remains
inert. Her back to him, her long white gown draped to the floor,
her head is golden lit. Yes, he knows perfectly well how she ends.
This is happening as before: "Let me see you," he calls to the
goddess. "I know you as only a child could know you. You are a
legend hung from a wall," he says, "a beautiful pattern, indeed.
What once was hidden is before me now. O, goddess, mine." As
he walks towards her, he recoils at once. A portrait witnessed,
staring out at him, taking his breath away. Behind the silver
glass on the wall, he *sees* for the first time; they are no longer
one but two: he is there but who is this other? He sees not one

but two: "That one's me, but who's this monstrous green …?" He stops, action and voice. Yes, there, in the reflection on the wall, he sees, the reptilian creature stares out, under water, but still in the perpetual glass. "I should have liked to ask of you, O, goddess: 'What is your verdict?' But there are other more pressing things to think about." The goddess's status drops; the goddess is surely lost. "This is no goddess at all," he cries. Any spectator would have wondered; anybody would have asked. "What on god's good earth is this?"

She shifts in space, in time: The goddess is resumed;
the system of glass disturbs the pattern.

"Are there two of them?" he asks, "one in glass and one in life?" He looks back, from the goddess to the mirror. "What's that?" He sees a thing ominous, of vivid green, with a snake's head, and most resplendently attired in a white silken gown. "Which one are you?" he calls out, so close that she can feel his breath against her flattened circular head. "Am I to kiss?" He looks upon her lips in life – But which one is real, the one before me, the one held in glass upon the wall. He looks away from what he has seen in the silver glass. Vermillion, they are, and red and natural, smiling at him, in warmth, just there parted to show her pearl white teeth. "You have not kissed me yet, dear knight," she replies. Nothing will come from nothing, is that what she means? "I thought," he can hardly speak, "you my goddess," he is tongue-tied, barely expressing his thoughts to her, his confusion: "And yet, you are two." The image of what hid behind the silver glass remains to disturb his equilibrium – that shape of vivid green, for one, that sharp forked tongue. "Look away from the glass," she cautions, "no truth is present there. It is but the duke's lies. He tricks us." For the moment, he has other things to say: "But I am there, but you are not. Look, O goddess. *See.* Your verdict?" She smiles, replying so: "But what is *your* verdict, dear knight? Are these not my lips here? O honourable knightly prince; my eyes too, the skin here; this raven-dark hair is surely mine too," she replies. "You see me here?" She lifts a nearby candelabra, bringing the light of it to her face: "It is but me, awaiting your own true kiss. You must see that, dear prince." And then she holds out her other hand. In this hand, she holds the silver rose drawn from the pail at the holy well as they sat on the crescent wall. He takes it, and looks again upon her visage, face to face. "But for how long?" Time is of the essence: "Do you not remember, my prince? From our meeting at the well. You swore allegiance to whomsoever holds the silver rose." Yes, that much is true. "He strikes his breast pocket," he feels coldness of the silver rose: "There are two," he says. "Not one, but two." Again, that number. "Two," she says, so you should know me; but we join the two in one, dear knight." Her ebony-black hair, as jet as golden, a cloak about her shoulders, as before; yes, as well as the time past. Yes, he murmurs: "At the well," he recalls; of course, the circular wall, endless and infinite, the silver disc of water. In life, there was a halo about her head, and she was dressed in a long white gown, so pure of white it seems translucent.

Her jet hair absorbs all colour and is presently drifting down her back from what seems to be a haze about her brow – her head shimmers as though golden.

He is more than aware of her extraordinary form, her pale white skin, transcendent in that gown pulled in at the waist by a jewelled belt with a snake's head clasp. She was surely a goddess who had come upon the world, or the finest of the ethereal forms, surely no human ever looked like this. "You will know everything," he hears, at once, the words whispered into the corner of his ear. "You see what you see," the words strike the shell, travelling inwards: In the circled silver of the mirror, he sees her now, he sees that monstrous figure. "Which one are you?" he asks. "Do not be afraid," she says the words are spoken so gently, drawing ever closer as she speaks to the young knight who stands upon his bare feet, wet with the liquor of red and pink roses. "I see you now," he says. Only us. There is no place for the reflection of any other thing. Their space is filled by the young man and his goddess. Oriane touches the prince's cheek, her hand is ice. "O, so cold." A shiver runs through the young man. Frozen is this goddess's hand. But the prince cannot take his eyes from her gaze. In the blacks of her eyes, he sees a young boy, situated there, reflected and still, as before. "You will kiss me," she says softly. "Kiss?" he replies; that is all he can say for the words are swarming, jostling, like ants. "Kiss?" He looks further into the black pools of her eyes, if that is at all possible. She moves her head towards his for the first kiss, for but a moment, her bliss is taken. Again, she moves towards him for what's owed: That's two of them taken. The final kiss, the third, is soon to be duly delivered upon her unseen puckered snaky lips. Her throat is white and soft-fresh. The woman draws attention to her throat, stroking it with long fine fingers. The young man looks at his feet, abashed, his own lips are fixed in a smile. He notices – a trick of the light, surely – that his feet are splashed in blood. But it is only the passage of his walking steps upon red rose petals; not of present blood, but of blood to come.

The young man eyes her alabaster bosom, it is without blemish, she eyes what was once his potential, now about to be achieved. He'll soon be worthless to her; nothing but blue death, stripped to shards of glacier cobalt.

One last kiss. The prince's blood pink plump lips are tempting, but only for a true match, not for her; these lips of his were wont to kiss once and twice, they will not have kissed thrice. This young prince will not ravage this false creature; no, he will not. The goddess is fooled. We are among words, or silence, but through this stillness, the truth remains unconcealed.

He hears the hiss again, opening his eyes as though

awoken to crystal and glass and all that shines.

"No, dear goddess," he explains. "Kiss? The thrice taken? "Not on your life. I know not why, but doubt is present in me – in this connection of one to two and so to three. You are near, and yet so far from me. I step back, dearest goddess, from someone who is not yet there, but soon enough will come. I must return, you see, to the gardens at the Green Palace." There is no shortage of words, that's at least (and, at last) perfectly clear. "He talks too much," the larger-than-life grass snake thinks, nearby, far enough away, no longer guide but watcher. "But what does the pretty prince say?" Is there something yet to confess? "I need not explain this to you, dearest goddess, most assuredly not. There is one who once waited. Under the ancient oak, he sits, patiently waiting, as if by my own memory. I should perhaps say: There *was* once, but the actual event was different."

He, alone, I once kissed. Only ever he and I make
two to one – for that was the promise."

The tapestry burns into his mind, his ears and eyes, hot and cold, alive and seemingly close to its end. "Turn," it whispers, "turn little prince," and turn he does: *Look back into the glass; the glass looks back into you.*" He looks: "*You see everything; everything seen.*" The silver, young prince, the slivering snake. There he is, accompanied in the silver glass by a livid green snake. "You are no goddess," he says, drawing his sword. Blood splashes his feet – in real time – he is no longer false, but true. He seeks the window, to see again through the soft gauze curtain, to somehow realise the scene which earlier captivated a goddess. As he looks over the dark and dimple-lit sea, he becomes aware of the distant forest he will penetrate again. He must return soon to the Green Palace beyond where the coming light will strike upon the trees in the garden, making the one who waited transparent, and then another; each life a leaf. "A place of hope and sanctuary," he whispers. Noticing the calm waters of the sea. Not so fast: a giant coil disturbs the soft waves, is suddenly seen, and then a scream rips into the fabric of what was calm and free. The Sea Serpent's ruby red eyes, seeking, seeking, and soon enough it disappears. Looking up to the indomitable granite foundation of the castle wall, the Sea Serpent can feel the presence of his love: "Serpentina, she will come to me. It's done! The spell broken. All must boil."

But isn't that Oriane running in her bare feet, her haze of hair trailing behind her like a dark cloak?

Chasing along and down the rough paved path, steep and strenuous; yet she glides as though passing along on air; she runs, refusing to look back, she runs, now or forever, she glides downward to the calm pale sea, seeing now the first rays of the rising sun. How so slowly it rises, how long it took to drop. But at this perfect hour, this most spectacular hour, for the first time, for the first time in hundreds of years, Oriane is returned to her true self: to Serpentina. "She is free, at last." The decrepit duke is watching from his sparkling cage, speaking aloud, looking down at the running female in flowing white silks. The duke sees only Oriane, floating on towards the first moments of red tinted sea, with strange shivers of blue and green, her hair a dark-golded cloak. But if you call them blushes, you may see unpleasant associations of red flesh: "Oriane, is that you?" the duke calls from his keep of crystal glass. But the flowing, haze of hair is not that of Oriane, as she is seen by mortal man or by woman; no, it is not. What looked so black is instead the golden hair of another. It is instead the beautiful flaxen hair of a prince. The Sea Serpent sends out a blood-curdling scream, but there is more of this to come. The self-same Sea Serpent who once sent up the causeway for the young prince to cross is about to be mournfully vexed. The monster who made it seem so treacherous, but that was but a ruse, is soon to be as mad as hell. "She returns to me, this hour of the rising sun. All will boil. This is the hour she is returned to the sea." But the monster is much mistaken. Serpentina is nowhere to be seen.

Two are fooled, the sad locked-in duke and the Serpent of the Sea.

Her disenchantment is overstated. At this very hour, her exchange should be set – to Serpentina – and her union with the Sea Serpent. But it is not done; it is put off once and for all.

Was she ever kissed? But once. And twice. Never the
kiss thrice taken; No, perhaps, not at all.

The duke smiles. "Will she return to me, one day?" He is bent and wicked, but old, and his appearance fools us; fooled him. He walks slowly across to his most magnificent mirror, guided by his trusty snake who has been with him as both friend and foe forever and a day – "My guide," he calls her, "my dearest guide." The duke greets the man he sees, an old man, bald with wisps of waist length hair, a face lined, a body crouched, his clothes are not fine but threadbare: "Hello, good fellow, can I help you in some way? I can be counted on, I assure you? You certainly look as though you have travelled long and hard. Speak up, I see your lips move, but it is hard to hear you. Of course, I will offer you whatever hospitality I can. It is so rare these days to have visitors. Your lips move … You *are* familiar to me." The duke then draws nearer to the ancient man, he sees his lips move as he himself speaks. "Who is this man?" he asks his companion snake: "Who is he, tell me now?" The ancient man's mouth moves, but no sound is quite audible. The duke's mouth moves, and the ancient stranger's mouth moves too, and for the first time, and the last time, the duke realises that this very moment is his life: "Am I the one trapped in this place of smoke and mirrors?" Suddenly, the other man recoils from this hideous vision, turning back within seconds to the starkest realisation. "You're me," the duke cries out. "Me!" He reaches out, touching the cold reflected face in the silver glass. "I'm old," he cries, "so very, very old."

The causeway is high, the sea recedes; the yellow and silver granite shines and sparkles in the light of the rising sun. That is not Oriane nor is it Serpentina.

Indeed not, the flowing, dark cloak is not that of Oriane, as she is seen by mortal man or by woman; no, it is not. It is the beautiful flaxen hair of another. It is the prince's golden tresses, the whitest of garments upon his body, gliding, floating down towards the sea. The young man is seen as a shadow ghost running, leaving behind bloodied footprints upon the stones. The Sea Serpent thrusts its head above the tranquil waters of the sea. "Where is she?" he dives deep, rising once again: "My Serpentina?" he calls. The young man halts in his speed. "I have something for you, Serpent," the young man calls across the glittering blue and green waters, washed through in the growing rosy light of a splendid early morn:

Dark-Light prevails in the coming of the day.

The Sea Serpent is presently silent, his head bobbing above the waves. "Do you hear?" the young knight roars into the air before revealing what he is holding in his hand. "It is here," he says, "what you have been waiting for," he shouts ahoy, holding up the head of Oriane. "Here," he cries, before throwing the green serpent-head into the sea. It stops still as though it has landed on hardened soil and not soft water. The big black eyes are open, reflecting nothing now of what has passed. Suddenly, the eyes seem to close as it sinks into the waters of the sea. The Serpent of the Sea screams for Serpentina; screams and screams: "For

Serpentina," he roars, but these cries are not the threatening kind; they are filled with deep sorrow and sadness for his lover in this life.

The forest is long gone, of course, but the mount
and traces of the moment remain.

A tiny island cut-off from the mainland. There was once a grand house at its summit; the Sparkling Castle no longer sparkles, if ever sparkle it did. The castle has more or less disappeared, and the house that replaced it has become a ruin. The battlements are only of interest to an archaeologist, the meagre drawbridge over the stream remains, the great escutcheon, impotent against invaders who have been and gone, if they ever came at all, are but the memory of a long dead knight. And always, just at the hour before sunset, a man's voice can be heard out at sea, imploring the return of this lost world. "You are the one," the duke calls, "dearest heart. 'Tis I, your own Penwith, still waiting for thee, my love. Forever and a day."

VII

A night without objects, a window onto the world, the
monstrous machinations of a circular glass, a porthole
that looks out at the blue, near turquoise, sea.

A crack to Malone's skull, another, then once more, to be sure.
A rolling pin, rattling the senses, what possible thoughts pass
through the mind of such a captive, I cannot imagine. Death
comes to all, of course, but not like this. Often I had to say to
myself out loud that I was not one of them, that I would one day
leave all this behind. The hospital staff horrified me, alarmed
me, especially when I felt that I would inevitably be numbered
among them if some visitor or passer-by saw me and half
unconsciously counted me as one of them. But it is over now;
some of us have survived. Miriam mourned Malone, not us, we
moved on with our lives.

O, the silence of the ward, the incessant
clock's ticking goes unnoticed.

Incessant, sure, continual, but benign: dividing the nights and
days, a metronome of certain ordered things, the moments,
which are never so long lasting, nor so well understood. The
silence, you see, yes, the silence; the silence out there in the
never-ending hallway; the silence, stalking the dorm, the next
room too, and the silence high up, crouching beneath the ceiling:
understanding, but never fully understood. We all are waiting. A
stiff breeze will come, blowing away time, and light, striking out
the shadows and then, and only then, will we see them. There
they'll be, waiting, yes, waiting for us, forever and a day. *No*,
comes the disturbing scream into the coming of night, with this
No availing us all for a moment to some kind of panic. It's
Crawford: No, he shouts, again, lifting his hand as though to
tend a blow to some invisible creature. And then he is still, quiet,

somehow soothed. He knows, of course, but accepts that things may come together. He gets it; he understands. The same Crawford, according to the shrink, has the mental age of a young child, a declaration seemingly belied by his present silence, his complete confusion, and his occasional outbursts of genuine sorrow. We must comfort him, alleviate the tears for his lost little friend, Guppy; and Duggan too is as silent as ever, and Roger Perrot calls out: Where is he? Where? and even Haines seems less keen on the perusal of shoes this final day, and every now and again one hears Watt, out of sorts, making a sound more whimper than roar. As he calls out, Guppy, Guppy gone. Feck's shake, playing down his own part in the injuries of the last two days. It must be said that Molloy looks tired and drawn. (They know, she is heard to say in the office, and with power, again, she says: They always know, a repeated line, there's something about death. They seem closer to the fragile boundaries than us.) Conclusions are bounded with continual verdicts, hardly any of them true: how Guppy was eventually found that night and by whom. The alarm was raised by Camier, or was it the night nurse? The night nurse immediately felt panicked, once he'd arrived, but soon settled after a series of deep breaths. Was that not it? This was his particular meditation, his approach to the ever-growing interest in mindfulness. Who had thought to look in the hospital laundry? Nobody was sure, but no stone was left unturned; numerous stones were left alone. Escapes from wards are not to be tolerated, the Consultant Psychiatrist stated unambiguously, ignoring the fact that the horse had already bolted. The complexity of a search party became more pressing – the statements hardly corroborated. The police are called, even the repetition of that numeral *nine* seemed strange, how so rarely do we ever do it, *nine nine nine*, and yet, so ever present in our minds, nine *and* nine *and* nine. It was Molloy who thought she could hear something. (Drowned, yes, drowned, who would believe it? she said, deciding to say little more. The body was not quite mangled, she dried naturally. This is no time for jokes, she tells herself, holding her tongue in public, neglecting to mention the spin speed.) Malone dies, is whispered about the place, Malone dying, unnoticed, seemingly; she seemed to exist for no one but Miriam, Malone dead. Battered to death, the words are unreliable, some masked attacker, ditto; the truth, in part, is there. You'd expect a high measure of physical damage after a period of time in an industrial washing machine, and a fast-spin against metal – there it is, the revolutions per minute. It was reported, and later repeated, again and again, by the morning shift at the laundry, that the body had been found half-in and half-out of the machine. As white as stone, one of the cronies said; Like stone, the other agreed; That's it, a statue. Nobody was allowed in, of course. Nobody saw any such thing. They were questioned, but what did they know? They were sent away – the laundry had been cordoned off; they'd seen nothing. The authorities were there, and the body was eventually taken away for a post-mortem on the causes of death. That is all we know. How Malone had got there or, indeed, why? How Malone managed to get in to the machine, never mind switch the damn thing on, nobody could explain. Was it suicide? Misadventure? The exact cause of this death, we cannot know. Murder? Was the ward now part of a crime scene? The world continued as before. Mallory came and went as quickly as he could. As he was walking off the ward, he commented to Molloy that the whole thing was a complete mystery: Guppy, he said, stays on the medical ward, for a few more days, he repeats, pausing for a moment: How on earth did he get out? What talk is this? The ruse has no end in sight. He'll be fine, the good nurse said, ignoring the final question. He'll be fine: Olwyn's checking up on him, which is not at all unusual, she pauses, this morning, she says: Without fail. This is not what was expected. His words are clouded, sounding out, sounding still, but it is noise not substance. She waits, the ward is lit, but everything feels dark and shadowed. You said nobody would get hurt. A change of tack is taken, words spoken under-breath. I said a diversion – not a charge nurse ending up in a washing machine, he whispers the words, but they are easily audible. That word again: *diversion*. He continues: I mean … I don't know where to begin. If we can get out of here without a GMC tribunal, I'll consider myself lucky. Or prison. Would Mallory fall? Are there witnesses at all? *We*, she said, responding immediately to the odd sentence. Who's this *we*? She pauses, angrier than ever. And what happens to *us*? The talk is cheap. Let us not be children, Molls. They both paused for a moment. The exit door seems so far away but it's only a matter of some yards. You know Darwin has some beautiful words. He paused again and then he recited:

> *The face of nature may be compared to a yielding surface,*
> *with ten thousand sharp wedges packed close together and*
> *driven inwards by incessant blows, sometimes one wedge*
> *being struck, and then another with greater force.*

I'll give you blows, she wants to say, you little cur – I'll give you wedges and surfaces that yield, you arrogant prick, she might have whispered that last part of her statement; she's perfectly unsure. Her mind reels but her brail is cotton wool, the words heep and gather, making sense to no one: All that matters is what matters – or nothing matters – I feel strongly tempted to inquire – the good sister, present and correct. Me, that is, Molloy. I want to luxuriate in the rubbish that he spouts – or spouted. I am in equilibrium somewhere, if I were not at this exact moment: as Murphy would say: *Do you get me?* I was hardly what you might call *on a roll*, but roll I did, in the manner of a true ball. I would discredit me, if that's what it took. Perhaps I was afraid, perhaps it was fear – and silence; the aloneness when you reach my age. My age, indeed; I was in my mid-twenties, but already I felt lost and, yes, alone – and well past it. I would let loose, roll on, let what could not be changed at least be altered somehow as though it were something that will have happened and not something that did. The one that happened to be me, that other one who passes for me. I have finished with this troop of lunatics by which I mean the *officials*. I am forever there. I am not now old, but they were the years and the days of yore; I say years and days, but here there are no years and days: only time. I resume years later, meaning that I was silent, for a long time. I can do this: stop up this noise, make the voices cease – wasn't that what I made Murphy say – poor old Murphy, and his glassy bird who last clocked him standing in shards outside a butcher's shop. All of this because he forgot to raise his arm at a bus-stop. Poor old Murphy. All of this – for a request stop. All of this for a signal; the facts are hard to bear. I have attempted to inject the contemporary into something long since forgotten, as the saying goes, into something long dead and dusted. Memory, notably. It was all of us, naturally – in the end, it was me, all me, just as I said it would be. Once I'd got rid of the Murphys and the Malones, the Mallories, the singular Mary too, all that would be left is the Molloys. Otherwise, it would be quite hopeless, making me waste my time, making me suffer for nothing, making me speak of them when, in order to stop speaking, I should have spoken of me, and of me alone, all along. What kind of creature uttered the final words?

Not a human one in any case, there are no human creatures here, or if there are they have done with crying.

The exit door was open, but somebody's nearby and unnoticed. What is there to add to these past particulars? Yes, Murphy was there. Only a few yards away. The large man is sitting in shadow, puffing signals from his pipe. He has heard it all: What is all of this? he thinks, he stills his breathing – Who *is* that? Not Malone, no; not at all. What is it he wants, opening the door? He has watched and remains aloof. *Camier, it is.* He wants to call out to him. *What is it you want?* Guppy floats out and away. *What is that …?* A flicker passes before the man with the pipe: That thing before me there? Can I be dreaming this, with my eyes open? Are they open? Is it Guppy? Yes, it is and I can see him better than I can know myself. Pictures and flickers, isn't that what they say? That is all it is. The end begins. He breathes in deeply: Pictures and flickers, he says, blowing out smoke in ectoplasm, quite unsure as to how he is configured: Pictures and flickers, is all. Sitting, or sleeping, or sometimes singing. It is so hard to tell what is what from what is made from the manifold. Who will be convinced of my substantiality? Seeing him there, thinking the reasons, the sounds, and the sweetness on all sides. Talking about rhythms and phrases of some time. Who's time? That shrink was doing the talking, talking out of his little blue lips, talking, talking, talking. He laughs, thinking of the doctor's ancient mouth, his white cotton wool hair, his words nevertheless pursuing him from the start. That's all it is, he speaks again: Noise and shamefulness. Rhythm, that's the word, and the name: Wilson, that's the name; speaking like I am a deaf man, or something else: Wilson, he says it, all the time, Wilson. I hear it all and these are the things I hear: Quite normal, he says, but not to me. You fool, I want to say it, but I keep myself to myself – You fool, I am just here. His cotton wool hair feels soft and springy. I see Molloy laughing; and me, smiling too. Ah, there it is – again. Can I be dreaming?' he asks himself – That was Camier, for sure, now whispering, somehow hidden, in the blocks of shadow. The trick is to make it stand still; the press of it, the rhythm, one minute, still, the nex... *I see you; but what is it you do?* This is no dream; that's all shored up. Pictures and flickers, but what it is it you do? Is it you at all? Camier opened the door to the outside world; he was also the one who smacked the kid in the face – once and then twice. Malone! Camier calls out, rushing towards her: ... Malone! The door – it's open – someone's opened the fecking door. Camier was out of breath. Malone was with Watt, about to change his dressing before he retired for bed. Who? Who's opened the fecking door, Camier – what're you on about? She leaves a blue Valium on the side-table nearest to Watt's bed. And Guppy's gone. Is he here? I've looked in the bathrooms. Nothing. Is he here? Malone replies quickly: 'Course he's not bloody well *here*. What would he be doing here, you daft 'apeth. Malone begins to look panicked. That's all she needed – particularly after the events of the last couple of days. What would decisive action look like? Should she sound the alarms. But how was the door opened? It's not possible, she said. It can't happen; there are systems in place ... Has anyone come in? All the world is falling, falling apart. That's what it feels like. No, no one. The door was open, he pauses, Stefan Guppy's gone. There'll be sackings. There's no doubt about it – no one's getting away with this. It's absolutely their responsibility to guard against any residents' absconding. *How*? – she wants to say, but can't return to that. *Why*? That's useless too. They've just bought a flat nearby. Malone can't get sacked. What will Miriam say? We're about to exchange contracts, crosses her mind in the instant. We'll be sacked, she says aloud. Camier's face is solemn, she can see that. *When*? That's worse. There's no time to think. Already two minutes has passed. I'll go, she says. Stay here, Camier. Make sure everything's safe. Even in the dim lit dorm room, Malone looks distraught. The alarms? he says. O, no; let's leave that. The night nurse is on his way – let me go first. I'll check for him – first of all. I'll go. Miriam's going to kill me, she thinks. God knows! And after all we've been through. The two of us in one place – why is that so strange. Love is love – O, Miriam. I'll fix this, I promise. I'll fix this. *I'll find him*, she says to the darkness. He'll be terrified, he will. How did he open the door? I can't think. Feck me, she says. Feck's sake, Malone, Watt chimes in, looking on the side-table at the glowing blue pill set there. Only one? crosses his mind, just the one – he'd prefer two, reaching out, necking it in the moment. We'll find him, don't worry, Camier. I'll go now. Don't fret. We'll have Stefan back in no time at all. You stay here, hold the fort. I'll be right back. This is not panic, but there is much fear on display. What shall I say to the night nurse – he'll be here soon enough. Malone turns, she smiles bravely, as though so much depended upon the future: Say nothing, for now, Camier. Say nothing, love, she says, I'll sort this, if it's the last thing I do.

VIII

*"It's just three kisses, my little liege man; that is all it is.
And then …" His feet feel queer, the odd sensation of tossed
rose petals caught between his toes, all red and pink and
wet. "What will you do? What then, my goddess?"*

"Our union serves the world – an emblem of cyclical becoming: together the loop of hope and ultimate good... Division … Division …" – she hardly makes a move; her language seems disjointed, halting: "If only – the earth…" she says, but ceases her words, as though disturbed, or re-thinking the worth of what she says: "You must understand this, brave knight," she's aware that she's been seen in the looking glass. "*Our* only hope lies in our becoming one. A circle of continuity, of all that is made just," she blinks, so odd in a snake. "In this way the oceans, and so the earth, remain sweet under our protectorship." Oriane is sure this youth has been informed of her, shall we say, "pedigree," that much seems clear – a *lamia* in exchange for Serpentina. He knows well the form she takes, of course. "But what of us, dear Oriane?" he enquires, shaking his golden tresses. He lifts his hand, his fingers spread to touch the form before him. He holds back his need to feel, he resists right up to the very last minute – "… You and the Father Serpent deny *our* existence in the world. What say you to this, dear goddess? You say so little about *us*." She calls for clarity: "*Us*? But what, dear prince, can you mean by *us*? By *ours*?" He replies, furthering his concerns: "Yes, *us*, *ours*, if you so wish. Humans, dear goddess, we humans. *Us*. This union you are so keen to speak of will thwart our growth. What if you frustrate our progress across the seven seas – what happens then? Two in one is unassailable – no human power could ever hope to compete. Each power meets its separate existence, its people, history; in short, dear goddess, its extent. In essence, you will be our undoing: you will be the death of us, our divisions confine us to the lands; we will never pass into the deep; we will be limited only to the surface. You come before, dearest goddess;

160

we come after. We are cognisant of your precedence: You come before – We come after. You come before *us* – therein lies the problem. We cannot cede." Her response is swift. "Our union is benign. You know this well, brave knight. You have been informed of this. We mean no harm. Even now I hear upon the waters near, silent seeming, and beyond, there sways a little ship. O, yes, I see it there, in silence, and, look see, the figurehead of she whose jet hair flows from her head to her snake's tail – a *lamia* – *lamia*, that is the name we are given. You see, too, don't you? Yes? You see, too." He pays but little heed to the seeming silence of the question . "You, goddess, you. You aim again to rule the waves. That cannot be" – she knows why I am here, passes through his mind – "We cannot be simply paid off by some false union, making you Mother Serpentina to the Father Serpent. This notion is nonsensical to us; it is incredible even to state it openly. By some talk of disenchantment made good by my human kiss – what is this? You may swallow your own tail, but that is all you'll get. Swallow away, false goddess: Swallow your whole" – he begins to laugh at his own cleverness, for that is what he takes it to be. He goes on: "*That* will be your own compensation – the union, the completion, the circle, not of two, but of merely one. Swallow your whole," he repeats the line. She shifts her aspect. The room is shaded and cool in the early spring light: birds about to sing, bees will buzz, a humming bird moth enters the room, feels the atmosphere's distress, hums out again to the freshening lightening darkness. "The seas will boil," she says. "Lands lost. In time you will perish, each and all. No human will survive: you must see this. Deaths, my brave knight. All." The young prince rests his hand upon the hilt of his crescent sword. "Deaths," she repeats. "And, yes, eventually, that will come: Deaths. This mad adventure can be halted. I am the womb of the sea, you know this, but..." – here she halts her own progress, an air of resignation in her wonderful voice. "Your mother...," she says, attempting to strike his heart. Must Oriane implore so? He will have none of it: "My mother suffered visions, Snake! Don't speak of the woman to whom all was lost; who but bore not me now but another lost in time; nothing else but that. In visions, she erred, what more is new. The tapestry made myriad promises: not one of these was kept – or she saw but dimly. Here I am, but even the Woodman knew nothing of my task to come. And the fair maiden: she faded to nothing – Came in dream, died in her dreaming. Nothing. Yea, again, to nothing." One last try: "Your mother" – she flinches from his hand, the fanned fingers seem huge, destructive, but his face deceives her. How so very beautiful he is, his youth, for she is as old as time, his callow youth. "Your mother," she repeats, "was shown the future in, yes, as you say, myriad ways, and forms and figures. Know this: The seas will boil. Lands will fill. Archipelagos will be engulfed. The cries, can't you hear them? Our continuous present, not the future. O, prince, but already in evidence. I am the other side of the infinite line – but alone – no, this cannot be. To complete the circle, becoming one, from what *was* to what *will* be, from being two to one again – One All. Kiss… – Her flow is interrupted, her thoughts swift and fast: "You came to release your uncle? Penwith? You came in search of him?" His look is one of genuine surprise, can she not see, flits to mind: "He is no uncle of mine," he said, a look of distaste in the mouth and amusement about the eyes, continuing: "Penwith came to kill …" She corrects this wayward prince, breaking his flow: "The duke came to care … He is kept here not by me – but by… by…" He raises his hand, Oriane flinches. "Come closer, Oriane. Come." His eyes seem so variegated, changeable, his skin so slightly burned, dark and white, his hair so fair yet a blackness alights about his head; his profile is that of an ancient statue, carved from the four corners of the earth: "Come goddess; yes, closer," he implores, his voice softening. "Hold still" – she closes her eyes, resignation, it looks like, resuming upon the instant to a bravery borne of desire or a sudden drive: "You have waited long, that is so true: Here it comes, goddess: the promise, yes – Kiss was, Kiss is, Kiss never shall be – with the curve of my sword's blade …

You waited so long: Here it comes – the final Kiss."

We see again, back to the beginning. We see again – we must go on. The queen's eyes, widening in stark fear; she looks across her chamber at the east wall ahead: "No," she shouts at the internal images, at the external patterns, which thread one final picture. "Not that," she said, "not my child. I see as if it were, as it will be." But there is more, holding her blooded babe in arms, slick with falling tears, her mouth moves, but the words are but whispers – she is too weak to dash the child against the wall unto death – "not my own child. Murder ..." The king leans in, seeing the horror in her eyes, straining to hear her last words – "O, there" – this young mother, holding on to her slick child for just a few moments more – "O, there," she sees in the brightest hues, the tapestry on the east wall – a young man, is it her own child? A rock in his hand, rising above his head, a boy of this land, born to the Green Palace. A rock is risen. "There ..." – her lips are trembling – her husband seems to be resting his head on her breast, obscuring the babe in arms – "There ..." Her view of the tapestry before her on the east wall of her chamber is far from hindered; she sees the speed of its alteration. A rock in his hand, at the lake side – in silence, he was hidden amongst the rushes. Strikes once, strikes twice, strikes thrice upon the king's head. The young man's cheek is spattered with the king's blood and royal-offal. The king's body is then laid to rest on the waters, gently guiding the lifeless body out from the lakeside, watching until the king disappears from sight. The queen sees this – she's seen all. The king leans in, watching with distress the horror in his wife's eyes, straining to hear her last words: "Death, dear ... You, love, yes ... water, dearest, the water" – she pauses, her face rigid in fear or its companion, total despair?

"... Murder ... Murder ... Murder."

What relief, that's what springs to the king's mind – not a moment of recrimination at all. Her last breath was for her and her true child, that's what he thinks: "I hear you, love of mine." The king calls out to her cold dead eyes, shining still: "Love of mine, I hear." Yes, shining still, staring wide across at the unmoving tapestry. "Her last words?" he demands attention from those who are gathered. "Her last words were:

'Mother … Mother … Mother'…"

"Hear me," the young prince says, "hear me, Oriane," and then he pauses, standing straight. As if thrice was a dream. Beyond the light of such dreaming one may see the passing fractions of partial light, the scenes of which are never blocked and shaped via sense alone, but are arisings and perishings, separations and disengagements, of land and sea. And then, just now, momentarily, a degree of connection and fuller engagement is made before the patterns become again. To what was seen, there's yet something else; some other matter of concern, or are we simply watching words and means? The gannets black-tipped wings of purest white fold into the creased sea, one, then another, another, lifting-up, passing by, disappearing, so suddenly. Now they are passed; a fulmar, grey and white, stiffed winged, is mistaken for a herring gull, corrected, instantly: "Is it not one life that I look back upon? Am I not one person – or so many ones passed – who distinguishes himself – herself – theirself – against all of these others?" The brave knight sees only the sea's breath from this high window, rising and falling. He leans slightly forward, as though he might fall. He again observes the rose petals strewn upon the stone flags, his feet, bare and slick with red and pink juice. Sea soft, a lake, it looks like, he recalls – "There has already been ample death, don't you see, goddess?" he wants to say – he hears as well as sees. The room, shaded and cool, shocks his eyes as he looks back. No way, no hope of ever altering the continual alternation of what creates with what must be destroyed – again and again. He craves his past, the image of the one he loved; perhaps he was needed only for some princely purpose. Here he is, a complete and certain vision; he chases the image, pinning him down, framing him, if only to gaze upon, and fondle the ephemera, for a moment or two. "Is that a patch of yellow," he replies, looking back through the window, as high as he, as her, as they. Has he heard a voice? He replies, nevertheless. A patch of yellow light, yes, waiting for him, a strand of brightest, silent, motion free, colour. Waiting, his decision, to wait, to see what else can be done – nothing, it's too late, far too late; his feet spattered red, but now not petals, pink and red, but the blood of a goddess, her jet hair resting near, indeed, tickling his toes. He feels he may burst out laughing. Tickle, tickle toes. Heading home, he sings out to the Serpent of the Sea: "a song for you, my mournful friend – a song for gathering mushrooms:

Her parting breast on mine she pressed, her head was like a feather O

And her lips on mine, but only twice, we both sat down together O

Together O, and her lips on mine do gently join

And we both sat down together O …

CHAPTER THREE
TUESDAY

I

*(It's like he's behind walls, she said, neglecting to elaborate.
Walls? I said, urging her to continue. She inhaled – exhaled
– not a sigh, but an issuing of smoke before speaking: Not so
much as a dicky, dear, she replied to someone else. Do you
follow me? Not a word she ever said was straight up; not one.
Follow? I asked. Dicky, kid, she replied, definitely dicky.)*

Like a sudden noise you hear in the dark, benign in the main,
but loud enough to make a lasting impression for a while. You
listen, so intently, then, nothing; not so much as a dicky bird.
(... no firm links, she pauses: To other lives, she says, her right
eye stung by a thread of smoke. But how could there be? I want
to say by way of counter. I let it go.) Guppy was a stranger to us
all, and alone: nineteen, at most (I should have been surprised,
she said, but I wasn't. She stopped suddenly. I was dying to
intercede with a wide-eyed response: *Surprised*? But my queries
were unwelcome.) Something very unpleasant was about to
come into our lives, ours alone, and that was that. Who can
answer for these things – who will ask the questions? Nobody
was in a hurry to stick their neck out. (... found like that, she
explained. There's not really very much more I can add? Malone,
dead as a dodo, she said, uncharitably.) Guppy was not alone,
not then, at least. So, the story went, and would be told again:
There's no holding him back, she said, suddenly he disappears
from sight. Escaped, she said. I say nothing, it makes no sense.
She repeats: It's like he suddenly disappears. A subtraction, she
says, a hole made in the fabric, she clarifies. This time I could not
resist: Hole? I say, fabric? Sounds like a Catholic wedding night.
She smiles, catches my drift, lifts an imaginary bit of baccy from
the tip of her tongue: The pattern is altered, she says, filled in.
An event, if you like, she said, then stopped. There seemed to
be an endless stream of tales about this silent young man. He's
holding something back, that's what it seems like, she said. I am
still reeling from the event she mentioned. Everybody believed

her. I began to feel we were all in on something. Like children playing – a late summer afternoon – happening upon a fugitive in the woods. They promise to say nothing. Sincerely, but we know how that goes. Words are set free – dicky birds. If not something so innocent, it soon felt as though we'd been caught red handed. But what led to the final act, the crime? What was our transgression? Life was anything but a solid substance, if indeed it ever had been. Minds now were reeling. Really? the veteran said, jutting his jaw: Nobody saw that coming now did they? How the hell did they all end up in there? None of us responded. That was yet to come.

What shapes are left behind by these unfolding events,
in the words we respond to? But the nub of the question
came down to this: How did Malone end up dead?

Camier tipped off Molloy. Camier has some nurse's training; he's not an auxiliary. He works with Malone; he reports back: I'll damn well show her, Malone was reported to have said – that's what Camier notes down – Does Molloy think I'm blind, or stupid? (More scribbling upon Camier's mind, a record made, later repeated. Planning what might be stirred and what shapes they would take.) It was all decided that day. What would be done in time, would be done without delay. What did we say? Nothing, of course, we said nothing. (Mum, Molloy had said, invoking past ages, we must keep mum. Mum!) We could explain matters, fill in the gaps, make good the thin sheet of empty spaces, but we didn't bother. All of this feeling, for that is what it was, *feeling*; yes, something we felt, an attitude, or vigilance, in the face of unfolding chaos. It wasn't exactly naïve optimism to imagine things would get back to normal. No, I didn't think that then; I am off when it comes to the truth. There really was no beginning to get back to, and no *new* normal, the *old* normal was still in situ. Maybe, I thought later that things could've been better configured. Fixed, somehow, into place. At the time, I simply wanted out, but it all ended in a jiffy so I needn't have worried. These were hardly what you might call the presentiments of nameless atrocities. (*Atrocious*? I asked. Bless you! Molloy called back, laughing at her own deftness: Like a sneeze, she clarified. *Atrocious*, I said it again: I get it, I said). Whatever you'd call it, we were headed there. (Not everybody makes it out alive. Isn't that what they say? Not quite: Only lovers, I wanted to say.) I'll try again, none was ever so true. (Quick sharp, Molloy said, interrupting). The situation was now one of considerable discomfort for everyone concerned. It all boiled down to Malone's stigmatising question: *How did you explain the door, Molls?* It was Molloy's sudden realisation that the standard had changed. (That's it, crossed her mind. Are they right, though? Do they have a point?) It was no longer half seen and guessed at. The waters had suddenly massed themselves, but when or where would they fall? There was that black shivering sensation that things had gone awry, but the feeling was ignored. *Where's Watt?* they asked, eventually making what can only be described as a tentative inquiry. Everyone knows that Watt is Malone's favourite, by far, she makes no bones about it. *What's happened to Watt?* Malone asks. (Here we go, flashes through Molloy's brain, lighting up various neuronal pathways.) Something snapped, right there, at the point of Murphy's outburst, and for one simple reason: Truth, or the lack of it. (We fixed things, that's what Malone thinks; a stitch up, that's what she thinks.) By Tuesday the whole door had been replaced and the only indication that anything had ever happened was a brilliantly patched square of lino bluer than the rest. The head of engineering, Mr. Garnett, had explained that the door was, in fact, faulty. The whole side-frame was replaced and painted. (We keep these in store, he'd said, by necessity: It is a particular fire-retardant door, he'd said, a unit of which we keep for such emergencies.) Everything was coming together nicely; patched up and perfected, and stitched into place, and somehow harmonious. (It'll all be water under the bridge, she said, you'll see. It'll pass, it always does.) Molloy seemed convinced, repeating her words: It'll all be water under the bridge. But for whose benefit? Her own?

Molloy's arrival to shift on the Tuesday morning was earlier than usual.

It was as if she expected to be caught in a web of her own making. The constraint of being among strangers alleviated itself while she read through the notes. Already, she has stalked the ward, looking for signs of difference. (What did I think I would find, an inner voice, niggling at her inner ear. Guppy, crosses her mind, the name, the all-eye of this silent creature. She recalls Mallory's words: He can't speak, and then she says aloud: You do realise that, don't you?) I found her sitting at the desk, the room was shaded. The night nurse had, at her insistence, left, a tad earlier than usual. The change-over had already taken place. She was reading Malone's notes from Monday's shift. All was well, it seemed. Mention was made that the damaged fire-door into the dorm had been replaced. (Like new, she said, as thoughts went surging round her head: You can hardly tell.) Garnett's report was there before her, it was signed and held in with a paper clip. He had omitted the fact that the door had been damaged by a missile, focussing instead on the hinge and the frame, stating that the door was to some degree faulty. Malone's written insistence that the door was *beyond repair* irked Molloy; seeing the words now written in black and white: Read that, she said. I read it back to her: *Door at left elevation to office, facing, ingress to night ward, was damaged by Murphy* [dated here], *as per notes of S. R. N. Molloy. Repair could not be effectuated and the door has had to be replaced* [date and time] *by Engineering team* [name of operative]... And so, on it went in this odd legalese, which seemed to suggest there'd been some sort of discounted transgression. See, she said, seemingly content with her conclusions. But there was a problem here, and a major one. But that's not Malone's writing, I replied. Malone's hand had that annoying affectation of making little circles above the 'i'. This writing was finer, the words put down here seemed measured and, yes, insistent. Molloy was well aware of this: Yes, she said, I thought of that. Malone must have dictated it to Camier, she paused, it's his writing. He's terrified of Malone, you do know that, don't you? Terrified! I took this to be an exaggerated position. Malone could be fierce but, surely, the word *terror* was going too far the other way. I played it down: It seems all right, Molloy, it's great, the door's fine now. But she was not finished. Did Malone really have to take it upon … Molloy paused here, her words were fractured with preoccupation – I mean the repair bit? Couldn't they just leave it to Garnett? He's saying the door was faulty. Wasn't that enough for them? All was fine, but something in Malone had, apparently, suddenly switched – what other explanation was there? Unease, that's the word I'd have used: Unease. (Something's up, Molloy said. I could hear her saying it, but I was not so convinced.) Nothing had happened, but Malone seemed curious, or angry, that they were being kept in the dark. I don't know, she says, it isn't certain, it remains to be seen. Malone's the problem. Her exact words: Malone's definitely the problem.

Within minutes of our departure yesterday afternoon, the biting comments commenced. The word on the ward was that Malone was – to quote Camier – Up in arms.

Screw the lot of them, Malone had said to her henchmen. To Camier, a small framed, handsome, youngish man of around thirty-six or seven years, and to another man, an odd fellow, reasonably well-set, of medium height, like Camier, and hard to judge in terms of years, but probably, like Malone, in his very early thirties. His name was Mercer and he, like Camier, was – so they say – terrified of S.E.N. Malone. Malone was railing against the world, rushing into the office, shoes squeaking as a kind of accompaniment to the expletives. Who the hell's done this to the dear lad? Then rushing the next minute out to the dormitory, seeking Watt, running a powerful arm around Watt's shoulder. Watt raises himself up from the pillows to accommodate the limb – Feck me, look at your face, kid, Malone calls out. In the eyes of the second shift, there was something underhand in all of this. Malone was hot on the trail, and yet even they were unsure as to where this path would lead. Malone would not expose, exactly, but they'd have to put things right. (I'm not a grass, crossed Malone's mind. But just look at Watt, Malone thought.) The world would be put back on its axis, a certain equilibrium was sought and, yes, somebody would have to take some responsibility. Fecking right, they all said: They'll have to pay. Malone, lifting the bandage from victim's head, said: It's only right. A nearby Camier felt duty bound to lean in, sniffing out the situation. Looks like he's been hit with a fecking axe, he said, to Watt's delight. Right, Camier, a righ' fecking axes. Feck's sake, Watt replies, pluralising the axe. Camier, apparently, was the one who looked pained. Change all dressings, Malone said to him, in an hour, and walked back out to the office. Then make a fecking record of it. This is scandalous. He's happy to make a record of whatever is required – he'll do precisely as he's told – I just did what Malone said, he'd explained when asked. We were going to pay for our putative sins, for our mistakes, for the woes of the world. For our attempt to fix things into place, that seems clear. What does Malone say *specifically* about Watt? I ask Molloy. I look at her looking down at the notes. Please! Don't remind me: that's all Malone ever goes on about: Where's Watt? How's Watt? What's Watt – she could hardly resist – she laughs for a moment. Who's Watt, Malone's long-lost brother? she asks – or what? Molloy looks back at the pages, to the biro marks, the fine lettering of the script, which are very clearly not Malone's overlarge hand. (Don't be petty, Molloy thinks, self-righteous, springs to mind.) She lifts her head. The light above is dim but her eyes look dimmer. In the notes? I say – omitting to mention again the discrepancy of the handwriting. I say, instead: What did they say about Watt – in the notes? She begins again: They must have seen what Mallory Jacobs had added to the notes. But not much else. She looked back up at me, throwing a pack of fags across the desk. Molloy can tell that *Mallory* was on the tip of my tongue; she could tell that I didn't want to say the first name of the doctor, that I didn't want to remind her of the embarrassment of yesterday: I called Mallory, Molloy had explained to Malone. She'd immediately regretted it, as soon as the word was out of her mouth. *Mallory*? Malone replies: Who the feck's Mallory? Mallory! Malone laughed into Molloy's face, it fell instantly, *Doctor* Jacobs, you mean. Am I right, Molloy? Amn't I right? That was yesterday's awkwardness. This morning Molloy's still sore. I took up the pack of ciggies and took one out, popping a fag in my mouth by way of a gag. I leaned in while she lit hers and then mine. Nothing much, she said, replying at last to my enquiry. Hardly a word about that. Really, nothing. Dressing, that's the crux of it; the dressing. Obsessed with bandages, all of a sudden, she says: Who knew? But that was the point, surely. Doesn't that seem strange to you? I asked. She puffs her cigarette, turning her face to the ward side window. I looked too. Yes, she replied. You'd think Malone would've milked it; but she didn't. You're right, there's something suspicious about it. The good sister looked vacantly out to the ward, still quiet at this hour. Then there was the assault upon Guppy. That was Monday, after we'd exited the shift, but we'd have to wait until this afternoon to find out about that.

II

Here, she halts her flow, leaving out these final words – "You who would wonder at each little thing, as if at every moment you were discovering the world. You who are lost once and for all."

No, of this, she cannot speak; nothing so much as spoken. "You who are chosen to bridge the great divisions." That much, the fair lady means to say. This callow youth – was he really so young? – is trying to move, to breathe, to avoid burning up; he is fast failing. "Humanity has developed differently there," the fair lady whispers into his shell-like, intoning with kindly voice, tickling his lobe. In this darkness, the discomfort of fierce heat is intolerable. He immediately strikes out his arms, attempting to rise, to fight, but to no avail – he feels himself sinking fast into the downy mattress as though into quicksand. The recollection of what he had once felt – as a boy – fades away as fast as his breathing. There is nothing to cling to. The outer world is lost. Why should he be dreaming dreams? He opens his eyes; he must see. A haze of luminescence surrounds this fairest of ladies, but begins quickly to diminish. "You must prevail this day," she intones; the fair lady is dimming, her shine, once so bright, is not quite what it once was. "Do you comprehend, my dearest boy? Can you hear me now?" The lady vanishes. A solitary man appears. Beneath the falling of the dew at dawn, the young man is sleeping under the protection of his grey steed. The Barbary, barely moving, still and darkest before dawn, monolithic and magnificent. This was the view the Woodman happened upon that very morning. He stopped and smiled and nodded to whom we know not. Yes, the forest's factor's here, his attention pricked. He comes.

The young man awakes, slowly, at first,
opening one eye, then the other.

"Dreaming," the young knight says, "only dreaming?" He smiles, repeating the line. "Abandoned," crosses his mind. "Or forgotten? Abandoned, it felt like." A moment – or aeons – it was hard to tell: once a boy, then a young man, now a brave knight. The fair lady, ever-changing, gone: "Just there," he said, as though addressing the passing of his dream. "Suddenly, yes, like that, she was old," he recalls: "Was she ever really there" – in the lines and colours, in the traces of uncountable strands, in the weakly made phrases, was she ever really there? "You cry because you cry," she said, but all was lost again upon waking. "I am lost to time," he replied, "but I will do as I am bid." How was this decision made? A boy was playing, but time passed. The Green Palace seemed to be floating in the distance, a long time ago. There he is: "I see it now, the tears welling up in my eyes, blinding me as I walked on." Without knowing quite why or, indeed, where, he quit a life of hearth and home. He simply upped and walked across the fields beyond the palace, out towards a life without hearth, without home. That was surely the very beginning, or some other end in sight. "I can't recall it," he whispers into the breeze, "my leave-taking. The Green Palace... floating... but when?" The unnamed creatures, and other hiddenfolk, flee fast and speed before and behind and beyond the steadfast trees. They have grown accustomed to the young man's eager form, which is beyond simple description, but never simply nothing. Was there no-one to have a care for what became of him? No mother – in death, forever absent from his crib – and then a father plunged into dark waters of the lake, a deep pool of despair. "As green as a frog, he was." The duke, his uncle, had explained to him, wiping away tears of laughter: "*What way was that ...*" words and words, he cannot hear, crossing one mind to the next, altering substantially as they go, "*... for a king ...*" the trace yields and is no longer true, unable to stick, flowing fast to some other depiction, "*... to die?*" The duke is struggling to speak, his laughter verges on the hysterical; stopping in fits only to commence again. "But what a send-off," he said, straightening his regnant chain, referring to the funeral. Perhaps he recalls the colouration of his dream, flickering just out of sight. The final moments of memory gutters as the final candle in a chapel, passing the cloister into ever darker shadow. There is an instant of ascent, a final plunge to darkness; the knight's past is lost and forgotten. All that remains is the recurring promise to himself: "Yes, the next time, I will hold on to my dream – next time I will not let go."

Through the metalled bronze of these indomitable trees – more like pillars – holding back the dark, he begins to see white light. "It is a line," he says, wondering if he's seeing a mirage.

"The dark light," he whispers, "of wood and glass and water." The Woodman begins to walk away from the young prince. "I knew you'd come," the young knight says. "Somehow," he says, "I know of you." The Woodman steps over a large branch, broken and bent, his axe hanging in a holster at his side. "Don't go," the knight calls out. The Woodman stops, turns, slowly settles himself upon a large granite boulder. "I go when I go," he replies. Then nothing. The Woodman falls to silence; so still, he becomes almost invisible to the human eye. Amidst the smoke that twisted in little whirlwinds from his pipe, he begins, slowly, carefully, to tell his story about a land beyond and far and away. "The bronze trees? The golden sand? The silver sea," he says, "the wood, the glass, and the water?" A question refuses to form: "The dark and the light," he whispers, his voice trails away, almost inaudibly perishing, and then arising. An incantation, it sounds like. "Before you, beneath you, beyond you now, one thing after another, now and forever heep." The other smiles, enjoying the passage of the Woodman's voice, which is both familiar as well as distant. "Woodman? I can assure you, I am not afraid. Say what you must say." The Woodman is enigmatic: "For why else would I be here, isn't that so?" That is no question, but the young man makes his reply. "Even though I cannot fathom quite where I am, Woodman." He looks across at his horse, as though for succour, before continuing with the words that made him bashful: "The place of my destiny must be here for..." The Woodman's voice breaks in: "There is a little more I can tell you." The voice is deep, resonant, filled with warmth and truth: "You see, I am a teller of stories, that is all I am. But the difficulty is immense." The Woodman hitches the thumb of his right hand into the belt of his breeches, his axe flashes an arc of the flickering sun into the young man's eyes. For a moment he is stunned. A little breeze shrugged in from the sea some distance off. The impression was of one immediate thing, a singular colour, constantly altering, but remaining somehow solid. The sea is entirely indistinguishable from the sky, they are whole and inseparable, without so much as a crease. One feels the whole world is but a matter of white light, and just then, as you observe, perhaps anticipating, a dark line begins to appear upon the horizon. Beneath us, beyond us, one thing after another, now and forever – arising and perishing. Instantly, the young man notices the oneness of so many things: the calmness of the chaos, flooding his mind, the wholeness of these fractions and fragments, restricting his reason. "The sea, the sea," he whispers, a sibilant song, a second voice, he hears so successfully. He looks down at his feet, the softness of the earth, he feels it; feeling fire beneath his feet, and then ice. An armoured black beetle ambles along. He stoops down, smiling upon the wondrous creature. He puts his finger out before it, but this serves only to oblige the beetle to turn around, changing its direction as though it had already been decided. "Was this fate?" he asks. "Does it come down to this?" A singular obstacle. He is no longer whispering. He speaks aloud, as if to the heavens passing overhead, as if in prayer to powers of human nature. "Fate," he calls out to the trees, the blending, bronzed, barks, the coiling Hedera helix, and the broken silver limbs, undead. And then he looks back up at the topmost window of sky. The speeding white cotton wool clouds beyond the canopy of festooning green, yellow, and red leaves. "How much was there to cast off," he says, his voice rising, "and forget?" The young man is a royal knight, a putative king; indeed, he has surely traversed the seven seas; he has fought and slain in pitched battles; crossed mountains and endless deserts – each pattern, altering, stitching together another time, and place, another place, time, and event. We imagine this to be the makings of his past life. Born to it, we'd say. Yet for all the benefits of his freedom and compulsion, this valorous knight was an orphan, his fair mother had died in child birth; his father, pining for a decade and some, before plunging himself into the depths of the lake. He was dragged from the water by his own brother, Penwith, one spring morning.

> *"What way?" the young man asks, "was that," again,*
> *"for a king," and again, "to die … To die." The words*
> *reheard, "for a king," but this time bringing enervation,*
> *"was that," pain, heat, and sadness: "What way?"*

The boy was called to his father's chamber. Yes, he recalls that much; he sees it now, an expanding amplification of an earlier opaque transmutation, progressing to near perfection. He sees it, imagining his father's death as regicide; the cold-blooded murder of a monarch. "What's that?" he calls out, but there is nobody to hear; familiar at once, and queer. That sound he heard, that voice: a sneering, laughing tone the duke affected with his lackeys. "Hardly the colour of a king." He can still hear his uncle's voice, remaining perplexed as he entered the room. Father, he wanted to say; father? He was not informed by his uncle Penwith that his father's face was a livid green, that his eyes were staring; a presentiment of shock, yet somehow serene. "He was perfect," that's what the boy hears. The king, wet and dead, but faultless in form. There was a smile upon his lips. "He was at peace," he hears. Freed from this life. That's what he wants to believe. "The king's now in the embrace of his queen." Mistress Bridges was heard to explain to the weeping scullery maids, the serving girls, and the youngest of the gardeners, all of whom were inconsolable. "Green," Penwith says, "bloody bilious, I'd call it. Like a frog in the mouth of a snake." His uncle made no mention of the king's colouration; the boy hears only this: "He's at peace, my dearest nephew. Freed from this life. Come, dearest youth; to your uncle come."

Passages unfold; recurrence paints these scenic views, and one wonders when it will cease, if indeed it ever will.

"My father? Dead," the young man's heart races in recollection: "Dead, you say, uncle?" Still questioning thought, the actions, and the words. Dead. Dead. Dead, you say? His presence, his loss, the king somehow fallen. In the embrace, they said, of the sojourning gods. Some such hyperbole. The boy hardly thinks of this, but his mind wanders, his attention is pricked: "Why is uncle dressed in father's clothes?" From head to toe in his father's attire – "with all the accoutrements of a king?" Worse still, he had the Royal chain dangling at his sternum. "The livery collar, uncle," he whispers the words. Penwith's hand reaches to it, disturbingly, caressing it gently, with his long white fingers. "Why are you dressed like that, uncle?" Suddenly, the boy's attention shifts again. The earth is not silent at all; all around the walls and the land and all about was groaning and weeping. "Our people," the boy says aloud, gaining confidence; yet, he knows then that the end had come. "My father? Dead, you say."

"Hello, little rabbit," he said, turning, dressed as a king, "I've been waiting for you – so long, have I waited. For you. Only you, little rabbit."

Running helter skelter to the tapestry, away from his uncle's hard crystal gaze, his shifting, sneering full red lips, calling to him: "Little rabbit, come now." That's all the boy heard, his uncle's words: "Little rabbit, where's your sense of humour." The boy rushes out and headlong to the late queen's chamber. The tapestry is not still, changing, once, again, again, once more, secrets told again, was that it: "They are moving, changing, all colours are shifting," he calls out, as though imploring the empty room to action. "Every move you make," he cries in vain to the patternings of the whole. "Every move." And what can he make out: "The young woman there," he whispers, "she ends in a snake tail." He pauses, looks deep within the presented figure: "There he is. There he is. There. And there's Penwith," he whispers, his voice hoarse from weeping: "Cut into the glass." What is the meaning of these words? "Look closer," he says, "locked into the transparent prison – his glassy cage?" You see it now? Yes, somehow, clearly, you can see it: "Look, and you will see right through the walls – is that it?" he asks, seeing deep within his past. "Is he dying? 'Ever Youthful' is his name and he is dying," he repeats – "Dying. Yes, the duke is dying, trapped in glass. And death." Were these whispers ever heard? Who makes the shapes, the forms, the patterns held up on a wall?

He falls; fails, weeping, weeping, feigns a weighty uprising;
filling out, filling up, weeping; going through life from
within, in silence, and with some sympathy.

He falls down. Away from the tapestry, hanging silently, shifting its patterns to accord for the change. He falls. This was not the first time; there'd been other similar experiences such as these; experiences which, by their very nature, proved beyond all doubt that this was not the first; that he remains on the brink of life and death, hovering between natality and mortality; that this was no ordinary world. From side to side, his eyes, seeking something, but what? No longer were things assembled by the ways of the world, or some such fashion; no, we can see his eyes are closed, but seeing, closed tight they are, which serve only to draw our attention to the pulse to the side of his head. "Say nothing." The injunction is heeded. "His heat," he hears the words, a feminine angle, his head thumps: "Look how he sweats, saturated to the skin," a woman speaking, a little stab of pain accompanies the external voice. "He burns up so." The fever rages within him, dredging up from deep below unknown, perhaps unsaid, images, trickling out from the wider picture of facts he had known nothing of; laying there or swimming or sinking to the bottom of the ocean; surfeited with himself, held drowning in deep water; waiting for the moment when he is commanded to live again; creating an orderly fashion, the proper sequence of which remains aloof; he starts, shivers, hovering between life and death, birth and decease – tossing, a fit of fury: "Calm, Master, please," Nurse Tink's on hand, *her* voice: "How you move, Master." And there, in heeps, and all crushed together, he is floating, hovering; at once his voice rises, then falls, failing fast: "Please, Master, don't scream," the voice changes, imploring him. This time it's Mistress Bridges' soothing tones, a massive homely figure, smoothing his hair back from his forehead: "We'll need more than prayers," she says; being nothing, altering, as the shadows moved behind them; being nothing, arising and perishing, becoming something. The figures drawn by the setting sun; low, a candle burns as he is burning, great shadows: "Such heat," he hears, a friendly light in the darkness; dark and light matter; friendly, muted, all of it, an order; nonetheless it is hardly nothing; his life, hovering; his death, slavishly acquiescent; surely coming, he makes no possible response: ceasing, endless things, once more forgotten. "Dying." His fall: Death.

III

Later that Tuesday, as our shift was ending and Camier's beginning, he slips into the office for a word. He is standing close to Molloy, looking as though he's got something on his mind. (Can I help, Camier? she asked. Well, there is something … something I think you should know. She looks at her fags on the desk: I'm all ears, she says.)

I think you should know something, he says, Guppy was *attacked*, he pauses, adding pathos to the unfolding drama, his emphasis on the assault. Her face is as stiff as a poker. Yesterday, he continues, after you lot'd left. The veteran auxiliary suddenly pops his head and jaw around the door, saying he's off – No wonder they call this a mad house, he calls out, closing the door behind him – resigned, dedicated, a touch of gallows in the words perhaps, but very little humour. The comment seems odd and distinctly out of place. Malone's yet to arrive. Molloy bids the veteran farewell, looks across the desk at Camier and says: Well? So, what happened? Tell me everything. Nothing could top the sink-flown episode of yesterday, that's what she thinks. (*Attacked* – what a word to use, she thinks. Her mind shifts and flits, speeding to instant conclusions: Is that what they're up to? Camier seems jumpy, she sees this, watching him. Her mind calculates: Getting Murphy to kick off again? Goading him? But why? It was not obvious why. In many ways it seemed a strange and dangerous strategy. What else can it be? Molloy replies to her own question. Malone means to get him, she says, quietly, inaudibly. If Murphy goes again, it's over. It'll be curtains for Murphy. That's it. This was not a proper answer: But why? she asks herself – again.) As the veteran reaches the door to the outside world, Malone's arriving on shift. He steps back to allow ingress, bowing in the manner of a courtly gent. Molloy clocks the exchange out of the ward-facing window. (Watch Malone go. Molloy cases the scene for a moment, looking out of the windows of the office: The back of a navvy, she says. The legs of a rugby player, she continues, under her breath.) We are goldfish in there, staring through the glass to both sides, day ward and dorm. Where does Malone get the energy from? she says. The voice of Malone is sharp and muffled at the same time, calling out to Williams who's walking over to make his greeting. But before Molloy herself hauls her bag onto her shoulder to leave; before Malone reaches the office door for the changeover; before Camier steps back, shrinking out of the way; before Molloy says: So, Malone thinks we've pulled a fast one. Before all that, Molloy encourages a full and frank statement from Camier. Tell me, she says, what happened? – I'm all ears.

(But Guppy, Molloy thinks, Guppy, of all people – there lies danger.)

Yesterday's fracas is fresh in all our minds, rumours are flying far and wide; the violence of it is leaking outside of these four walls. Chinese whispers are heard all about at St. Anton's. There's little to get wrong: Murphy's outburst, Watt's related injury – the whispering holds. Would it all return to normal? Don't be ridiculous, somebody said, the old veteran, possibly, our doomsayer, jaw-jutting, gobs off; Olwyn made do with her reliance on *unusual* things; Cloud cuckoo land, Molloy would say; and Malone was, as usual, but more so than ever: Fecking furious. (What a small voice, he's got, but what a time to make it big. Tell me all.)

Guppy had been meditating. At least, that's what it looked like, Camier begins to tell the tale.

He was sitting on the blue linoleum in front of the office door. Yellow light flooded in from the high windows at his left, giving the impression that he was floating on a pool of water. A guru, at least, that's what it looked like. His legs were not quite lotus shaped; his cerebral palsy marginally hampered this level of flexibility. His right leg was held out and triangulated upon the ground as though he was about to dip his foot into shimmering water. The other was tucked under him. His shoulders were held high and wide and his head was steady, topped-off by what looked like an aura; in fact, it appeared closer to the lightening of a head-hugging halo. His hair looked paler by comparison, the white exotic face was brushed with a certain stillness, his eyes were wide open and blue, the stare provides an eerie expression, his half-smiling countenance suggests he no longer needs a room, or firelit walls. There he sat; a protest about something. He would not move; he seems hypnotised by the wings of butterfly, unobserved by the others, his own dark eyelashes flicker. He was not often stubborn; in fact, he seemed to not *anything* us at all, if you get what I mean. He didn't *anything* us – or anything at all. This skewed some people's attitude to him: He's a creepy cur, Malone was in the habit of saying. None of them can stand him; Guppy gives Malone the fecking heebie jeebies, as they say; there's no secret there – Camier attempted an impression of Malone at this point, rounding off with: You know what Malone's like. Cur, that's the word, cur. Molloy laughs, not recalling Malone ever having said *heebie jeebies* or *helter skelter* or, for that matter, *cur*. But Molls is only too well aware that Guppy is ever watchful. (He sees too much, she thinks, far too much – the little cur.) Camier, pleased with his short impression, carries on with the events of yesterday afternoon. Well, there he was, sat on the ground, refusing to move. He is momentarily distracted. Molloy will urge Camier to continue, to which he easily accedes: It was only then that Camier's own short and gangly frame came into view, his arms, his legs, his jet-black hair, his friendly face is suddenly fixed into something serious and forbidding. He tried to joke Guppy out of it: Are you meditating, he'd said, or what? You're like a fakir, he continued, laughing to cover his concerns. He approached slowly, speaking gently as he did so, his voice seemed hoarse. Up you get, kid, Camier had said. Guppy made no response. He asked after Guppy's needs, imploring him to stand up or at least move away from the office door. Please, Guppy, he said. Please, he said, enunciating the words under his breath, *do*.

He looked back at the office, looking through the glass window, then darting his attention back at the prone figure who seemed to be floating on the bluest of water. At least that's what it looked like. Guppy seemed entirely unaware of the slight man standing above him. He glanced for a moment up to the high windows. The light streamed in and made a cone of orange upon the walls which were usually a cold yellow. There were sharp lines of noise rebounding throughout the ward. A burst of hideous sound, seemingly from nowhere. But Guppy remained incredibly still. The television sounded throughout the day ward – Camier forgot to mention that. But it did. It was this cacophony that pricked Guppy's attention, looking up at the box on the wall, fixed between two high windows with whitened, glossy bars, an opening at the top of little more than two feet. There was no breeze that day on the ward, it'd been hot, it'd been close. The high volume of chatter emanating from the tube was beginning to make itself known; bothering and hectoring. Not one of the residents was regarding the screen, but would move fast away as though the din physically struck them. They were susceptible to chaotic disorder, responding bodily to the raised voices. Williams was rocking in his chair but he was not smiling, faster and faster, he rocks. His sleeves are rolled up on his shirt, not because he's hot, although he is, but because he'd not so long ago cleared away the cups, the saucers, the plates, and bowls, following afternoon dinner time. It was later in the afternoon; it wasn't that late, Camier said: Not that long after you got off shift. Yes, it was definitely not late. I'd changed Watt's dressing; I remember that much; an hour later, I guess. Molloy remained silent; she did not want to scare the horses, but seeing Camier looking around, fearing she might lose him, she began to encourage him. After dinner? she said, do go on. Molloy and Camier are in the office alone: it's changeover, and the conversation would normally be led by the nurse and the team coming off shift. Usually, it's quick. Camier suddenly alters his attention. Malone is calling out in the distance, shouting out to Williams. They can hear Williams call back, laughing, his broad smile showing the gaps in his teeth. We only had Camier to go on, his shift was not our shift. He refused to move, Camier resumes, do you see? He just wouldn't get up. Molloy checks the side window that looks out onto the ward, she can't see Malone. Someone screams – it's laughter. Not Malone's. I see, she replies. Then what?

This is how this moment will pass.

A knot in his mind, for what else could make sense of Guppy's revolt? Response; not a bit; movement; not a breath; care; seemingly not a one – Guppy sat as serene as a Buddha, floating on blue ice. Murphy had eaten his meal and was smoking his pipe in his usual place near to the exit door. He was a free man, released from the holding cell. Silence provides an element of contrition. Two men from Engineering had come with the fire door, as arranged. Murphy watches them, making inaudible comments: These men bring bright things, hanging in the sun; these men are like words in a book, a good book it is to read. *Thank you*, I must say it, *Thank you*, *again*. The operatives are quiet, their respect is not the fear of violence, no, not that, although they speak only cursively to the liberated Murphy, still clearly feeling the effects of the earlier administered Chlorpromazine, their timidity is drawn out by what they take to be against nature. The physical is not so much the concern; it is what they understood, at that time, to be mental. The patients contained and constrained here are *mental*. Of course, the events of the late morning have not been forgotten, how could they be? The word is détente, if any of us had known then what it meant. Murphy's outburst, unseen by the other shift, is evidenced by the damage to Watt's face. It is referred to a great deal, particularly by Malone. There is none of the false hope of one our shift. (Say nothing, she says, if anyone asks. Nothing. It'll pass, Molloy'd explained, it aways does.) There is only the keen affront to the dignity of the other shift. (We'll make them pay. Scandalous, it is, Malone will say, what else can you say?) Murphy had been so quiet, so silent, that he might have been abducted. His pipe smoke, rising, radiates a shroud or a cloak, and his puffing of white miniature clouds, for that it what it looked like, was all there was to be seen of him. Silence is the word. Silent and contrite. There it is; that promise was false, it teetered, it toppled, it fell into deep water, but we were all unaware of it then. Engineering is done within the hour – the patch of lino comes in for much begrudging admiration. Malone says such warm things, mentioning to the two men, along the way, that something was awry, but left what it was hanging in the air. Malone was strategically placed, apparently. Malone taps finger to the side of her nose, winking at the men who smile, awkwardly, then pull faces behind Malone's back. Looming large across the great space of the ward, the workmen seemed discomfited by Malone's proximity. They looked dismayed, trying out short replies to Malone's so-called … *flies in the ointment*, for that is how it was put. Murphy was a little out of sight. The partition obscured his presence, but you could hear a few fragments of words in a rumbling baritone every now and again, muttering, perhaps he was singing, or reciting something: She lit the candles, she did, all yellow, and blue. The sound is deep, it is rich, he continues: I was hiding, pretending not to see; she lit them up, I blew them, in one breath, *O, Murphy, my son, that's good luck*, she said to me. He looks up, as though interrupted. There was a great deal of movement going on around him. Human bodies are shifting here, reaching there, some sat and waited, others made shapes and sudden sounds, and then two of the bodies left. Activity and the brutal voices, alien, transmitted from the television set bolted onto the wall by the high windows. Yes, already the tables had been cleared by Williams, and he was rocking in his chair, his shirt sleeves rolled up in the heat. Every now and again someone called out, a screaming or a slapping, and the transmitted talking heads kept droning on relentlessly, jarring, adding to the general melee of the later-afternoon. Duggan was standing around, occasionally bending at unknown ghosts, then making faces at the palm of his hand. Perrett, still dressed in his blue boiler suit, suddenly screamed out in his high-pitched voice but, apparently, not out of ill-sorts but because he'd been calling out to Williams who provided him with an immediate smile. Williams waved his hand for a second from where he was seated and laughed at Perrott. Watt is wrapped up in a bandage. He is the invisible man when he wants to be seen – while one speaks another peeps – unwrap the bandage, and he will disappear from sight. Poof. Samuels eyes a beaker of water. Haines sniffs the heat emanating from a kicked off nearby hobnail boot; the boot suddenly vanishes, along with Haines. What's all this? Mercer called out, exiting the office. Malone could be heard laughing. Their face was smeared against the window, gurning, apparently indicating the method of attack, pointing down at Guppy:

The Buddha of Disturbia, she said, a laugh
that falls like a stone. Little cur.

Malone apparently clenched a fist and raised it up to the world: Let him just try. Their spectacles tapped against the window as though in warning. Malone looked like they were inside a television screen with the sound turned down. You could just make out the safety lines of metal wire running through the glass but only if you looked closely. Outside, the television was in full throttle, there was something distorting about it, something loud and insensitively white: I turned, you see, Camier explains. Guppy just wouldn't get up, Molloy, do you see? Camier explained to Molloy that he'd turned, alerted by a human form: Mercer pushed me out of the way. In fact, it was done gently, but with a familiar physical contact. And then it started, he begins to shout, Mercer, that is: What the feck's this, man? Mercer asked again. What's the fecking wrong with you, man? Somewhere else, life goes on in the ordinary light of their sun, but not here: Camier attempts to say something, to provide an explanation, but was instantly cut off. What's this? The fecking wrong, is what it is, Mercer is shouting, repeating the odd phrase. He said it again: The fecking wrong, man; the fecking wrong … He leans down so that he can engage Guppy's angled leg. He yanked the leg up and the high pose was broken, a mindless riptide at the bent limb. He lurched back as though about to be ducked into water, his leg, being raised into the air, was rigid, but as accommodating as a stick. He flew back, a heavy thudding sound, as his head struck the icy-hardness of the blue lino. Guppy's head ricocheted, a hate-filled slam-dunk. His head flew back like a rag doll. He leans up, quickly, his face impersonal; angry looking with its rigidity. No longer lying upon the blue pool of lino, his leg is lifted, again. Mercer is cursing him; the once haloed head suddenly connects again with a dull report. Guppy makes not a sound as he is swung round and dragged back towards the door to the dormitory. Malone can't be heard through the glass, the sound is muffled, but it looks as though they are screaming, hooting with laughter. Their lips purse, we know Malone's saying a sentence that contains the word fecking, but it remains merely implied. Mercer begins to act up, enjoying his own performance: Move, you little fecker … You worm. You dodgy clot! He does not slam Guppy's head again, but he wants to; he really wants to slam the shit out of the little cur – he wants to harm him; this is not blue, it is unadulterated red. Mercer's voice rises with effort of his stagecraft.

Mother … fecking … cur …

Malone is there now, at the office door. They've moved for a better view, looking out, not merely smiling at the spectacle before their eyes, but crying with laughter. Malone is surely cracking up. Big time. Guppy? Malone says, the voice rising, as though seeing him for the first time. Just you fecking wait … you … little cur … Malone is shouting out the words, competing with all external noise, the television screen blasts, but Malone fights against it: Just you ... fecking ... Stopped in their tracks. Suddenly, an interruption. A voice deep, and resonant but, more importantly, a presence of some magnitude, was making itself felt: Hey, you, Murphy called, hey, don't you bother pickin' him up by his feet. Hey! I won't say it ... Fix him down – Now! I say it ... Do it now. Or you'll hurt so bad. The words suddenly halted. Not another word was said. Mercer had his free hand on the handle of the door to the dorm, his glee that Malone was nearby and watching is lost. His intention is to – was to – drag Guppy away. He became as still as the cone of light thrown up on the walls, distorting the yellow to an orange glow. Murphy, his very self, advanced, his pipe held straight out of from his gripped teeth. It was a replacement from the ward store, like the door had been to the other side. You see, back to normal. There was a slight rip to his shirt that had not been mended. No need, he would insist, nothing is perfect on this earth. You see this? He puffs his pipe: You see this, he repeats the phrase: imperfection. He is surrounded by smoke as though he is walking through smoke. Eyes distant, his movements still sluggish, ambling, the liquid cosh is wearing off, as accustomed as he is to heavy medication. There was to be the sound of a lash, the sound of a slap to Guppy's head and face, but that is what's to come – but never arrives. Murphy's heart is racing, he feels wide awake, breathing deeply, ready to pounce and pound upon the offenders; somewhat incongruously he's still puffing smoke out to the side of his mouth, making what he is saying hard to hear, but no less terrifying:

You are hardly awake,

you little see-through people.

Murph's mind races, but his words are clear: Sometimes when someone beyond shouts that there's cake on the table, and them little candles burning bright as can be; remember it; remember these days; hear them, and understand. The presents put up on the table, ready and waiting for me to arrive; putting on my face a look of shock. Remember it so well, and rush to blow out them candles. Every one of them pat me on the back. *Happy birthday, son*, mother say. Murphy begins to laugh, quietly, to himself, it looks like he's crying, standing there, all alone, as he is, thinking of his self as a child, but it is more than thought – it's his heart breaking. And then he laughs. Mercer begins to look horrified. Murphy's laugh is gentle, small; his shoulders, however, are massive. Malone too is terrified. Murphy laughs again, continuing: And some one'd left the door open and I had to pretend that I never see the things inside; mamma lighting up the last little candle, some pink and some of them blue. They burned so fast. I pretended not to see, the door pushed over again, and I am hearing them call me: *Murphy, boy, come here, there's chores to be getting on with. Murphy* ... They're only pulling my leg; she doesn't know I've seen them. Going around lighting and arranging things, all for my eleventh birthday. Don't know now what was the presents,

but them little candles,

burning fast, pink

and some of them blue.

Remembering them so well. I blew them out in one go, and everybody clapping and carrying on, and pulling faces. *Make your wish, Murphy*, they all cried, and mother: *Make it, son, make good.* But what the wish was, I can never tell because all wishes are secret. Ah, it was over in no time at all. I remember it so well. Eleven, that's all it was. And that was that ... Murphy halts his murmuring. He looks closely at Mercer. The pipe was now glowing red from the bowl, smoke chunted out of the side of Murphy's mouth. He'd said his piece. Malone closed the office door, sliding back into the recesses of the shaded room, then looking at Murphy through the glass, she said: I don't want him fecking getting me. We'll have to be careful – I don't want him getting me; *somebody*, but not fecking well me. He is now around three yards from the office door, standing there, his shoulders broad. Mercer had already begun to move; little by little, he puts

Guppy's foot down on the blue linoleum, treating it as though it were an incendiary device which, in many ways, it was. Help 'im, fool: what is this? Mercer put his hand behind Guppy's back as the young man attempts to get up, and away. His face was flushed and red, the blue of his eyes was vivid, but they were bloodshot from the blows, the jarring, the slamming of his head not once, but twice onto the hard ground. His yellow hair was stark and shone in thick gold loose curls, no expression at all on his face, his blue eyes, fiery and staring. He gets to his feet and seems to float away to the left side of the partition, heading in Williams's direction. He stopped. But remains on his feet. It was just a joke, man, Mercer says to Murphy, unconvincingly laughing, shifting his shoulders from side to side, an odd dancing manoeuvre, then holding out both palms at his hips. You know that, Murphs; we always having a laugh, me and you; you know that, man – You know that. Murphy made no further reply but, looking intently at the blaring television out of which tiny people were shouting from a house on a river that looked like a stage set, he said: That telly's splitting our heads, you know that? What you gonna do about this dastardly noise? It's making me sick. It makes us all sick. Then there was silence. Malone was caught short, shutting the door to the office as gingerly and as cautiously as they might if they were fearful for their life. Murphy looked away from them. Mercer joined Malone in the office as soon as he had switched off the sound on the television, pointing the remote control up to the box on the bracket. We'll get his back up if it kills us, Malone whispers to Mercer. He'll go, you see. Am I right? Tomorrow – their eyes lighting up – Tomorrow night, Malone clarifies the position, and almighty hell will break loose. Am I right? Tuesday will be a special treat – *for someone.* Am I right?

Watt could be heard, only just, calling out for a different shirt, holding up his trousers at the knees as though he wanted to show off his bare feet.

His bandaged head is exaggerated; he looks partially mummified. A plume of smoke emanated from Murphy's mouth. He resumes his place, sits down. Guppy drifts away, no emotion shown, no nearness, no distance: nothing at all. Until, just then, he walks back, his awkward gait, his face red, but, still, as though floating, blue eyes fixed, yellow hair standing high on his head; he came back. Then, Camier said: Guppy went and sat down right beside Murphy. Just sat there, looking across at him. It was like he was going to say something. Camier stopped there, thinking about what he would say next: A few seconds later, he was gone. I went out, headed over to Murphy, to check on him, like. Camier stops. Starts: And then he says to me, that Guppy's like a little angel. That youth. That's what Murphy says to me. Molloy smiles. Camier goes on: He says to me, Lord knows, a little angel, and no mistaking that, and then he looked away. The *angel* bit sounds weird to my ears, hardly something Murphy would ever say: *little angel*? Really? The whole thing seemed off. And was that an impression of Murphy; was that what that was? An impression. Malone was one thing, but an impression of Murphy? The incident was not recorded in the daily records. At changeover, according to Camier, Malone barged into the office, refusing to look at the night nurse coming on shift: All quiet, nothing of note. Read up on Watt, Malone had said, there's been trouble. Murphy ... The word is left there, not as a name, but an explanation – *Murphy* ... Can you think of anything else, Camier? He looked startled: No, nothing, Malone, he'd said, nothing at all.

We are returned to Tuesday morning: as you know
Molloy's arrival to shift was earlier than usual.

It was as if she expected to be caught in a web of her own making. (What did I think I would find? Guppy crosses her mind, the name – All Eye, she calls him – the name passes through her mind, up and out, unheard. The all-seeing silent creature, she

193

recalls Mallory's words: He's non-verbal, he can't speak – You do realise that, Molls, don't you?). I found her sitting at the desk, the room was shaded.

The constraint of being among strangers alleviated
itself while she read through Malone's notes. Already,
she has stalked the ward, looking for signs of difference.
Camier is yet to speak – a shift must pass first.

On Tuesday morning, Guppy appears unusually sluggish, but there are too many other things to think about. There will be unseen bruises to his head, but there will be nothing visible of note upon his face; his eyes are bloodshot, that's it. We return briefly to the place where we began. You may recall, Molloy's arrived at her shift earlier than usual – she's reading the notes. The handwriting discrepancy – Camier's fine hand. Molloy's super-cross. Did she expect to be caught in a web of her own making. Or stymied by the ongoing constraint of being among strangers? Molloy was becoming incensed as she read through Malone's notes. She'd already looked around the ward for signs of difference. (Did it really happen, she whispers, I mean, really.) That Tuesday morning, Molloy is well angry, stubbing her cigarette hard into the office ashtray, sparks flew and burnt out instantly. Did Malone really have to take it upon … Molloy is repeating the line she's just spoken to me. I mean the repair bit? Couldn't they just leave it to Garnett? Not a chance, that wouldn't be enough for Malone, now would it? It's early, Molloy's been in for a while. Suddenly throwing her bag across her shoulder, readying herself for the bathroom: Be back in a mo, she says: Only women bleed, she continues. I blush, and she laughs – It's only natural, she shouts back, call me Mrs. Blobby if you must. I suddenly notice the impression of kitchen porter's rolling pin, pressing against the bag's tan leather, shaped like a rather large dildo – I mean to make a joke, but I lose my nerve. What've you been doing with that? I want to say, poking the dark impression made by the rounded wood. Or perhaps: Ann Summers's stuff's getting bigger and bigger – Who knew. I kind of say, half-heartedly: That's from yesterday … the rolling pin … You've forgotten to put it back, but I trail off, leaving the last words in mind, unsaid. Olwyn was going off shift, that's what happened. All was suddenly calm. She's got the wooden rolling pin in her hand. Is this implement a means for own protection, given the events of the morning?

Christ, Olwyn, what on earth are you going to do with that?

The kitchen porter looked down her arm to her hand in a slightly unhinged way: O dear, Olwyn said, then laughed. Isn't that *unusual*? The reply is swift, and funny. Well, somewhat, Molloy replies: It's certainly not *usual*, she means more, she wants to indicate that a rolling pin is a very *odd* thing to carry around the ward: I was meaning to roll out some bread rolls with the boys, Olwyn explained. Rolling pins are not to be sniffed at, Molloy replied. Well, it comes in handy, the other joked, but I never sniff them. The kitchen porter laughed briefly – Leave the jokes to me, Molloy thinks, but says nothing. Olwyn continues: But handy, she hits her palm by way of demonstration. I bet it does, Molloy responded, seated behind the desk. The kitchen porter's about to leave. She says she'll take it back to the kitchen. She wants to know if there's anything she can do before she goes. We can see her glancing through the dorm-side window of the office. She can just make out Watt. He's lying back, and she can see his slippered feet at the bottom of the bed. The bloodied burgundy shoes will be replaced (That's a promise, she'd said to him. A promise Watt. And let's get fresh clothes for you. That's it. And then rest.). It's fine, Molloy said, you're going off shift: give it here. I'll take it back. Molloy looked at the wooden contraption, feeling it in her hand, she too slaps it against the palm. You're right, Olwyn, it's got some heft. Definitely not for sniffing, but, in some way, heaven scent. Molloy appeared drawn by her own witticism, but made nothing of it, making do instead with dropping the rolling pin into the bag at her feet. I am about to make my joke about it, but I am transfixed by an incredible sound. It stops, but then begins again, in earnest, echoing throughout the ward. What's that? I say to Molloy. O, she smiles, it's only Williams. The ward's empty; just Molloy heading out to the staff bathroom, an early morning light hovers as though it's dust: Haven't you heard it before? she asks. My eyes are wide, especially given the time. Williams? I reply. It is always the same song, that's what they say. Yes, it's Williams. Soon enough, the echo of it reaches me, the beauty of the baritone. Williams is singing, deep and resonant, repeating the same line and then not quite scatting, but continuing with wordless enthusiasm until he reaches, once again, the chorus, that one line he sings perfectly, again and again, in that beautiful baritone voice:

We all live in a yellow thubmarine, a yellow thubmarine,
a yellow thubmarine. We all live in a yellow thubmarine,
a yellow thubmarine, a yellow thubmarine ...

I leave the office. I am nearing the toilet block now, Molloy is now behind me, heading to the staff bathroom and I have passed her. Williams's voice will treble there, and that is the point. He loves the echo, she calls after me, which accompanies his voice. Williams turns, a perceived shake of his physical being. Is he twenty-four? – at most he's twenty-five, six years older than me. I am staring at him. He is smiling as he sings. I think I am smiling too. I am aware that I am bigger than he is, but his presence suggests that I am no match. He seems hardly to move an inch, just swaying, his long arms at his side. I am staring at him. His presence is as silent as a shadow and yet his voice soars. He is smiling as he sings, watching me rather acutely, at what he perceives to be my own, well, shock at what is happening. His movements feel effortless to me. I want to say, real; yet it is more than real. *It is more than real.* And, yes, then he smiles, he is swaying, hardly moving, entirely soundless yet soaring, his vibrating shoulders are the only true indication of his joy in the moment. The ward is presently silent to all but this voice, rising above this ungraspable present. Everybody hears, everybody knows, everybody awakens to this sound. His voice reaches all parts of the ward. All are listening, knowing it to be Williams who's singing. He is there, as young as ever, he is no longer there: Williams's own whereabouts is bathed in bright reflected early morning light – yes, like dust. Nobody seems able to fix words onto the world. Nobody even tries. Instead, I feel something is happening to me, or to the other who passes for me. I was too attentive to know who was this *me*. I wondered whether the tears would have fought through closed eyes, but then how would I see? Welling's the word, from nowhere, salting my skin, darkening my lashes, sentimentalising the moment. What the hell's wrong with me, I whisper, the voice filling my ears, touching my skin, making me smile. What on earth's all this talk of light and darkness; when has this ever happened before?

IV

The young man is suddenly confronted with the sparkling blue sea.
"The sea, the sea," he says the words in a whisper: "Again, the sea?"

He is mesmerised by the small silver and white fishes that skirt over the lee of the waves. They seem drawn precisely to where he stands, looking out at the ripples as they form and flow and disappear. The sea is as still as a lake. He wants to scoop them up in his hands, he wants to throw them up into the air: "the fishes," he whispers, "look carefully: see there." Then at the shore these fish disperse yet again and arrive in semi-circular fashion as incessant forms or as markers of some essential delineating littoral. His armour begins, for the first time, to feel cumbersome and heavy. He calls out in anguish. How his metalled mail cuts into him: "I am burning," he calls out, "burning," he calls again, "burning, I say," a voice swept away by waves or by decree, landing shallow on the sand. "It's no good. I am forced to return – it's no good," he shouts with urgency, or almost, with despair. "It is surely not possible to reach the other side. I cannot endure," he calls out. Alone, no he is not alone. "Well, without doubt, there can be no *tentative* advance," the fair lady explains, "that is *abundantly* clear." Nothing will come of nothing; she whispers into his ear. "Nothing," is the word he hears, "nothing, you say? But I cannot move! I can no longer breathe," he wants to reply, "nothing." His voice is halted, he feels himself pulled under, deep beneath the surface of the sea. "I wish to go under," he cries, the invisible currents pulling him along, wishing him, "to come again," speeding him along and across the profound depths of his breathing. "I am aware," hot, sweating, calling unheard, away and away, from his own private being, "I am aware." And so, as though in spite, he pulls this outer armoured shell away from his mortal body; a cuirass, if ever there was one, the breast-plate as inert now as a silver turtle resting on the warm sand. Behold him, the man he is, standing in a pure white cambric shirt and jet-black breeches, his sword, sharp and silver, swinging at his side, a fierce cutting crescent. It looks of the hour – the shirt is in such condition it might have been fresh laundered that very morning ("You are quite right" – the fair lady's voice is abundantly clear – "are we not all so simply covered in buttoned cloth, beneath which there is but soft flesh and bone?") His sword too is new forged as if just that moment lifted from the heat of the furnace. ("Hold fast, this fierce iron, my lord, stay your sweet hand, strong knight, the time will come.") But all of these impressions are false, first and foremost, for he has travelled far and father time has taken its toll. "Hey, you," he shouts, laughing at the spectacle. There, rolling on his back upon the yellow golden sand, his beautiful grey Barbary stallion, making the most of the light and day. Away now from the closed world of the forest where things turn still to bronze pillars and fallen sylvan wood rest as the corpses of granite stones. Where there are things which move, which should not, and things which should not, move; and where familiar faces, lost to unfamiliar forces, known, unknown, are loved, then equally, and immediately, despised. The young man's eyes were captivated by a huge rock structure that seemed to hover above the horizon of the ocean-line. From this obscure rock, there came into view a castle: "A moment ago," the young man says, "there was nothing but mist. Nothing. Only whiteness," stark and bright, his eyes half closed against the light, "but there it is." It was earlier shrouded, that was all. The sea fog has burnt away, leaving behind a picture of the castle upon the huge black rock. The silver and white waters are splashes of paint slapping beneath the huge curtain wall, giving the impression of a singularly existing monument. "Just look," he says, "out there; just look, at the base of it all," he calls out to his horse, at the point where the island tumbled into the sea. He is pointing across at a line of terraced cottages where the servants of the great castle must live in peace and tranquillity. "How do I reach this place?" he said to the soft, burbling breeze. "How can I cross the water to reach the rock?" he asks again: "It seems an impossible task to reach the great castle."

The ever-repeated mirages of the world at large that comes and goes and keens and cons and calls in strangers from the shore. The light lulls, but it promises much.

"Young one, you see only what or who there is for you to see, and you know only who or what there is for you to save. Yes, 'tis Oriane." The fair lady begins to age, her haze diminishes: "It is Oriane who sits and waits and prays for salvation from the man she knows will save the earth from shame." The fair lady diminishes, her breath against his ear feels not hot, but parched.

In the castle, Oriane grows impatient: "He is near," Oriane speaks, "he is close," she continues. Oriane's guiding snake's nearby, listening to the words of her mistress: "I can feel him," Oriane whispers, "I can taste him,' she says, flashing her forked tongue out of her warm pink lips, "I can taste him."

"How may I cross?" the young man asks, but to whom? Alone, he steps forward, guarding his eyes from the hot sun in pellucid skies, blindingly cerulean, crystallising the yellow sands to shimmering solid patterns. "There's something out there," he said, his heart racing, thumping hard against his chest: "I can see you," he calls out to the giant, twisting, figure, slipping easily through the waves. A huge green monster, vivid and smooth, rises and falls from sight. The creature advances, for some short time it surfaces; out the sea it rises. The fierce being peers at the kingly knight with its deadly ruby eyes. The creature of the sea is looking upon the young man on the land, a grey Barb close by, standing tentatively at the shoreline, alone and unsure of what lies ahead, and, indeed, what it is he sees. "Yes, I can see you, monster, still as can be, I see you still; though as yet I know not what you are." The slate grey steed, usually steadfast and true, suddenly reared. The young man is quick to take the reins and calm his friend, for that is what he is, a friend, and companion.

Once settled, the young man looks back at the disturbing sea. He steps toward the shore. Now, nothing. "Nothing," he says, looking back at his horse, "there's nothing there." He knows how to soothe fear and impatience. "All is well," he says to his horse. But what is made abundantly clear by the busying waves, the swell belligerently coming his way, is that he is not mistaken. There something dark and dangerous dwells in the ever-altering waters. "How to cross," he whispers, "with that damned creature, lying in wait?" All is not as it may seem hereabouts. The water tranquilised; the waves roll upon the shingle like a chain followed by a weak booming sound, an echo of ages. "Deceptive, all seems so strange." He refers to the present calm over yonder on the horizon. What is the secret? What should I know? ("Oriane is kept against her will," whisperings in his ear, images unseen in the keen light. The fair lady's words, recalled: "She is imprisoned by a cruel and very old man who goes by the name of the 'Ever Youthful' Duke. He feels the pressure upon his young chest, but speak he will into the obscurity: "*Duke*? You say … Did you say, *Duke*?")

Indeed, she replies, lie still, young one. Be attentive to the remains of the day: you hear what you hear – I say, again, the ageless and ever youthful duke. This is how he pays for his paperwhite skin.

"Each must pay," the contract will be sealed, each much pay. But ageless, he remains. The future debt is not clearly set but surreptitiously, even furtively, agreed. "For youth – *everlasting*," are the words the duke hears, folding around the circular shell of his ears before heading in to mind and matter. But what is the price to pay for this rite to the pleasure of dewy freshness? The skin might be taut and white, the eyes might be clear and crystalline, but the interior of the man must surely be corrupted, bleak and black. "What care I for what lurks within?" he is said to have said. "We are all but surface, do you see? That is all that counts." The duke reasons with his own inner voice. The 'Ever

Youthful' Duke forever dwells in the castle which rises from sparkling seas. He was once a man of extraordinary wealth and fame, style and panache. A man of learning and enlightenment, a renaissance man of unassailable literary tastes, as well as a scholar of the alchemical arts. All of these were his, but there was something more, something the duke had been missing, and missing sorely. Ever-youthfulness in his own life time. He will pay a singular price, as must we all in life, but the meeting of minds, on this occasion, must be made, in some way, to coincide, bit by bit.

> *"Duke?" he says, "did you say the duke, fair*
> *lady? Did you? Damn his eyes."*

Not immortal, for that cannot be given, but a precious corpse would be left behind at his death. In life, he would have the vigour and strength, the dewy freshness of a young, young man; a life sentence, you might say – but that is not the price, but, then, what is? Simple: the enchanted one must be kept within her castle keep and so, in this state of incarceration, never can she conjoin with the Sea Serpent as her true self. Their passion is planetary poison – the seas will heat and boil, the earth follows suit, all must perish. *Simple*. There was one small matter. The duke could not for the life of him work out the myriad locations represented on the surface of the tapestry. To begin with, where was it meant to be? Was it many places, assembling, accumulating, whole to part, part to whole; or one place only? "How can I follow the coming and going of it all?" he said. "What are the directions of this flow? Damn you," he called out with extreme impatience: Damned thing," he shouted, at last exasperated. His anger immediately exacts a response from the tapestry.

> *"With the day, there must be Oriane; at*
> *night, so close to Serpentina."*

"Oriane, you say. Ah, yes, is that her? The beautiful woman there? I can't quite make her out. This damned chest is in the way. No matter. And me, is that me?" But he is stopped in his too thorough investigations. The tapestry intervenes, whispering so forcefully, bringing a deep concern for something more than composition.

> *"With the night, there must be Serpentina;*
> *by day, so close to Oriane."*

"Oriane, you say, she must remain. Ah, yes, I see it all now," he says, observing the pattern-change, the invisible made visible. The way, the pact, the ever-youthful life ahead, is being revealed. "Yes, yes," the duke calls up to the tapestry, looking quickly to the door of the queen's chamber lest he be overheard. Not so much as one bit at a time, but as though figures were forming and differentiating from out of a singular mist, progressively, diffusively. "Yes, yes, I see it all, each piece is made true to me. Keep Oriane? That's it? The castle keep! All well. Speak again," he says. The tapestry is enigmatically silent. This silence is not good enough. The duke seeks affirmation: "Yes, yes, I see it all now. And my payment?"

> *"With the night in you, continuously day; with*
> *the day in you, continuously night."*

"My youth," you mean, "the day in you? Yes, yes, I see. The light, everlasting in life. All true, there I am, ever youthful as I stand proud. The day *in me*; the light. Yes, yes, I see it now. It's so clear." And whatever it was, it suddenly perished, was instantly lost to sight: "It's gone," he calls out to the concealment, seeking now for its hiding place: "It's covered over," he shouts out, a frantic call made to the east wall. "Tell me more, tapestry, whisper again. Promise me. It seems now so opaque. One last word, please do." And so, the pact was made, the contract done, with the vainest of all men. The deal of dew and youth was struck with the tapestry who whispers, once, then twice, indeed, thrice – to show the ways of come what may, and so directs the ever-youthful duke to his ever-youthful destiny. "Upon condition that I keep close within the castle this thing, *your* nemesis: Oriane? Is that it, tapestry, whisper again. Promise me. Just one word more."

The tapestry is whisht.

Without adieu, the Sea Serpent with hardly a sound falls beneath the dimpling waves which percolate upon the shore, a sound of falling silver coins is heard all around, then the echo. "Chains," the young man says, "it sounds like chains."

V

*Soon it'll be dark. The wind is picking up; it's parky enough,
that's for sure. Thunder and heavy downfalls of rain are
expected by nightfall. Gusty winds coming in the direction of
northern France are already making themselves known.*

Molloy's head is tilted, her nose is raised toward the ceiling:
What's that thing called? she shouts out, pausing for a moment,
sniffing the air: You know, when you think you can smell the
saltiness of the sea? I say nothing, she goes on: The experience of
it, you know what I mean, like day and night, or salt and water –
the brine combined. Do you know what I saying? she asks. A
moment later, she continues: You can't really smell the wetness
or the saltiness, they're scentless. She pauses, sniffs for effect:
But you experience it, do you follow? She stops, a short laugh. I
ignore her ruminations for something fresher: It's fifty miles
away, I say, but she's not having any of it: So what? I smell what I
smell, she replies with just a hint of harshness: Like an invisible
shadow, she says, nothing's really real, yet everything's an
expression of its reality, do you see? She looked around, nobody's
paying much heed. There's only me listening. The ward's light is
indeed somehow blue, a structure unfolding. Silver blue down
the wave of incoming light, something like that. She is silent, her
eyes are blue, like the sea, a sea of osmium-blue; blue frames the
ward, the balls of hydrangeas behind the high windows are lit
and lifted across the walls, dyeing them right up to the strip
lights, which have little or no hope against the power of the
delicate yellow sun, hidden somewhere beyond, making itself
known in heat, spilling down through shifting blues, or lifting
the earth to new heights of silver. Over the rocks and far away,
Cornwall, she recalls, and there the light is rising, the sea is deep
blue and pure white in the vigorous breeze, serpentine sprays; a
huge rock suddenly rises from the waters, grey as can be,
glinting as though the quartz in the castle rock is sparkling. At
the base of it all, the cottages shimmer in its shadow, the

background is a steep ascent, like a mountain, a stiff hike up, at the very least. You can walk over to the island, she murmurs, when the tide's low, a yellow and silver causeway rises, yes, she says, hearing herself as though underwater or in some panic to catch her breath. Those were the days, the boat took them across to the island, the tiny harbour there, where other tiny boats fought with the dimpled waves. The causeway was hidden, she whispers, they promised me, she says, that I could see it, cross over on it. But there was nothing – only the sea. We waited at the great wall down the steps from Marazion town, the boatman picked us up. There's a nip in the air, he said. Good weather for kites, he smiled, winking at my mother, pinching my cheek. Like an invisible shadow, she says, repeating herself, the words from a moment ago. Nothing is really real, she says; I smell what I smell. I wait until she has finished: But we're nowhere near the sea, I repeat. Thinking on it, she turns, looking me straight in the eyes. She says: You smell it too? I don't, of course: Kind of, I say; then, I relent further: Yes, just there, I say, inhaling as she had, breathing in the breeze blowing through the half-open windows. You see, she says, it smells like freedom, doesn't it? The sun throws dark wedges of gold and orange segments onto the cold yellow walls of the large open room, extinguishing one's blues. The sun's impediment brings shadowed darkness amongst fits of bright, penetrating light. It all seems so clean, she said, looking about her at the ward lit with a shifting, fantastic existence. Before long she's breathing in a Benson and Hedges. Two dear friends, she calls them. I look at her, waiting to hear her repeat the refrain: Smells like freedom, she says. It's like that Carry On film, she continues, changing her tack. Which one? I ask. She's lightened her mood again, brighter, but, really, I hardly know her. Come now, she says, the one where the Sid James says to … O, what's her name? She looks up to the ceiling, then shouts, Désirée. That's it, 'Désirée! That's it, she knows: Dubarry, I cry out, breaking in. And the Black Pimpernel. She laughs loudly: And he says: *Come, my dear, let's take a walk in the arbour*. And she says. Again, I'm ready to swoop: And she says,

Blimey! *I didn't know we were so near to the sea.* Yes, I say, rushing in, interrupting her line. I loved the Carry Ons as a kid. It's Joan Sims' film. That's it. That's the very one, Molloy says, and then she screeches. Never fails to make me laugh. Cockneys, she says, like most of this lot, she indicates those present and absent on the ward. Sid James is the Black Pimpernel, isn't he? (We hear what we hear.) That's it, I say. I've just said that. She muses on this: Did you? she says, and then she repeats the line: Blimey! I didn't know we were so near to the sea. Then she stops, once and for all, and puffs on her cigarette.

> *Nothing exists all by itself; you need someone else to make it work; to help alleviate the pressure.*

Don't lose your head, kid. That was it – good advice for us all to heed: Don't lose your head, kid. But what if there is nothing at all? Am I talking to myself? All the words we put down; all the written words in all the libraries of the world; all the books and all the scriveners; in all these fragments and fractures, we seek just one book, or perhaps just one word. Who was that? There is nothing to add. They're all done and dusted. This point is not made. What is it, then? And yet time and again we come away with nothing? That's not a question, I say, speaking these words aloud. I then become self-conscious. I am alone. Did someone hear me? Am I now talking to myself? To cover this, I begin to sing, quietly, as though searching for the words. I go, *Th-at's not a-a-a questi-on*, making it sound authentic and then, realising that I have not been overheard, I stop. He's like a ghost, she said. The way he moves. Grace, that's what I mean, she explains. A ghost? I say. Well, he's so quiet, she says: He hardly makes a sound. Non-verbal is one thing; he never makes a single sound, she says. Silent, I suggest. Nothing, she says, not so much as a dickie. A pause, her thought diminishes, a weighing of her conscience: But he sees everything, she says, I don't think he misses a trick. Sharp as a knife. But, yes, quiet.

To finish the moment, to find the journey's
end in every step of the road …

I entreated sleep to come. Counting up. Counting down. Was I too high after the day's activities? Too low. A vixen, that's the explanation you gave – for the harpy scream that terrifies us in the night. He meant no harm. That's what I tell myself. Wilson's, I say, by way of explanation. Watt's fine. I listen closely for a sneeze or the striking of a match. I know only too well that nothing can be seen or possibly heard. It is dark, and I see into the black of night, but a single colour, that of zero, which is perhaps reassuring. I am required only to count: *One*, that's the wind, blowing out the curtain, not a ghost entering my room this night; *Two*, an owl hoots, resting yonder on a barn; *Three*, a dog howls, scenting a passing cat; *Four*, soot falls in the breast, gathering as black snow, that is, zero plus one, black plus white; *Five*, you inhale, breathing halts a moment, relents, outward passing, the patter of rain heard, winding down the pane, out of sight, hiding its meaning; *Six*, the sound of a clock, ticking, ticking again, without an end, or is it the patter of rain; was it; is it, even then in a solitary room without a hint of mistrust; *Seven*, a tile shifts, dropping from a roof, skirting down to the pavement; *Eight*, in and out, pain makes itself known in a very puzzling sense of dizziness, out and in; a rattling chest near death; *Nine*, if that is what it is, sleeping ever so deeply; *Ten* … the sea, waving or weaving, the loom lifts, weft-faced on the eastern wall, promising what becomes us, warped and distaffed, falling, backing away; he or she or they who are to stand before an abyss in a completely secure position would not be able to back away, but must remain to see nothing more than the picture of a ghastly and chaotic re-birth, upon which so many of us pinned our hopes. That's enough for the day; enough of this salty aroma, no more talk of the sea; of that mediated by the sense of smell exceeding its own function: the wet and the white in the water are sensed somehow but scentless. No; *Eleven*, the far-off foxes, a screaming vixen locked. Really, that's the truth. I raise my hand to the wall; it is dark and I am somnolent, but I am convinced that the walls are running with damp or with slime; *Twelve*, dew and grass, sopping wet, we stride on grassy floors, rose petals are blood red, dreams come to us without interruption; enclosing us like stones islands, penetrating the smells of sea and salt, and amidst the screaming everything's sodden. Time to go in. I turn in my bed; awake or asleep; in or out? I return my hand to my side; I cannot see my fingers in the dark. I guess, by *ten*, I was out for the count or earlier when the victims were, at the very least, fundamentally justified; *Thirteen*, that behind the madness, method, perhaps even malice, lay hidden; there is always method in madness; *fourteen*, there is no fourteen.

VI

"In no way, a figment of dreams," he says. "Day break – At last."

The Woodman is walking away from the young prince. He calls out to him: "Which way, Woodman? Did you say?" The Woodman is soft upon the ground, it seems improbable that this large man could leave nothing but the slightest trace. "Before you, beneath you, beyond you now," comes a voice both familiar and distant. "You are leaving?" the young man asks, "but the day has just begun." The Woodman steps over a large branch, inert and silvering upon the earth. "Woodman?" the young man inquires. "I am not afraid." The axe swings at this side, his hand steadies it while he settles himself upon a large granite boulder, so close to the yellow strand and the blue sea. "If kissed three times upon the lips by the one sent, a bond is made and one that cannot be spoken of. Listen, young man! The oceans will boil and with them all humankind, but only if the bond is made. Do you hear?" Amidst the smoke, twisting in little whirlwinds from his pipe, he continues his story. He pauses, puffing on his pipe, before the incantatory sounds from his resonant voice rises high into the crystal-clear orders, before he tells tale of rocks and sands and days feeding on the treasures of the night, before he brings these seeming far-off lands into the nearest proximity of a kiss, a kiss, a kiss. The young man struggles in the heat: "Kiss? Am I here to kiss? Kiss?" The radiation of light from the sand, disturbs him. The shining shapes, arising and perishing, are making this and then that before his very eyes. "Oriane," the Woodman hectors the young man. "Her name is Oriane. Can you hear me?" The young knight knows nothing of his purpose and much less of this apparently imprisoned creature. "Oriane," flits across his mind. He was going to burst into laughter, bend down, feigning preoccupation with something at ground-level. "The armoured beetle," he says. Bent over, he must concede that there is something there that he could not see; forms are for real, after all. "Nothing." He sees it now, expanding, an opaque transformation progresses. That sound the young man hears, that voice once heard, so long ago. The sneering, he recalls, the laughing duke, standing there with one of his lackeys. "Hardly the colour of a king," he was calling out. Held by a familiar figure, one seen loitering by the lake in the tapestry – waiting, or so it seemed, for the king to arrive, the boy's father; captivated, he was, for a moment, by the black and white down combined in the soft grey plumage of a diving loon. "A magical creature," crosses the assailant's mind, a mind momentarily removed from its task, noticing instead the pale red colouration at the creature's throat as though emanating from a wound; suddenly the loon disappeared into the water, hearing, it would seem, the footsteps of the king walking on the lakeside footpath.

"A loon," he says. The bird dives into the depths of the water, suddenly reappearing a moment later, the palest of red pours down at its throat: "An omen," he whispers, his full red lips breaking into a smile – "for him," he says, his voice trails off, hearing now the tread of a noble king.

"Your father is drowned. Did you hear … Well, did you?" The young prince remembers the message: a perfect recall of his running in, and then the hideous jolt of confusing his uncle, the duke, for his father. "Father," he had called out. This passage of time's been sent packing by the corruption of dreams. Worlds of times and tears are lost or lessened. To elucidate that which would harm him so, to pay allegiance to the magical mechanism at work in a brain, never softening to its doughty prick – now that was a task too far past to contemplate or yet to come. What were the figures displayed to these clearest of eyes? "Who lay in wait, up there?" Hiding, but stiff in the tapestry. Yes, hiding just beyond the lake; listening for the foot fall of his father. "Yes, yes; that was surely the man's intention. But that was then and we are now."

The island struck out of the calm blue sea like a giant black rock.

"A moment ago," the young man says, "there was nothing but mist. Nothing. Only whiteness," stark and bright. "How can I cross the water to reach the rock?" he asks again. To unfold once more to other things, in time and in place, at once there, solid and shimmering, at once lost, fast and hidden. "Yes, there is a way across," the Woodman speaks: "A causeway appears upon the falling tide of day, as though waiting for your arrival; only for you." He must wait until the causeway is clear, unencumbered by galloping waves. "To go too early spells death," the Woodman will more than intimate: "To go too late, the same." But the young prince does not know this just yet. But he will. Upon the words of the Woodman, he will know it well, and will greet the first tastes of bitter loss. Is he asleep, upon the yellow sands? The soft sun warming myriad reflections, individually the sand stones are but tiny black fragments, not gold at all, but other-coloured, white and brown and black and yellow gold. He takes a deep breath into his lungs, breathing as though for the first time: "Is the sea frozen?" the young man asks, his voice barely audible, "can I simply walk across the stiffened water as rounded rocks and stones? What can possibly stop me?" The Woodman calls out to the young man who seems more intent on what is simply present and passing, and on silence and sounds, than on hearing. "But you must not kiss Oriane. No, that would be no task at all for you: You must not kiss her," the Woodman calls out to him. The Woodman will soon be leaving, falling, falling away. But for now, he is present and smiling at the wakening young man; the waiting is over. "I hear thee well, good Woodman, I hear your words," he replies. "But why should I go?" The young man has just seen the scales of the Sea-Serpent circling, recurring, in a shift from the surface back down to the depths of the waters. "Why should I go, Woodman?" The Woodman sighs: "What answers have I for you, young man? None, for I am but a storyteller; I am sent with one singular task and one solitary warning." He is no longer asleep on yellow sand or forest litter, no longer held in primal dreams: "Who sends you? How were you asked? What is it to you, Woodman?" The question is not unexpected but good answers are hard to come by: "Who, how, what? Mortals and gods, of course; they must somehow be revealed. The earth and the sky. Two in one and one in two," he replies, the staccato delivery is decidedly dodged. The young man has yet one further why: "That leaves only the question of why, Woodman. Why?" Who asks *why*? – is it only the young? – "You will be led there, that is true. Somebody or some other guiding *thing* will come to you. You will be led, that is true: *but*, I repeat: You must not kiss that dreaded creature. Kiss that creature not once, not twice, nor thrice, not ever. Or she will return to the oceans and to the bond of the world's torment, once and for all time." One question, he said, now he asks two: "But why *you* Woodman? And why should *I* of all people have this end?" The reply is swift: "Are we to do nothing, but wait? Await a moment more pleasurable? This is not the time for waiting, my young friend. That time has passed." The young man feels the effects of the heat and flops upon the ground. He picks up a handful of sand. "Falling," he says, "nothing remains in my hands, all falls through my fingers." He looks across at the Woodman. "There's only earth, everything returns to the ground; there is no sky. All is always falling." Falling, yes, falling, the Woodman smiles: "Because it is you; it is you." He hides his smile, for gravity's sake. The young man's not pleased: "But that is not to answer *why* Woodman – you must have more for me." The Woodman smiles again, his teeth are white against his burnt skin, a parchment of all times, and lives and futures: "You must be akin to the summer rose," my dear friend: *Without* why. You go because you go: Without *why*." The Woodman pauses, and smiles at the young prince who is surely listening intently, his hand held out, his eyes seem closed against the rays of the sun. He holds the palm of his hand out: "Nothing," he says to his empty hand. "Nothing remains, do you see?" He is falling back, slowly his own body is attracted to the softness of the yellow sand. The Woodman's voice rises, calling out before it is too late: "Heed this warning, young man: The Sea Serpent out there awaits you: awareness is all. The monster knows you are coming. He and the duke are tasked with Oriane's keep and ongoing incarceration. But that is but a trick. And *why*, you ask. *Why*?" The Woodman halts his explanation: "Need I sum up for you, young man?" But the young prince is asleep. "The creature of the sea must never be allowed to become disenchanted, for it is only a trick. You must refuse to heed the words you hear. Oriane is her name and forked words are her currency. O, young man, hear me." The Woodman lifts his hand, pulling a few threads from the un-mended tear in his shirt. "The day has come," he whispers. "The seven seas will be boiled and devoured; nothing can be done. Only earth and sky and mortals and divinities can save us now." The Woodman begins his return to the forest, passing on, as time will: falling, falling out of sight in to the darkness of trees. His homesickness will be remedied by resuming his place in the forest, heading back to his homestead from which he came. He sees his wife, she waves, smiling, coming towards him for a kiss. "Dear heart," she says, "you look so very tired." He must let her know that he has failed in his endeavour: "The day has come, my dearest love," he whispers to this wise woman. "The seas will be boiled and devoured; nothing can be done. Only a God can save us now."

> *"We are called. There is more yet to tell. Can you bear*
> *to hear me now? Time slides. Yes, I must go."*

The young man awakes, slowly, at first, unsure of his whereabouts. Hours and hours have surely passed, the numerous minutes bred from the broad daylight, returning as seconds in the depths of the night. "Dreaming, only," he says, "only dreaming?" he repeats, without getting any further forward. Not a bit of it, he thinks, the nihilating knot of the moment; not a thing from the past; no longer isolated with his body; never known, nor wished for. The Woodman leaves not the forest, sits not on yellow strands. The trace gives up, yielding, and is no longer fast nor true. Perhaps he recalls the heavenly hues of his dream, flickering just out of sight, above the earth now; all is soft, and bending. The water begins to pick up. "The sea. The sea," a sibilant song. The waves begin to expand and express themselves without the so needy concomitant wind. The sou-westerly breeze we have come to expect refuses to rise. There is no sign of threatening storms. No harsh showers to hail from the prevailing wind; none of that, but presently absent. No dark clouds, no crouched figures, no; only the concussion of the waves. All is presently still – or so it seems. The sea is sparkling waters. Yet the swell is rising, and unfolding, now singing staccato. The young knight looks again for that huge circle of life that lurks out there in the deep and dark beneath. "There's its tail," he says. "I am sure it must be there, lurking, waiting. Is that it's vast fin? Fin?" He recalls a day (was it yesterday?) when he was confronted by the serpent in the sea, stalking him, watching from the waves with vicious ruby eyes, disturbing the little white horses, the disappearing sails, the murmuring lips which lapped towards his feet. Today – if indeed it is *today* – the creature is hardly in evidence. "Fin?" he says, "the tail? Fin," he says again. But the water moves alone, turns and twists in a display which one could only attribute to the discomfiture of its very own making. Turning. Turning. By some magnificent mechanism, turning; slowly, yes, slowly, something appears beneath the welling waters, lying in the depths between the shore and the island. "What are those yellow shapes?" the young man asks himself: "What is it that rises from the sea?" It looks like granite stones are coming up from the waves. Out of the waters. "Rising stones," he calls out, *"rising."* That they too are gradually perpetuated – for what other word is there? – as though patched together right before the knight's eyes, unnoticed, it seems, by his steed. Let us not forget our grey Barb. Rise the stones will, and the grey steed pulls and shifts, smacking the right leg down upon the sand with some agitation, hoof splashing against sand and sea. And the young man calms his horse. "Hold back," he calls gently into its ear. But the horse is intent on crossing, not pausing. *Right now*, hoofs striking into the yellow stripes of sand; *right now*, to the castle on the horizon, standing high on the huge black rock; *right now*, galloping into the waves, making haste for the causeway revealed by the receding tide. "Halt," he calls, "halt," he cries. The horse cannot be held. The grey steed is fiercely eager to cross, to gallop on. In panic, the young man mounts his horse, throwing himself up and over. And there they take to the water. But the causeway has not risen to its proper extent, the level upon which they might safely pass has not been reached. So suddenly, so fast, so soon, there is further successive changes of place, or pace, as hoofs fail, splashing too soon, and soon sunk. The sea is hardly unsubstantial, turns, turns again, unsettled, and bitter-sweet, and though the day is calm and still and smooth and sure-golden, the water is suddenly held within a rising storm. Darkening sky and land. Without delay, the two are stranded. Man and horse. Darkness gathers. They have set off too soon. This is forbidden, but the two are lost in the contest. And the yellow granite road is deep below, the tide needs to recede further, to expose the stoned causeway. The Barb horse's hoofs are denied contact. And then, just then, from out of the water comes the sea monster. Wild screaming is heard, a fearful blood curdling sound. The Sea Serpent has been waiting, waiting, for impatience is his friend and his foe. The progression of the causeway is not yet complete, not risen yet to its fullest extent, it is some precious minutes away from its final construction. The sea-road to the other side is not right for the crossing.

> *And the giant sea snake is there to take his just*
> *desserts and his poisonous tongue's desires.*

This most dreaded creature, guarding the slip of sea between shore and the black hulk of rock, glides below, under water and deep with growing desire. Now hidden beneath the once loveliest purls of sparkling water, now as black as pitch, he lies in wait. But not for long; undulating there, slipping silently, an unearthly, sudden scream. It falls back, disappears as though formless. Silence gains, back, rising again, striking his vast tail into the sea. This hideously libidinous creature screams. Storm made. Waves rise. A chance-like apparition of death, screaming, screaming, rising high out of the coming of white-foamed froth. He rages at the grey steed, and the young knight, lowering into the shivering, bucking waters. Quick-sharp, the young man has his sword in hand. He swings at the serpent and he cuts him deep. And he can taste the salt water, and the stinging within his eyes, and he can hear the roar of the waves within his ears. But all of this is drowned out by the screaming of the giant snake curling and coiling and vanishing deep within the waves. The causeway still advances. The wet granite rocks arising. The two are all at sea, but still and steadfastly they make their vain attempts to reach the other side. The horse and the man struggle against the vicious waves, which drag and dredge at them. And once the causeway is true and fully exposed, the two will cross in peace, and calm. But, no, the time was not right – the time has passed. The grey Barb was too eager. The bitching, so brutal, waves have come from nowhere, advancing, again, ceaselessly. All is dark, as clouds shroud the sky, and the glittering and the Sparkling Castle cannot be seen. The direction of travel is altered and who knows what is up or what is down when all seems black and blue, and bruised, and bastard-dark? The giant serpent rises once again from the deep of the sea. O, yes, here they are, huge fangs with mouth held wide, O yes, my beauties – the monster slashes at the grey steed, who winnows in such a frightful tone. Teeth slicing through the white shifting lines of the waves, cutting into its beautiful soft grey darkened-by-the-sea. The blood sweeps out and colours the white horses, the spume turns red. The knight somehow swings his sword again, but it feels heavy, lead-heavy. Again and again, he cuts deep into the serpent's scales which seem more like an armour. The snake-creature cries out. The pain is but joy and ecstasy, an extreme pleasure is wrought from the water-weighed blade of the knight, slashing his scales, initiating his darkest green body with delightful cuts. Blood spurts out from beneath the young knight. His trusty grey Barb is fighting to keep afloat; the giant serpent swoops again at the dying steed, failing and falling now. Her companion struggles to remain in the saddle; the animal is struggling for survival, to breathe, for both of them to somehow live. The road advances, tide receding, rises still, the causeway's almost there. Too late, by far, too late, the two have already gone. The grey Barb is beginning to go down, but attempts with great effort, one last time, to throw her friend, yes, her friend and companion, upon the granite causeway, risen now to its fullest extent. The mortally wounded horse sinks into the dark of the briny sea. The Sea Serpent dives down for his prey, to feast upon this grey Barb, so cut and so well and truly bled. The monster knows well that the human is saved upon the yellow and grey stones of the causeway, as he was meant to be – his horse little more now than a fancy feast: "O, to glut on delights of this grey Barb," the Sea Serpent thinks; and thinks more: "The young pretty prince safe upon the island. He will kiss and he will kiss. Yea, that quaint lad will thrice kiss!"

VII

Someone shouted, a dull sound it was, but they will not be heard.
Not by me – or by you: we feel for them nonetheless, enacting
in some way their present state of fear, the danger to come.

Assuming that they were a part of life, all things regulated by the authorities or accepted by the state, even the events falling within his own destiny, were justified by someone. This someone means him harm. There's an unwritten score to be settled, that seems clear. *Damn it all to hell, Murphy will blow.* That's hardly the mantra, but the words should be heeded. Three bright lights are lit for the high windows, darkened by the night. The flickering fluorescence of each one is hardly picked up by the eye. Soon enough they will be dimmed. I look along, looking in, a solitary wanderer, one who looks back: alone, perhaps in the company of others. Who knows. Whatever did it matter. We seek to know the meaning of this disturbance. Then we shift along to the other lighted window, minding puddles that have gathered on the other side. There it is, at last. What we have been looking for. A hunched, large figure stalks the ward, coming out of shadow. A dim light is made out there in the office, but the night shift is yet to arrive. Is it us, bobbing up and down, before the high windows, looking from side to side in at the becalmed ward? No, it is not us for we are here – not there – in an altogether different place. But we must somehow stand as witnesses to the coming danger. We must be there. Somehow present. The puddles from the summer storms hardly make it an island, but what we see has the power of a lighthouse, the lights turning, darkness, returning light. What did it matter if the island was small, that viewed from the hill it was only a strip of black rock, rising between the white of the gulls and the silver-blue of the sea? Or a prison, perhaps; the convicts are held and managed by the proportion of an old physician, easily distracted the rising cry of birds which dwell in a place far away.

But we're nowhere near the sea.

Calm, but about to be quartered – hung and drawn. We are back! And hidden in the substance of shadow. There is movement. Large and dark. Transposed as we are from an early shift to a later one. We then hear that word. That somehow wordless question: *Guppy*? and then again, *Guppy*? We look back. *Guppy*? we say – so many Guppies made to bloom by something from without. Now this one we see; this one will not ask you where or when but how to escape the long and everlasting corridor which leads to sudden death. He's departed. All that's left feels faded in candle light. A dull yellow light that throws to low-relief the partition's oblong shadows, dancing there in the day ward, angular and sharp. In all three high windows, the light is lit in a strip. But all we can see is a dark and large human being. Hunched and enormous, with its arms outstretched. A quite unnatural stance, you'd think. But it sees what we cannot because they are there – and we are not. We must be vigilant, and we are; remaining, so very fearful, to observe the world from the perspective of their eyes. We fear to put ourselves in their place. Beyond the glass, the bars, the three lit windows. Beyond these promises of light, there is something we cannot see. Beyond are the sounds we cannot hear. The creak and screech of their rubber soles on linoleum, they are aimed at the target, their prey. This putative example of what we call care. This young man, this Guppy, will be rinsed in cold water and left like torn paper, floating, floating, falling to earth as fragments – or fractions of our humanity. He is an evasion to our questions, a refusal to answer to that stalking cry: Gup-py? Gup-py? Someone is moving away, not from us, but from this night. The night has fallen and so falls out of sight. The moon is but a slither, throwing silver light, luminescent and true. This will be the night they caught it. That falling emblem wrapped in such valued revenge. He will make no reply. He will not obey. They make it seem so simple, pivoting around on their heel. Disturbed, but not for long. For but a moment. Camier returns to the dorm. This someone turns again: Ah, Camier, they say, you're back – where've you been, lad? Their arms are moving, sowing seed, that's what it looks like. And then straight out before them in sleep-walking mode, or a trance; a parody of Dr Frankenstein's monster: they are alone, seeking the prisoner, the whole space of the ward seems theirs: hung, drawn, quartered. Punishment permeates, the conduit's close. He's here and now. His ungraspable and inexpressible fear. Perhaps there, just a flicker in the brows, conceiving the unfolding incident. Guppy limps effortlessly out towards the water closets. A poor hiding-place upon which to watch the huge hunched creature pass by. Hope. Eternal. Springs: soon enough the night nurse will come, lights will lower. He will be permitted to close his eyes once more in night-peace. Guppy waits, standing behind the door of a cubicle. Yes, the nurse from the night-shift will come. He is on his way. Guppy waits. His crooked leg vibrates. He hears something, and his heart responds. The question which bears no answer:

Guppy? Guppy?

His breathing stills. He is aware of the squeak of the soles of someone's shoes. One after the other. It stops, they're sniffing – surely, they can't smell him, stopping, and starting again as though following a scented rag. A heel squeak's a warning, coming closer. This is not the night nurse. Guppy is to be made to pay for the transgressions of each and every shift, for every slight they have themselves endured: *This is my life*, they scream within; an internal explosion. *Mine*, can't you see what you are doing? To *me*? This is *my life*. For all that is solid, or shifting, for all that is finally defined, Guppy remains the price of this *me*. He is the *mine*. Miles away from home. Was it ever thought he had a mother, a father? They don't care. Were there perhaps sisters, a brother or two? The same. All the bars of their incarcerated cage

– and rage – will fall as shadow on Guppy's luminous face. He doesn't even recognise me; the voice is but a whisper: But he will. He'll damn well remember me. I'll make sure he does. His inability to look at the intruder which, to the other's heated mind, denotes a total lack of recognition – or care: But he will, they whisper, as they close in on him, he will. A long shadow falling along the way to the water closets, climbing along the walls as they walk. Hidden behind that flimsy door. He steps back. His leg, bent, a-quiver. He staggers. He falls onto the porcelain mount. The lid is up. He feels for just a moment the fierce cold of the porcelain through his legs, right through to the bones of his behind. He could keep falling, falling down into the cistern, into the subterranean water and out and away. Freedom is elusive; cold it is. How have things come to this? And where are all the others? The residents, the nursing staff. Where are all the people in the world who can help? There is nothing we can do, of course. We are not there – not in person, at least. But we hear it, watching hunched Malone covering the whole space of the ward in a few long moments. Following him, following, following their scent. We believe this, we truly do. Here and now. We do; we believe it. From these times, theirs to ours; these long-lost times. Malone is the monster, right? Our attempts at hearing through the dark night is in vain. Not waking as if from a dream, nothing so extra-mundane as that. But in our thoughts, which come to us, across the years. In time, yes, in time, we bear witness. Not yet. Year after year, the passing of each thing into something else, the whole world is not changed, but differently formed. In the blankness of our minds an astonishment is made with intricate profusion. Of all the myriad events which led to this. The cold water, floating, floating, the fragments of Guppy are not changed; they're differently formed. The lost and presently losing years; how many years of conjecture; how many years of replaying the same story? Out of the black and yellow and silver mutability of this precise moment there is yet something alive. Another spring passes into a single summer's day, a purity was laid out on the fields as wide eyed and as watchful as we are, but what is there to see? Something for us to hold onto? Perhaps. A part of Guppy which we must keep intact. I have told you. Now you know. We can keep hearing. All of us can hear too. Here it is – that one single question as they open the door of the cubicle: Guppy? Gu-ppy?

… So there you are?

And so he was.

VIII

The sky is sought by the golden sun and the erstwhile dark of the clouds is burnt away. Wind which brought up the silver waves passes on, leaving behind a deathly, swaying silence.

There is a deathly, swaying, silence. The young man roars out into the vast expanse. Then halts, listening; the Sea Serpent has disappeared, falling out of sight. There, again, his head rises up out of the depths. Sound and silence. He calls out to the water, inhaling brined air, aware of the incessant inner din of his own mind. The loss is felt greatly, from the safety of the solid path from where he's been thrown. This is anything but quiet. The last gesture, his horse. He'd roared into the galloping waves, calling high for his horse: "Cornubia! Cornubia!" But, nothing. "Cornubia." Nothing. Suddenly, the water is crinkled, percolating softly. He remembers that winnowing into the frothy waters, the waves had enveloped her, once and for all. Silence again. In vain; his panicked calls are heard: Someone is alerted. The sea returns to calm and blue, pale blue silver. He is standing alone at the castle-end of the granite causeway. What now? Will he be led up to the castle, sparkling up there on the rock? The manic creature screams, high-pitched, at the young man: his eyes of ruby red, his teeth like daggers, but these weapons were held back. He could have cut the young man to shreds. After all, the youth is mortal, and his beauty is ephemeral. "How we have waited for this moment." This is the expressed yearning of the Sea Serpent; his own long-awaited anticipation: "… he comes – At last, he is there." This is the precise moment too of another's decision. To follow the intertwining threads that lay loose around the edges of his mother's tapestry, a memory of shapes and forms and figures. "Hold true," he'd called, his arms pulled by his thrusting horse. But once, and again, has he not already seen this time in the tapestry? Consider the animal as if it were a human being. Insight: Death. And now, and again, here he is upon the causeway; and, yet again, the grey Barb goes too soon: "The stones are coming out of the waves," he shouts. Out of the waters. "Rising stones," he calls out, "rising. A moment, only ... to go." The horse will not be held. He knows this. The grey Barb is eager to cross, to gallop on. In panic, the young man mounts his horse, throwing his leg across the creature's back. And they take to the water. One last time. The road advances, tide receding, but rising too slowly, almost still. The yellow and silver stones of the causeway are *almost* revealed. It's too late, by far, they have gone too early. And as the horse sinks, he lurches one last time and throws her friend, her dearest companion, upon the granite causeway, fully risen now. The horse drops, sinks fast into the dark of the briny sea. To be gone where she's most moved to go.

The young man suddenly awakes, looking up, now leaning on his elbows which are sensitive to the prick of sharp stones, he takes a deep breath.

He notices at once that the forest is now situated on the other side of the sea, blue as osmium. The little silver waves are rising and falling, curling out of the blue, as though in sleeping breath. The yellow sand rests beneath this curtain of dark trees. "I have crossed," he says, "I am here." His exertion tells on him, a toll paid, indeed, now lying on him, and the fierce heat fixes his mind on the fever of those earlier days. *When I was a boy*, he recalls, a tear suddenly blurs his sight. "Blue," he whispers, "blue? As a boy." The hot sickness that followed his father's death. "I am amazed," he says, "that I was able to make a complete recovery from the world of that fever. Somehow," he says, "I found my way back to familiar things. As a boy." The young man stands, stretches his arms to the sky. He falls back onto the pathway. "Rest," he says, for just a moment or two. He feels the strain at his neck, his chest feels constricted, his throat is dry. He looks out at the sea; panic suddenly seizes him. "Cornubia," he cries out the word, an enquiry of sorts: "Cornubia?" The granite causeway stands proud and as true as a patch of yellow fabric. The wandering glassy castle looms large above his head, too high to be made out clearly. "I am on the other side," he says, "alone, but here, at last," he whispers. The seams are seemingly weaved and sown back together, loosening, tightening their grip, even while the young man strives to tear its fibres. "I am here again," he says, weeping the loss of his companion. Then squinting his eyes against the sun, he repeats, "I am here, at last. O yes, here am I. But who knows the reason why …? Why," he calls out to the waves: "O, why?" Over the causeway the young prince did rush – headlong as it rose. The grey Barb, impatient, reared and rushed towards the target. "What choice did I have?" he remembers, but to mount up fast and fly over the watery stones. The Sea Serpent sees precisely what he's been waiting for. "They're here, at last: *he's* there." That damned creature attempts to send across a wave to dislodge the young man, wave after wave, then screaming, screaming, to such a pitch. That ear-splitting sound enters into his very mind, deep into his cortex, and seeks therein to destroy his sense of perception. To no avail, or so the young man thinks. The causeway cannot be breached by the sea creature. The huge, hulking stones, appearing to rise as the tide falls, are firm and strong; yes, it is true, the tide recedes and then returns. He cannot know this, but he is safe within the confines of the temporal crux. The time of the tides, that is, will cede, leaving behind, block by block, the yellow and silver granite causeway. "O, yes," he says, shifts his elbows, one at a time, for relief from the small irritating stones that are digging themselves into his skin. He looks across to the other side: "I was there," he says, "not long ago, but now," looking for any disturbance of the sea, "here I am." The brave knight was thrown upon these rocky foundations. The huge black rock upon which the castle rests is now just ground and not black at all, but a sparkling grey. In time, he must take the long, strong, walk up to the very top. But not quite yet. No, for a moment, he rests upon the stony ground. Eyes closing, his voice quieting: "Somehow," he says, "I found my way back to familiar things. As a boy," he says. Exhausted and distraught, ashen weak. His eyes are closing, his face he rests upon his angled arm, he soon passes into a deep sleep. "The fever broke," he says, "when I was a boy." How long ago? He asks as though to the waves: "How long?" For a moment it is as if his flesh turned to unfathomable particles. There is no sequence, but all at once occurring, driving him upwards before the wind, fragments of him and fractions of the whole, rising high on the wind, ascending above sea and stones to cloud and sky.

*Clouds are ever turning; clouds are shapes in
the sky; are shadows on the ground.*

Rising to his feet, he stands there, well below the bedrock, alone but seen, spotted by a shaft of sunlight. The Sea Serpent espies his prey from afar: "The young pretty prince is safe upon the island." He dives deep, returning without delay. "He will kiss, kiss, kiss. Yea, that little lad will kiss!" The young man begins to make his ascent. Far off, in another place, the tapestry is swirling and adapting, shifting and turning, assimilating light patterns within the darkness of the past. "Yes," he replies, "I know the way to go." And that way is showing – *Up*. He feels bounded by towering, over-hanging flowers, crowding-in, abundant, separating and merging, clinging haphazardly and tight to the rocks. The stranger has been noticed from afar. Yes, the young man is always being watched. An emissary soon comes this way. The brave knight must be brought to Oriane. "Look at the patterns," the young man says. Look how they are changing, the shapes and colours, unfolding, making landscapes and mountain ranges, and people and skies. Again, but he knows not why, he feels so very homesick, terribly in need of what once was familiar, defying recall, holding true only to the distance. "Look at the colours, the blooms, the flowers," he says, "clinging true to the rocks," as though arranged by the hand of some majestic creature. "This is too much for my eyes," he says, "the scent, overwhelming." The myriad colours, yes, here and everywhere, as though placed on the huge rock by an equally huge hand. "Am I here?" he asks. He is still, so still, but alive, yes, alive. "Look at the shapes, the growth of forms, the fast figures," he says: "You only have to look. To see." Just out of harm's way, the bubbles of sea spray fall like dew, waves chop at the surface, surreptitiously biting at the island, eroding its earth-hold. One day the castle is reclaimed by the sea, the rock now risen falls to hiding-sand beneath the waves. All will fall. This castle's national trust will one day be lost for all that remains of time. "Yes, just there, it moves, drops, stone upon stone, into the sea." Turning from his elevation, he begins his climb up the broken lesser trodden road to the castle. "It's like I am hovering above the sea," he says, looking down onto the water and across to the forest, underlined with a yellow strand. He shields his eyes. "Gone," he says, "all gone." He begins to laugh. One palm obscures the world from afar. "Nothing is bigger than these five fingers. My palm." The sea is sparkling waters. Yet the swell is rising, and unfolding. The knight looks again for that huge circle of life that lurks out there in the deep and dark beneath. "Is that its tail," he asks, "or a wave in the sea?" It is surely there, lurking, waiting. Is that its fin? "How small it looks from here." He recalls a day – was it yesterday? – when he was confronted by the serpent in the sea, stalking him, watching from the waves with vicious ruby eyes, disturbing the little white horses, then as disappearing sails in the distance, the murmuring lips which lapped towards his feet. Today the creature is hardly in evidence, "Fin?" he says, "Tail?" A breeze swarms over in a belt of irritance, then falls back; there's a chill to the wind that brings shivers down his spine. The Serpent of the Sea twists through his domain, his head appearing above the water-line; his ruby eyes intent, staring at the escaped prey, filled with ire. The creature is desire for death and destruction; the creature *just is*. But also, surely, there is fright and dismay, for soon enough a union will be forged; the Sea Serpent's lover is released back into the seas, and to the mayhem and to the death of the material world. The very next moment that creature, like its lies and deceit, disappears to the deep: The creature *just is*. There will be no observers of this, none. The earth was nowhere near the sky above. It had dropped completely away, fallen, and so lost to all sight; all knowledge; all being gone. Black is lost, white too, all colouration is dismissed; all fear of aging, all hatred and abhorrence gone; love too, inseparable, close knit with our human anxiety; all joy exalted, inexact, all ground upon which we hold ourselves up, and below, cut down; each and every wandering which seeks the simple question.

"I understood, but why?" This why *is brought to incongruity; this excess of light is also the moment of our night.*

"Day break?" the boy asks of the fair lady. "Day break, at last," the fair lady replies. In the garden were the golden orbs of oranges and the intoxicating scent of early spring flowers, many of which are set within their glossy green foliage, held in relief against the distant blue of the sea. The high garden pays little heed to season. There, in addition, bunches of grapes hung, or strewn by our invisible hand, these pleasant little balls of fantastic jet bijoux, dangling in trellises, leading the way through the scene of this sculptural and spectral site. Is that a well? There is a circling wall upon which a young woman is seated, looking down into the glassy water. She seems taken by what she sees reflected back at her; at what she is: snake, and only snake is what she is.

This must be Oriane.

IX

You could make him out in shadow as firm as a fist of flesh and bone. An ominous shadow: shifting and spinning within the present feeling of space. He cowers: they will strike him.

It's as high as a mountain, he says, looking up. Darkness is thrown. The shadow has fallen. A sharp sound is heard. A strike at him, thudding against him. You like that, do you? The stranger's voice is familiar, but sounds queer, isolated from its usual charm. A strike, harder, the cur gets it, but heads are hard. Looking at the palm of their hand, at the fair face before them, beneath them; the shock on Guppy's face is comical. He begins to laugh. Two more blows to the head, as hard as hell. Cur, the stranger says, fecking cur. Their physique strikes fear into the smaller one, his arse cold against the white porcelain. But Guppy cannot hold it; involuntarily it occurs. The stranger's harsh punches and sharp slaps come as a relief. God knows why. Punishment, a misery to be put out of. Anything is better than this. *What's that terrible stench?* A sound echoed on porcelain, rebounding around its circular sides before striking at an endless pool of water, rising again, then arriving at the olfactory system of the stranger. Jesus, he says. Really? The stranger cum interrogator is momentarily perplexed, indeed, he is stunned. Christ, he says, completing the term: You've dropped your guts, Guppy. Jesus, really? The stranger steps back somewhat, but there's very little room to move in. Guppy stares up, those vivid blue eyes of his. No expression, but we might deduce, not a little satisfaction. *Silence.* Their intent, infrangible, but as vague as vertigo, and yet as true. Guppy is dazed, his chin drops. The figure steps back, but there's very little room to see their handy work. Guppy smiles to placate; to let the stranger know it's all right. All is well. No words issue from the one seated on the cold white porcelain: My fingers trace behind the shifting world, the words are there, white; Or is the shroud white? Or the bread I sink my teeth in to? My teeth, white too? I cannot see the words,

230

but hear them, yes, eating themselves into this darkest night. Guppy is silent; we know not what he thinks. Firm ground is soon felt, as mind passes: Another? they say, you little rotten cur. You stinker. Mind passes into mind. This mind is more than meaning, more than truth. It was something coming; it was presence itself. The singularity of death and darkness. They relent. There is time. Out of the depths of space and time and words he is multiplied and dissolved within this water closet. From meaning to something meant, from truth to something just. From all of this to something which rears its once hidden head. From an echo of his own physical lack of stature to this hulk of striking, aching meat: Man. Out of the depths of darkness springs forth a pale, blinking kid, nineteen years at most.

He is sought because they think he means everything.
He is ceaseless to them – a means to an end.

He is the direction of their sins. The stranger steps back into the darkness of the diminished night. The door to the water-closet slowly comes to, leaving a gap of around six inches. Freedom is his. Freedom. Out of shadow. Who was it, the stranger, the one who, walking away right now, seems intent on not being seen? Disappearing from sight. They can't be. They are. Guppy reaches his hand out, the door kept ajar by around six inches. Watching them walking away. The short hallway back to the ward is lit with an eerie blue light. He waits. He stands. He leaves. Suddenly feeling cold but somehow safe. His eye tickles from the earlier harsh blow which fell on his brow. He wanders out of the cubicle, a long short walk to the day ward. He feels confused, disorientated, but not by the flickering blue. By violence, the blows he received to his head. He can hardly breathe but he will set out, alone, with no hope of escaping from one of the high windows. An impossible task, as will later be testified to. *Not even a contortionist*, Dr. Mallory Jacobs will say. But where are the records of the inquest: *An unusual death, to say the least,* stated the good doctor, *something of a mystery.* How the hell could he get out. *A mystery,* the doctor will reply, *a complete and utter mystery.* All the doors were apparently locked; the windows barred. Only Malone and Camier were on this late shift; Mercier was off sick in much the same way as Savage's skirt. You've got to show off a bit of leg, she says to Molloy, sipping her drink: What's not to like? she says, laughing out loud. Whoever it was who walked away from the cubicle, hardly making a sound, will be soon revealed. For now, we call this violent stalker, the stranger. O, yes, there it is: the hideous squeaking on the blue lino as they stride away. But these sounds are deceptive; they are hardly conclusive. Guppy floats out, safe and sound, not a flicker of expression or emotion on his face. Just there. Just there. *It is open.* My fingers trace along the cold wall, the world shifts, beckons me. The door to the outside world. *Open.* He must think these words. He must see this state of affairs: It is open.

The exit door to the outside world is open.

Left wide to the world. Beyond it, in what seems such total darkness, is the endless corridor. *Who cares?* He must think this. Whoever cares? Is this England, he hardly knows the meaning of nationality. If it is, he must think, no one hears you scream. The longest corridor runs and runs and runs the full length of this Victorian edifice. Yet it offers hope. The exit door is open. The stranger upped and walked away, squeaking as they went. Headed towards the office, so they are, neglecting to look back. Heedless. The young man floats out of the door and away. The exit door was open, but somebody is nearby. This someone has remained unseen. Yes, he was there. Only a few yards away. The large man is sitting in shadow, puffing signals from his pipe. Seen and heard some bits at the surface: What is all of this? he thinks. He is watching but he remains aloof. Guppy floats out and away. What is that, a flicker passes before the man with the pipe, that thing before me there? Can I be dreaming this, with my eyes open? What's there, really, but pictures and flickers? That is all it is. He breathes in deeply: *Pictures and flickers*, he says, blowing out smoke in ectoplasm, quite unsure as to how he is configured and then presented to the audience, a phantom's here: Pictures and flickers, is all, he says. Sitting, or sleeping, or sometimes singing. It is damned hard to tell what is what when all is said and done. And what was it about the eminent one that troubles him. *That shrink was saying some things about me?* What was it now? See me thinking the reasons, the sound and the sweetness. Talking about rhythms and phases of some time. Who's time. Him talking, talking out of his little blue lips, talking, talking, talking. He laughs, thinking of his eminence's ancient mouth, his white cotton wool hair, his words nevertheless pursuing him from the start. That's all it is, he speaks again: noise and shamefulness. Rhythm, that's the word, and the name: *Wilson*, that's the name; speaking, acting like I am a deaf man, or something else: *Wilson*, he says it, all the time, the same *Wilson*. I hear it all and these are the things I see. *Quite normal*, that shrink says, but not to me. You fool, I want to say it, but I keep myself to myself – *You fool, I am just here*. His cotton wool hair feels soft and springy. I see Molloy laughing; and me, smiling too. Ah, there it is – again. Can I be dreaming, he asks himself, whispering, somehow hidden, in the mist of shadow. The trick is to make it stand still; the press of it, the rhythm, one minute, still, the nex ..., and him all inflated because he's the big boss doctor.

Wilson, that's him saying it,

but, you know, no one bosses me.

Not you little man,

not this strange one passing here,

squeaking the floor with the shoes on their feet:

I see you; but what is it you do?

This is no dream;

that's all shored up.

Pictures and flickers,

but what it is it you do?

Is it you at all?

Night falls. Its fallen, at last.

The ward is silent, the night nurse is due soon. But not quite yet. The staff have abandoned ship. The ward seems so close, shadowed. The barred windows are blinded by darkness, reflecting the inside of the day ward like a mirror. It is black outside. The transparency no longer provides a system of relief. The whole of the windows, twenty-four in number, in each dormitory have a portion of their height, about two feet, working on a swivel, so as to open to any desired inclination. But there can be no escape, not from these windows. The top of this swivel-light is constructed as a cast-iron hopper-shaped frame, glazed in front and ends, but left open about two inches wide at the top, the opening being covered with fine wire gauze. The lower portion of all the windows will also be constructed so that the middle part, about one foot in width from top to bottom, can be unlocked and turned upon a centre, and thus a flood of pure air be admitted when desired. The windows were left open that night, it was close, night was falling, but it was stifling, humid and hot. And nobody can squeeze between the internal white gloss bars. The bars are regularly painted in glossy white. They are sometimes hard to notice, but it just might be possible, somebody said, for a small nineteen-year-old male to make himself small enough to squeeze through and gain access to the outside world. No, Garnett explains, it is not possible; no, not at all. The only inexplicable answer was: Yes, but only contingently so. Anything is possible, after all. Forget it, another said, not on your life. Forget! Forget! How to forget? From a far-off palace,

Green it was, verdant, you see, fine, there pipes a bird, as though words were spoken, a language of sorts, but birds' words, threaded on a wall, in trees, sounding nevertheless; red roses winding away, trailing the terrace walls and there hedging hides the rabbits who, breaking cover, dash in disparate ways, directionless, it seems. And then, over there, some yonder place, watched from afar, he saw the loon dive deep, a momentary flash of red at the throat, his father was followed; walking in step, a pathway discovered too late. Struck, struck, struck, when so softly your brow is bleeding, colouring your front in red, a king is split, floating away on the water, down deep, as though turning, as though asleep: Why father, when so softly your brow is bleeding? Throw legends to the wall, let dark curses rise above the trees in bird flight, till their wings are burnt and they plunge into the deep. But already he has gone. The exit door was left open wide, you see. Murphy waits, pipe smoke rising, he waits for the coast to clear. But doors are easily closed again.

X

The young man awakes, suddenly; rises to his feet. He looks
about for his grey steed. "Cornubia, Cornubia!" he calls out,
yet again. "Lost, my bringer of hope; denied." The young
knight feels for a moment as though captured in memory.

He looks across the expanse of sea, to the other side. "I passed
over that water," he says, "upon rising the causeway. Too early,
too soon, too late." His voice is hoarse, his chest feels hollow:
"Now Cornubia is lost – and his absence admonishes me."
The castle set high upon the sparkling waters is high above
him, shrouded in its customary mist. He can hardly see the
turrets which strike at the sky, hidden now in murky white.
The glassy mirrored walls are no longer in evidence. Back on
the shoreline, he sees the yellow strand stretching far into
nowhere, the wild woodland is fallen into sentries of bronze
pillars. "Impenetrable," he says, "the darkness. Yes, it is there,"
he speaks as though to the soft breeze: the forest, the bars
of trees which stretch back for miles and miles as one single
dense landscape. So deep, but fragile, so dense, impassable, but
somehow vulnerable. "There is smoke rising from the forest," he
says, his voice is little more than a whisper, his throat parched.
A dark shadow there, yet penetrated, yes, penetrated: "Who is
burning the woodland?"

Surely, there can be no way back to his
homeland. The only way is up.

He can make out that damnable monstrous creature, risen from
the depths, throwing itself down, bubbles form, vapours arise as
though from a cauldron, stark whiteness envelops the soft, the
fragile, blue: "The sea's boiling," the young man says. "It's
boiling." Above him, he can descry a stratification of rocks or
slabs of shining slate, large slivers of schist, one temporal flow

built one upon the other. "Look at all the time," he says, looking up, wiping sweat from his brow. "All time is there. All – and yet our own time passes the moment we grasp it." He has crossed the sea; the causeway rose and will again fall like a stone. "The causeway has disappeared," he says, looking down. How, for a moment, he walked upon the waters; from afar, that's what it must have looked like; a man walking on water. His horse is lost. "O, Cornubia." Still now, silent and calm, the sea; bit by bit the day before – was it the day before? These days? He does not ask this but, still, it is there. The question of when and how re-etches itself upon the frail wings of his emotions. "I have crossed," he says to himself, his voice is soft, barely a whisper, "to the other side." He is coming to, slowly, waking from all his efforts. "We are always in peril, always in a bad plight, just on the edge of destruction and only to be saved by invention and courage." He feels a gnawing absence. His horse, yes, "O, my comrade. Cornubia!" He calls out again to the waves. "Cornubia torn, destroyed, ruined in the sea." Silence. But there is more to come. Looking beyond the sea, he sees someone: "Is that a man, between the beach and the high black trees? Is he waving?" Something feels hidden to sight, or is it that espied figure who is lost? But whatever it is, it must somehow show itself. He hears his own words: "Is that a man?" His own voice, a sound he knows so well, is unfamiliar: "How long have I been travelling? O, how lonely I feel. My home, how I sicken for it." He thinks of his father, drowned, his uncle held in glass within the tapestry's fabric, merging, changing day after day, shifting, and turning. "Dying duke, the duke dying," he says. He thinks of his dear mother, lost too, never truly known, her fate to die in childbirth: "Mother," he says, the woman whom he knows only from the tapestry upon the wall of her chamber: "Dearest mother," he says the words, imploringly, "forever lost to me: Mother." Yes, he has crossed, but he is not a free man. No, he is not. At once, he feels restricted. Something is busying itself about his legs. He is being tied up as if by a rope, quite unable to move freely, he can hardly stand erect, twisting his own body, to locate the restriction, he almost falls back to the stony ground, but he stands true. He sees, very clearly, almost immediately, that an iridescent, over-large grass snake is coiled about his legs. This is like a dream, he thinks, managing to pull out his sword, swift-like, at his side. "Be gone, you damned creature," he calls, raising his sword, still prone, with thoughts to slash at the snake. But he does no such thing. It is clear the creature is benign, hardly struggles, just coiling itself around and around the legs of the young man, moving slowly up, advancing towards his waist, its skin is soft and fine. The young knight no longer moves, but remains rigid, still, silent. So intently is he watching the grass snake, advancing over him, that he drops his sword, unhearing of the clang of metal onto stone. The larger-than-life grass snake is winding its way slowly towards his chest and upward bound. Until it stops. The creature stares straight into the eyes of the young man, face to face. "You are here for me," the young man asks. "Should I follow you?" The largest of silver grass snakes speaks not a word. The two are there, seemingly held by the sea on one side and closed-in by a forbidding wall, strewn in wild flowers, rising, up and up, to the main walls of the castle. To find nourishment for their vari-coloured shrubs and flowers, the blood-red-centred bromeliads, they rise on rock, climbing up granite walls, seeking freshwater and soil for their survival, away from the shore, the heat and the brine, they arise and perish from the heights of the circling crows. They have their way. Eye to eye, the snake seems to be smiling. This cannot be. There is his little tongue flicking out, then returning from whence it came. The large black eyes behold the young man's variegated ones, occasionally seeming green, then amber, dark curling lashes top and bottom, the soft pure skin, white and unblemished. The prince is fixed upon the snake's black round eyes, totally black, but with a square shaped light. The snake is looking so intently into the prince's eyes that the young man becomes lost in the power of the creature's stare, each of their eyes mirroring the other. Who's mesmerising who? – who dictates the game of seeing whose light is yet to reach us?

You will never see anything worse than yourselves.

The creature, without further ado, having apparently introduced itself, uncoils and twists and returns to the feet of the young man, filling the knight's heart with cold horror. "Yes," the young man responds, "I should follow you." He walks, feeling something amiss at his side: "My sword," he shouts, striding back, retrieving it from the rocky ground. "My sword," he says, a glimpse of his face in the blade. He feels lost, stricken in a day-time dread, a day-terror. That something sought is forever lost. For a day, or forever and a day, he cannot tell. "I thought I understood why." Indeed, he feels it, in his heart he is aware of its thump, a madness, it feels like, a fight. A fright; he must follow the larger-than-life snake. His memory is laid out flat on green fields of his homeland, high on the steeple of the chapel, skirting the surface of the lake, a skimming stone, a fast-diving loon hidden in the depths, signifying death: Green, he was, bloody bilious, I'd call it, a frog in the mouth of a snake. What a way ... Wide-eyed he was, finding fault for feeling this way, feeling that; weeping in the garden, under the old oak tree, striking his head against the bark, the head gardener's son at his side, sizing him up; ever so watchful, he was, do you recall, entirely careless as to how he was transformed in the tapestry, or wasn't. To do as bade, of what was done, or thought, by the beholders of fate. To save someone from themselves, to unloose the world from globes and bubbles, and ever-ending serpentine spirals. "It fades so fast," he calls to himself, casting his voice for his hearing: "Think, damn you – if only I could think." The guide snake is out of sight: "Where have you gone?" the young man calls out, looking back to the stony path that appears to twist and turn behind him, before him. The large grass snake stops, looks back, and the young knight follows. "To know the cause." His mind strays again, struck now by simple following. Marred memory strikes into the present moment, is brought back, laid out flat, stretching far away into the future, no longer past at all, or so it would seem. The loss of his beloved companion, the grey Barbary horse. He has put Cornubia out of his mind, but surely not. "Cornubia is lost." The crossing on the causeway, his own near death, the horror of the Sea Serpent, the screaming, the onslaught of waves, the slashing at the creature with his sword – and suddenly the silence. Surely, he recalls his journey here. *Silence.* These overwhelming pasts of his life consume him, nagging at whole regions of doubt. Through the columned wood, dark and obscure, he rode his Barb horse. The whispering trees were understood, the earth was soft and plump, and there were large silver stocks and crooked branches that had fallen from the trees, from the oaks and sycamores, from the ashes and the birches, from the beech. These lay so softly still, in repose, or sitting up, as though they were humans at rest after weary toil. There and not there, the appearance of convivial friends, coming to be as comrades for the knight, his eyes now closing, his heavy lids dropping beneath the darkening space of the sky, an obscurity reached only through and beyond the tips of this sylvan wood. And all about him were the unnamed creatures and other hiddenfolk: "I have seen you before," he says, "and before" – and the earth around him was strewn with golden coins, somehow fallen, but if you made any attempt to pluck one up would simply quiver and vanish and appear elsewhere. All of this recedes into the past of the tapestry on the east wall of his mother's chamber: a place where things are dealt with differently, a place that exists only in the neverlasting reaches of time. No, these places are far distant memories. Today is otherwise. On this very day, the largest of grass snakes is leading the knight up a steep incline which leads not only to the castle keep but to the hour and place of his destiny. "You have come, for me?" she will exclaim, a voice that reduces him to tears. "What is this?" she asks, the tears dashed away, an answer is vouchsafed, but it is perfectly unclear. Time passed, as it must, as one said it would; some cleavage in the darkness, a separation of mind and body. Look, just there, as the sun rises, a spark of recognition, twisting her face in the glass, making her say something which might just save her. Nothing will save her.

The sun moves through strength and zenith towards the moments when it drops like a golden stone. The West from where it perishes; Easterly risen; the whole is two halves.

It rests awhile until restored and spins into rude health for another day. The east there; it rises; the west waits. Daybreak's passing, the earth hurtles by, east to west, *vice versa*. The knight and the larger-than-life grass snake continue their climb upon the rugged path, steep, steeper. The ascent is hot hard work. Time passes, as it must; peace descends, the shadow wavers. The young man becomes ever so thirsty; it is the salt from the sea, he thinks. He stops, halts a moment, his nose he raises high: "The sea," he says: "Hey, Snake, can you smell the sea?" *Silence.* But there is no rest, no spring from which to slake one's thirst. He holds his hand up to the falling sun. The fan of his fingers eclipses its rays, hiding the red to pink burning sphere, warming his hand. "How I remember his touch. Against my cheek, the first time. The first time." The guiding grass snake stops, occasionally, slithers and slides and hisses, looks sideways to censure the young man's sloth. Though he still advances, light as a bird upon the rough-paved stones. So steep and strenuous, he refuses to stop. The young knight sees before his eyes, a time before travelling, before the long road of mortal denominations: "How long ago? My hand. His hand. Our touch." He is here. The head gardener's son had rushed to him: "Sorry, Master," he cries, lowering his head. "Yes," he says, how he remembers him, but distantly. "The same as you," the head gardener's son had replied, then laughed. "Within days, they say. My mother nursed you as she did me. Wet, they call it." The head gardener's son, laughing still, looks down. "I hear his voice," the young man says, under his breath. He came to me. "The rabbit," he said. "Your uncle killed it. He killed the thing." He drops to his knees. "But that was so long ago," he'd replied, laughing now at the recollection. With an open hand, he touches his cheek. The young prince could hardly breathe. He must have thought me angry, but quaking, yes, all these things. "Hold true," he whispers as this singular feeling fades fast, "I want to touch you." The head gardener's son's face so close to his own. Another moment comes. Another moment comes. The young prince's face, so open, so honest, and true. "You are beautiful," the head gardener's son says, as the young prince brings his hand to the other's hand and holds it there, against his own face. Their touch.

"You are beautiful too," the young knight whispers into the breeze.

He does not feel hunger, no, he felt no such pangs. But that earlier thirst we mentioned lingers longer in the mind than the smell of the sea. But in thought, all foreign things are made transparent, absent, the doubt of two things are merged, fading to grey, to black and white, and suddenly wiped clean in the thunder of his mind. Spirit is absolutely free here. Present and past are the same, but the past is the same as the past insofar as it is in the present a different matter – a memory made in the moment of reflection. How can you appear in a mirror, me or you, mirrored in certain identity with its mirror image? How should we distinguish the past as it is reflected in the mirror? The past, the reflection, is and remains the other, but only with respect to the present. "O," he cries, but his voice is slight, dried out by the salt in the air: "O," he repeats, "my head," he says, "how it splits." The weakness of his limbs, the determination to reach the top is all-consuming. Whitest of marble steps, the rocky path transformed: a spiral of them, twisting out of sight. These will finally lead him, very easily, to a well on a terrace, a holy well, enclosed by a circular wall about its perimeter. He is unaware of this; it's the thought that counts, thoughts which neither moths nor thieves can penetrate. But there will be water there, fresh water, and a carved wooden pail. Turning, once again, turning, his foot strikes the end of the spiral stairs, a terrace flat and true, a surface glassiness. The knight will soon enough rush to a resting place, a reflecting place, where he will sit and while away the water in the well.

*Time and presence here cohere, but there are paths
and pails and perspectives aplenty.*

"What are these," he asks, holding the pail up to the light – "are they snakes?" One after the other, swimming in shiny, silver glass – not glass, but silver-added to the wood. Snakes abound, around the pail, inlaid to the wood grain. "Look here," he says, but words are lost in what is hoarse. "Craftsmanship," but the enactment of words is merely thought. The pail is real, carved with the skill of ages. Precious snakes stretch around the structure of the wooden pail: "Such skill," he says, "who is responsible for such work?" Sun fallen fast; his face feels as though it is glowing. The well is deep, very deep, and the strands of lichen, and long delicate weeds, are as arteries in the water, threading to the depths to determine the imminent state of things. For a moment, he looks up and away from the well's water, turning his body, listening to the streaming waterfalls, making their way down from the higher castle terraces. "How it all looks so small. It's hard to believe it's even there," he calls out to the faraway world. The snake guide, looking back, seems to nod, aware of the young man's instability. "Look, the broken coastline is twisting around the sea; it gets lost into the far distance." The guide snake has lost interest. That's what it seems like. "O, and how the forest has disappeared into oblivion. All is so soon gone away, fading into the darkness. Am I lost, Snake: answer me." Then into the depths, a bright lit pool, held within the circular wall. He will look down into it, he will; a silver glass disc reflects his face back at himself. "There I am." He laughs, within the shining circle, a double arc of quicksilver dimpling and distorting the young man's features. The prince recognises himself, but only just: "Is it me? I seem so much older, no longer the boy as once I was. Is it me?" For a moment he's unsure, he looks down at what was once the purest white skin, now bronzed. The curls of hair falling, tumbling around his face, seem bleached too by the sun. Those variegated eyes are surely his, yes, he realises quickly that it was only he; a solitary face looking down into the still water of a well. But a strange feeling, numbing him, weakening his resolve: *No human can say what a goddess is.* Consciousness is it, or a growing, a gnawing, a deeply felt tiredness, stealing upon him: *No goddess knows.* The wooden pail with the inlaid silver snakes is dropped, shaking the still water, obliterating the reflection of his face. He fills, and then retrieves the carved pail, which his haste makes weightless. For a moment, all he saw was the silver snakes swimming in perfect circles. He drinks from it fully, slaking a thirst which has been sorely tested by the salt in the air. "The sun has well and truly set," he says, placing the pail by his side on the wall. "Daylight down," he says, looking out from his vantage point. An orange golden orb, once seen so clearly over the waters, throws back the last remnants of its force, dipping away into that pale blue shadow as it died another day. "Dark light?" he says, with big shadows behind him: "How I dream of sleep." The knight hears the hiss again. "From where?" he asks, and when he turns, he sees a thing most thing ominous: "Snake!" No, not his guide, the grass snake, slinking away, suddenly lost to his sight. "Snake?"

XI

There are dark shadows wherever you look, geometrical
shapes taking hold, fleeting and fast. No, they are
not disfiguring, but watching them felt, on the
whole, like falling upwards and outwards.

The roads were all silent, a branch tapping the pane above your head is hardly heard, if at all, and as the night drew on a mantle of silence seemed to thicken in the dorm room, running down the walls, onto the beds, hovering just above their physical beings, a night hag squatting on a chest, the dim lights fighting a losing battle against the immeasurable waves of darkness surging all around them. Just listen; there, can you hear it? The tentative, unmeasurable, sounds of slumber and sleep is all. There's nothing to fear. It's a little before the night shift's here: *Look, is that Watt?* No, not tonight. He rests, injured, still stoic, of course, but his head hurts when he lies on one side. And Murphy? Yes, he's there, in a chair by the door to the wide world, puffing on the final embers of his burning chamber. Can you see him beyond the grey smoke in the dimmed lights? He'd watched as the door was left ajar, the figure then walking away. That's what it was. An emotion formed, rounded itself, broke for a moment, disappeared, only to swell again. *Where's the right in that?* he says, his voice seemingly inaudible. On a night like this, you can hear twenty different sounds – and wasn't it Molloy who could hear the sea? Muprhy'd watched the stranger unlock the door, and walk away. Whose very name? he says, whispering, I forget. Who told me? Enough of this, he says, his voice deep, resonant: Once I was lost, but now ... He hears the voice in his head, the one he knows well, and is familiar with: Dim it is, and so dreadful. The fear of sudden sounds can seize you: *I'm listening,"* you said, *"I prefer it that way."* There's that voice. Perhaps they're right, after all. A straight line, you need. There is order, yes, it resumes, it never fails to come back – the order of things. *Toe the line*, you said, *it's easier that way.* They'll never catch me – never. That was my reply. He puffs, quietly, silently: They never stood a chance – *You can't leave*, you said, is that it? *You're too afraid to stir.* But I'll make the best of it. It is high time we wake from our slumbers, feel something, whatever it is. They were standing, a huddle of people, laughing. *I'll tell you who I am*, I said to that man, hailing us. Remembering him, walking the streets, calling out to the people, paying him no heed. *Repent*, he cries, naming us *Friends*, then counting us, one by one, that's what it seemed like. Too many faces and not enough names. Each one of us has several. Faces, not names. Then comes the grave warning: *That night is far spent, the ...* but we paid him no mind. I stopped for a little minute, looking at his face, his eyes, which were closed. He appears tried and tested, his skin was lined; he looks sick, weighed down with placarded shoulders: *Who could be strong*, he says, his eyes wide now, *and refrain from murder*? Well, what a thing to say? What a thing to do? But he has more: *Who can bear the gaze that we encounter*? he calls out – *How would you repel the scrutiny of your killer*? he says to us, half-closing his eyes. And I am thinking, it's not his look I'm fussed about – what if he's packing a blade! Faster and faster, perhaps. Do you get me? But he's badly restricted about the shoulders, front and back. He'd be unable to make his thrust. And then I laugh: he'd struggle to get the switch out of his pocket – damned fool, never mind make a hole. But this ancient man has more for me to hear: *Where is the petition in that*? What a question – and aren't we always asking for some way out? And there's him saying it. He smiles, puffs on his pipe. Murphy sits upright, smiling at the thought of the knife lost in a breast pocket: And then he says, preaching to all who'll listen to him: *We must remove whatever is false.* Wasn't that the line? *And be real.* That is not it. What was it: *Every time you take it off, some bit of the disguise still clings to us*? Was that it? Murphy's voice is like a continuous flow of sound, everywhere and nowhere: I says to him, *Who am I*? I called out from the crowd. *Can you say who I am*? That's what it was: *Who am I*? I ask him, and the man says, calling back to me, *I will never blot out your name*, and then to the crowd: *Never will I blot out his name*. And that was that: *I'll tell you who I am*. I am still calling out to the man, the preacher man, hailing us: *I'll tell you my name*, but he paid me no heed. From that moment on, nothing.

> *Murphy puffs aways, watching as the shadows*
> *passing: I better see where this leads, he says. Better*
> *see what names there are that pass this night.*

He evinces little or no particular concern that Guppy's just walked out of the ward wearing little more than yellow pyjamas in the of flimsiest polyester cotton. He seems unconcerned that some minutes later he's followed by some crouching figure. It seems, for a moment that Murphy's entire attention is piqued instead by the nearby sink: I'll find a way out of it, he says, staring, watching, unblinking, as the glass globe drops green soap onto the vitreous white. Within these walls, I have no preference, he whispers to the erstwhile white of the porcelain. Watt is already in his dorm bed, deep in blue Valium dreams. Haynes is sniffing on a promise, and dreaming of shoes and pretty feet. Williams is still and silent, hidden under a single white sheet. Perrot and Duggan and Samuels are as quiet as barques under moonlight. I do not know how, Murphy says, quietly, to himself. Or why, watching there as Guppy exits, floating out of the door to the wide world. Or when. Guppy looks left, looks right, but there's no road to cross. He walks in the direction of the hospital laundry, immediately lost. Each yard that passes, another year is felt. He will soon enough reach his majority and, one day, his century. Each year that passes, another step is taken into the unknown. Guppy steps out: and, yes, he floats, a flickering flame in yellow pyjamas, passing into outstretching shadows. Where's Murphy? All that's left behinds is the hovering smoke from his pipe. Something's there, Guppy feels it, surely; looking back. We see only ghosts, or shadows. Now we are blind to what unfolds – the kid is an arrow aimed and we are absent. Who's that crouching figure? Somnolent walking, here in the semi-darkness. Dim it is, and so dreadful, Murphy says, unsure of his way. Three people passing along a shadowed corridor. One with words, one with worry, one with wonder. No praise for this perfect indifference, no words can save us. I see some strange things – then nothing. *Order*, you said, *toe the line*, wasn't that your caution? Wasn't the door suddenly ajar. There's no point harping on about it – follow the scent, and seize the moment. Guppy is young and moves with grace, as youth must, and will. The young man is genuflecting. That's what it looks like. The effect of floating and waning in this shadowed place. He adapts to our image of what we want him to be. Guppy is somehow independent of the world, not scornful or angry, but present. The time is out of joint, they say, but he remains. Each year, unknowing of the other. Each year, the darkness. Each year, the shadow. You'll have to name them, Murphy whispers. He looks down, he is wearing slippers, but he can't quite see his feet: I know it because I feel it, he says, his voice rumbling in the dark, dim-lit corridor. The windows to the side are usually so bright, so fierce that you would need to shield your eyes with your hand, especially against the brittle summer light. But it is night. The thunder storm has come and obliterated all hope of the waning sun. Otherwise, surely, he'd be seen, and they'd recite some trite line. A fellow resident, perhaps, or an auxiliary, alighting a ward, would say, *I was under the impression* ... Out there, alone, she would say. *This will flare up*, the passing auxiliary would exclaim, *this must be reported*. Words would be said, but were not. What can Guppy know of this? Around us, in our mind's eye, in what we can no longer hear, let alone see, the years have passed, and stretched these moments into about half a century. These years later, subtracted from all matter of multiple things: *out* of the dusk of a summer's night, *out* of the blinding light that's passed, *out* of the trees in the strong breeze, *out* of the wet fields, *out* of the darkest night and, *out* of all of this, an *out* and *out* deluge is the only way – *out* damned spot.

Who could be strong, and refrain from murder?
What a thing to say, what a thing.

The young man looks back. There is not so much as a flicker of recognition on his face. I can't even bring myself to, Murphy says, listing in the distance. Guppy's not seen, he's far off. Talk to us anyhow and we shall be thankful. Eyes staring out from a face, large polished buttons, fixed in the dark. Does he have any idea where this shadowed road is leading him – the endless corridor of his life amounts to one hundred and forty yards. Nonetheless, he walks on, as summer's night miraculously overcomes and engulfs what once were the yellows and the reds and the golden lights of day; now subdued, blotted out, darkness rolls up, rushes in, and blows out all the candles. Lost in the shadows, in the shadows he is lost. To say another word, make another sound. The light lessens as night falls; the sun is sinking fast. Lost in the shadows. The red and gold that earlier shot through the glittering windows onto white walls and dark wood, onto pillars and posts, tables and chairs, and the people in preparation for their beds are no more, but once were. In the shadows, he is lost, but what sense can be made of this? Along the ever-increasing corridor – a seemingly everlasting tunnel, growing out into the diminishing depth of an ocular pupil – jet black, then, but empty of all content. One hundred and forty yards in length, an endless void, it feels like. He holds out his hand to be held, the finger tips find only the coldness of a wall to touch. It feels wet, the walls, fluid, or somehow overflowing. Guppy's eyes are now accustomed to the night. The walls are shimmering. It is warm, yes, humid, and heavy. The radiators are cold. He smells the night, the reek of spectral sulphur as young as freshly cut grass, and he breathes, deeply. His fingers lightly touch the wall, the wooden wind sills too, as he passes, and just, for a moment, he stops; what, to catch his breath? That is hardly so. He turns again, looking back. The crouched figure is there, nearer now, their shadow lengthens. He notices this strange figure for the first time – he is not alone. Now, he knows. Nearer and nearer, the dark light comes. He looks, for a moment, out of the window nearest to him, it too is open.

He recognises a distant figure, the rain has past,
the tarmac is full of night light.

It's Molloy, he sees her. It's Molloy. Molloy. A thunderclap, he hears it, but pays it little heed. Guppy looks up at the crack of possibility; floating up, away, and away into the darkest night, rising high above the streets and houses, the grey slate roofs of estimable dwellings, over and above the sighing fields, the farmland, downs – over all – all over. It remains but a crack of hope, if that is what it is. It's Molloy. Molloy. Molloy is seen in the distance, he'll hold fast to it. Suddenly, he is there, yards and years seem to have passed; what age is he now? He reaches the doors to the hospital laundry. An industrial scale affair which responds to something in the region of sixty tonnes of washing in a single week. From Elizabeth to Victoria: The linen, conveyed by trucks from the patients' blocks, will be brought into the receiving-rooms, passed into the washhouses for either sex, and washed and dried either in the grounds or on the steam-horses, thence passed into the laundry, and folded, mangled, or ironed, as may be necessary. It will then be passed into the delivering-room, and there sorted and given out at the slides to trucks in the lobby. From reign to reign, it was calculated that about eighty female patients were required to assist in the laundry, and, as great loss of time and inconvenience would arise if these were compelled to return to their respective blocks for their meals, a hall for dining has been placed close to the laundry, with a servants' mess-room adjoining. The laundry is unpeopled at this hour, as you might expect. Guppy cannot know that this is his destination. But he must go on, without anyone, or anything, but him – or so it may seem. There are no ideal conclusions.

Under the double doors is a strip of faint light. Our single hope would be to hold the darkness back; let all the madness and metaphors take a back seat. That would be one way to bring an end to it all: he hears it, he hears it not, but he will not fight it.

Gup-py? Gup-py?

There must be fear. How else can it be explained? There must have been some hope of survival. He would hear Molloy's gentle tones, calling out to him – she would take his hand. As I say, we speculate at our peril. Instead, he hears the voice, cooing and calling out to him –

Gup-py, Gup-py.

Molloy has gone out for a bevvy with one friend. In other words, she's nowhere to be seen – not here, at least. Savage and Molloy – AKA Saveloy – a testy term, coined by some wag upon espying the two exiting Wong Li's chipper. It stuck – not that anyone would say it to their faces: behind backs and closed doors only are they *Saveloy*. And the two are laughing, and complaining, in equal measure: the goings-on are told again and again in hushed voices (The sink, she whispers to Savage, right off the bloody wall. What! Then flung across the ward. Really!), but the conclusion to it all is not yet known (Thank the lord it wasn't the kitchen sink, d'ya know what I mean? counters Savage. Everything but ... Molloy screams back. Immersed in the shock of the comment, the two laugh loudly.) Under the skies darkened by unseen clouds, on the roads, the pavements, peppered with puddles, reflecting what's not seen. An expression of alarm? What can it be? Who could tell Molloy, sipping her last vodka and soda, that death stalks the corridors of St. Anton's at this very moment? In that very place, once known as the Metropolitan Asylum for Chronic Imbeciles. Perhaps they were free to say any old thing; perhaps not. Molloy leaves Savage at the roadside to the front of the Queen Victoria public house; they're high on drink but well-lit would be the better soubriquet. Molloy heads back to her hospital digs – Saveloy splits – Savage to her cottage. The pavement is wet following torrential rain and there are puddles dotted about in the road. I might disappear into one of these, she calls back to Savage, jumping across a puddle. Imagine, she begins to laugh, leaping over a small dark pool of water, then another, as she reaches the other side of the road. Well, she's tired after the early shift and she bids farewell to her friend. The veteran had been sitting up at the bar, waiting for a go on the pool table – he looked lonely, a little disreputable, on the outside. He swivelled round, smiling with that jaw jutting, and winked. Savage and Molloy waved a weary hand or two. Breathing in the fresh air, Molloy makes a joke about her shoulder bag: The weight of it, she says. What the hell have you got in there? the other inquires, prodding the hard shape with her fingers. Don't ask, Savs, Molloy jokes. Her mate lives at the other end of the High Street, in a small cottage, done out all nice and cosy. They keep calling back at each other, their voices echoing across the distance, aided by the flow of temperature inversion. The last sound is heard but the other is far out of sight. The final waves give way in the deserted street, punctuated by pulses of soft orange light spilling out of the cast-iron lamp-posts. We might concentrate all manner of innocent people into just one place, into a single lifetime, into two or many more than three. But where will that leave us? With three solitary lives – or just one more. All care is thwarted, no matter how hard we may try. And care – where does that leave us? Most of the staff did their best, that's what Molloy thinks, looking across at the darkened orange bricks of the institute building. (We troop around, watching like hawks, oversensitive to the clattering, the stamping, anything moving behind our backs. *Quick, Perrott's fallen. Hurry, do*! One after another, taking our turns on the bathroom rota. *Hold the flannel up to your eyes, Haines*, and so he does, splashing your feet. *Come on, lads, let's get sharp!* We bounce and we tussle, making beds, bringing tea, administering medicaments, doing what we can and what we can't, and, in the end – We call it care.) Thoughts flew through Molloy's mind as fragments and fractions. The puddles she jumps are deep, she's decided, a false step and she'll disappear. The road, black and mechanical silver, is endless, mist rises of it in puffs of watery smoke. Yes, they said they were coming, said Savage, earlier in the night. The forecast is on, for a change. Summer storms, Savage said.

The cooler air after rain feels fresh, Molloy
breathes it in, deeply, exhaling loudly.

(Let's be friends; let's patch things up, she wanted to say. The other seemed less than amenable. It's all the same to me, Molls, came the odd, insolent reply. And that was that.) The street is deserted, the whoosh of a passing taxi comes out of the blue. (What are the ins and outs of anything? You're either in … thoughts trail off). Savage's voice fades to grey, no longer interrupting the flash and flow of her thoughts. Molloy's head swims nicely from the effects of a few vodkas (plus one for the road: This fecking road!). The one she thinks she'll regret in the morning as she suddenly veers off for a moment, avoiding another of the dark pools in the street. Little does she know, as she wanders into death door. She halts her approach at the lane into the hospital. Breathes, deeply, the petrichor of fallen rain on earth, continues, steeply, her way to the walls, the doors, the walled-in, the unnameable. The moment of truth, the hope of sanity, all flying, floating, the fractions and the fragments. Who knew that walking back from the pub after a few bevvies could be so perilous. Her mind swims, she breathes deeply, fractions and fragments, is all, but she is clear and fine. I can hold my jink, she says to herself, then laughs: Drink. She stops for a moment. Jink, then laughs again. Let's be friends, she wanted to say. It's all the same to me. Fractions and fragments, is all.

XII

The younger man looks across at the other man before him:
"Do I know you?" the old man asks, "have we met before?"
His lips are trembling, defying the stark palsy of the eyes
staring back at him. "You're ancient," the young man thinks,
drawing nearer, but is too kind to say. Suddenly, the young
man recoils from this hideous vision, turning back within
seconds to the starkest realisation. "You're me," the duke cries
out, "me." He reaches out, touching the cold decrepit face in
the silver glass. "I'm old," he cries, "so very, very old."

We inhabit the wide world where a bough turns into a forest, a lonely knight into a crusade and a single hanging tapestry becomes an entire multiverse. It is a world without reason; it is because it is – it can be no other way. No door is discernible, no windows or walls; it's glass, all glass, filling the chamber with myriad coils of translucent snakes, writhing, rattling, rising, tormenting his very existence. Surrounding the pristine duke are wall- and floor- and window-filled serpents, captured serpents, hungry serpent, and fierce serpents; some are docile and still serpents. The duke is a snake charmer without flute or claim. "Music," he calls out pathetically, clapping his hands, "where are we without it?" Those hands holding on to what looks like life are overlarge and knotty. This *what looks like* is the depths of the chimerical crystal. I used to so enjoy my morning walks, he says, perhaps it's a little chilly, a tad misty by the lake, but ever so inviting, the water's clear, somehow soft, the red throated loons are diving, hardly a ripple made at the surface. He lifts one of his hands to his face, drawing a line across his cheek, his eyes darken: "Then send me sickness, surfeit, and so die. I have seen death many, many times, faced it too," pausing, momentarily, "– the strain of so much dying is killing me." Surely, he is drugged; hallucinogenic powders, or elixirs and opiates, carefully balanced over a blue solution, are administered to him, silently yet regularly, in a place apparently without exit. He sees them; he sees them not; he sees them. "Don't move," he cautions himself, fearing that he might be tempted to seize them, antagonise them; distressed, he turns: "Which way is up," he cries, "and which down?" Suddenly aware of himself, walking on the ceiling, on the walls, the fragile-looking windows – from the highs to the lows, from one side to other, the coils of snakes, writhing, rattling, rolling, inhabiting all four corners of this crystal cube. "They are all, and everywhere," he screeches, as much out of frustration as fear: "Everywhere. What is a man to do?" On walls, across the transparent ground, joining with him, entrapping him, seizing him, are all manner of distressing snakes, weighing his frail body to the ceiling, to the ground, the windows, pressuring, pursuing him, striking at him, biting him. There is no mission here: the snakes are as captivated and mesmerised as the ancient man himself. They have no purpose but their own survival. "All is glass, it is all glass," he cries, "blinding me," as the light refracts to myriad, prismatic colours. But that is surely inconceivable: how can he possibly escape such pleasure upon the instant? How can he quantify, nay qualify, his time, and place? "I have so many enemies. I beg you – I implore you – show some mercy," roars the duke. Quick thinking: "I will elude them," he begins to calm. "I will get out of here, escape this horror. Damn that unnatural woman! Am I not a man more sinned against than sinning?" He is a cultured man; he thinks himself a king. "That woman is no woman, but a tiger snake, venomous, filled with poison. She will kill me!" he cries out, pathetically. He is no king, and killing a king makes you not a king, especially when the tapestry turns, shifting little endless threads. Weave, weave. What?

The storms, rains, cataracts do not arrive. He
swims in light and cold luminosity.

He is present and absent, reflected upon the solid surfaces of his keep, unable to put himself out of their reach. They multiply, these images of his past, his present, his future merged in what will have been. Memories from different times are brought together, placed next to each other, exposed one after another. They are the multitude that count as one, a writhing mass which serves only to shatter these illusory detentions. "I am an elderly man of, what, nearly sixty. My diamond year, that's what it is. Ah, just there: I see me! Hardly twenty-six, perennially in jade." And yet, he is subsumed and tormented by his youth, his relative beauty. "It is a solitary essence of a single image, somehow an ancient man with the reflection of a youth's face." Pristine, indeed, a senescent child but, by his own impression, a relatively young man in years; yes, he is trapped in each and every mirror, as they jostle and seize his unfolding image, fighting each to each for the pleasure of the refraction. "Ever-Youthful, wasn't that what they called me? And who are they, and where are you now?"

It was a contract, also known as a meeting of minds, an agreement signed in shattering glass and sliced veins.

"I beg of you," he cries, "end this now. The contract is frustrated; let us strike it down." But there is no end in sight, and the voice issues from everywhere and nowhere. They say: "Many have come, dear duke." The walls are whispering glass: "All have failed," the whispers strengthen, intoning: "Many mortal men have climbed the Mount, followed their momentary guide, walked the travails of moon lit night and morn broke day. All have failed." In human years, once he was noon, then darkness came over the whole land of his being. The face is egregiously lined in white shadows sent into the recesses of the caves of his skin. "Roll back the light, old man – and see." There, at last, he is revealed. The snakes writhe at the corner of his eyes, out of sight, but seen, briefly, floating, translucently. They scare him, come upon him, slither about his ankles. "Don't bite at me. O, my lady, please, make it desist." The old man's sight is dimmed and dull with age. There, you can see his stooped back, his knotty feet, the gnarled, yellowing toenails. His hands are veinous blue and appear huge against the emaciated wrists, the arms, which run up to hollow shoulders, seem overlong, and his jowls hang like skin curtains. His bare head of lustrous blond hair is but a pate, scabbed with bites and stings and burns; he is as bald, most certainly, as the proverbial coot. The threadbare strings that remain now rest upon the shoulders of his night gown. As he walks, he stalks about the room, reciting poems of his youth, in a deep incantation of his life, his memories: *"When in disgrace with fortune and men's eyes,"* he calls, but fails to shift to the end of the following line: *"I all alone beweep ..."* He harks back to an earlier time. "Was it a boy, that once I knew ...? The heat of the day took him away. Was he not transfixed?" Weakly, and alone – is he above the earth now? "But a boy." Fear no more, young child. *Fear no more the heat of the sun.* "All lost, sent away, his life taken into the deep." His desperate pain abates, if only for a moment. He is alone. "The Sea Serpent took them," he says, "as they crossed too early upon the causeway." He'd watched as they were washed away, looking out from his glass chamber, out to the wide world at those who might save him. "A young knight, it looked like, a grey Barb horse. Devoured! Is any of this true?" he asks. *Haply I look on thee ...* I did not look upon you so. "Had I a wife?" he asks. "And children?" He places his hands up to his face. Looking out from the gaps in his fingers. "There was once a boy. Yes, my kin. But ... What became of him? Fever, that was it. Fever. And death ...

Fear no more the heat of the sun ..."

This cage of mirrors, inescapable. Above and beyond this earthly world and yet, in this glass, this hall of subtraction, he is younger, younger still: "So handsome, my lord, surely the youngest man at court." The king's court, once filled with laughter and with friends and children, is no more. "What is true?" he asks. But these pasts, and these parts, which he has lived, and played, are now no longer true. "What was it then?" All lost, and taken, for the duke prized his youth over all else. "Why must you do this?" he asks, a simple enough question. "It is not known, dear duke," she replies, "I have never been aware of any other way. I do it because I do." Was he all of them? Man and Woman? Human and Inhuman? Was he one and distinct? He did not know. They sat there, together, while all else was banished. All is lost in this wide world. "I could not stand it, not for another moment," he cries, recalling how disturbed he'd become to see his brother's son growing so strong and so brave. "The true heir," he whispers; "a future king. Killing a king makes not a king. But another king lives long." His vigour, his strength. "O, brother! Our own king washed away. To find him so, drowned: Dead – my dear brother dead." No such end for he, the duke would be led here. "Why was I not put into the water too? To die like that – a king!" And so the duke happened upon this meeting of minds. To be ever young. And all else is lost. "Was it the tapestry? It showed the way to me. Opaque, yes, but somehow clear. It showed the way – a moment only – but sufficient. A lake, first, that was it: 'Be ready; ready be,' it whispered to me, 'readying you for the king; the king readying for you.' Count what's read, I think it meant. And then the fair lady; that promise – and my youth. 'You only have to kill the king, dear duke,' you said. Was it all but a dream; these dreams we are made on?" But there is a snake, in the shape of a woman, who terrifies him at night. "Many have come," the walls are whispering glass, "all have failed," the whispers strengthen: "Many mortal men have come, all have failed."

The duke is waiting, not hiding. He knows she will soon come to taunt him. The same as it ever was: digging her nails into his fair skin, licking him with her forked tongue, kissing him with her harsh little lips.

"O, duke," she calls to him, "Dearest duke, I am here. Here am I, at last." The duke tries to duck out, to look away, to make light of the difference we make so much of. There is nowhere to hide in this hall of fragmented lacerations. Among the colliding multitudes of lost or veiled lands, there is only flesh and blood: "My, my, you look so young, dearest duke, so handsome, how do you do it? What is the secret of your everlasting youth?" She laughs loudly, mirthfully, her raven hair falling about her livid green face, as she flicks out her vicious forked tongue. He sees her present enchantment. "He is coming," she sighs, watching the little old man cowering in a corner of glass. "He comes," she says. "Soon he will kiss and I shall be released. I and the Sea-Serpent. Union. And death. All will boil. Union," hardly can she breathe, as she speaks: "And death," her voice deepens, "only One must be. Union." The duke is mirrored to infinity. He is enclosed by books and atlases and globes all mirrored to forever and a day, and each and every repetition is a lie. The duke is but a crone, looking and feeling his way around, pathetically, but he cannot, nor will he ever, exit this dreadful cage of mirrors. Now or not at all – no, never. "Tell me?" he shouts, then softening his voice, barely whispering to the hideous one, being as polite as he can be. "Tell me, dearest One, how can I get out of this space of glass?" She laughs, licks her hard little lips, tastes his blood, and then she says: "It's been a long time, my dear duke, ever youthful child that you are. How the bargain turned bad! Yes, it's a very long time, and I have often asked, 'Is *he* my prisoner, or am *I* the prison?' But you know the answer, dearest ancient one." She raises what he knows to be her talon hand. She strikes at his loose skin, slicing him, just a little, but enough to please. "He is coming," she says. "I will soon be free." Forked tongue licks quick-sharp the lines of red. "O, don't rip me," he calls: "Please, don't rip me." She laughs. She enjoys toying with such little men. "How should I respond?" she asks, running her sharp tongue across his face. "He paid the price," she explains, "as all must." His eyes are staring ahead: "Who paid, dearest one?" He placates; she doesn't care a damn. "Did I not call out to you: '*Destroy it*?' But my nocturnal screams were not enough for you. My fair lady, sent in dream, was ignored. *Ignored*. And before you, your brother: 'Tear it down: O, King,' I hailed him. He did no such thing. 'Your whore-queen,' I said, 'wrongs you,' but he was not swayed, refused to hear. 'It remains,' the fool relented, 'it remains.' But you drowned him, did you not, dear duke; your only brother. You did the deed." The duke cries out: "Alack for pity – I lifted his majesty, my brother, from the lake. Nothing more." She flicks her tongue again, wishing it would cut. "And how he weeps now," she replies – "Through all eternity." She kisses his lined, emaciated face, lifting the hand he cowers from. She rips through his chest, more than enough to please: "He knew my words: 'Burn the damnable thing,' but the fool failed. The tapestry's tale unravelled and my green snake's tail was revealed to that little brattish boy." She watches blood dripping from her enchanted hands. "The tapestry boy must come. Kiss was. Kiss is. Kiss ever shall be: I will be free – The tale is told. The tapestry loses ground." Oriane begins to laugh, so loudly, too voluptuously for words, a sound as true as dreaming, a tentative advance, carried beneath the surface of a scream. And then, looking upon her quarry, torn, pricked, and plucked at by sensations, she says: "Once were thee, dear duke, now there will be he!"

XIII

*Guppy knows it's her out there in the distance, jumping
the glass discs set into the road. He can see her: a puff of
smoke was an early indication; the flash of the flame,
flint and gas and fire – then a puff of white smoke.*

This is a life. It has to be straightforward. But it isn't. This is
how it is. He sees her, out there, coming closer. Molloy's walking
along the asphalt path towards the orange brick building,
bringing his heart to his mouth. Hope. Then it ebbed away. She
stops for a sec, firing up a cigarette's end, smoke rising from
her mouth. The lighter leaves an after-image upon the glassy-
surface of her eyes. She looks out, inhales, throws the strap back
onto her shoulder. She stops. Someone's looking at me, she says.
Who? An odd sensation coming from somewhere, but where?
Nowhere, she replies. She looks up, inhaling again, blowing
smoke, squints her eyes across at the building before her. There's
the double doored entrance that she will pass through on the
way back to her digs. She stops, off the road now, walking
towards the hospital building. Is that Malone? she asks herself:

Malone? says Molloy … Molloy? says Malone …

She can just about make out a large form of something familiar.
There, in the shadows. She stops to watch the strangeness of
it. Molloy can see Malone on the other side of one of the high
windows, bending down, somewhat stooped; really? Really? Is
that Malone? Crouched over, as though looking for something.
Can that really be Malone? But why? she asks, squinting her eyes
at the weird loitering apparition, walking through the corridor.
Why? The darkness is relieved by eerie wedges of orange and
brown light. She feels the pressure of the night. Then comes
another rumble of thunder by reply. It cracks above Molloy's
head. A summer storm of some inordinate electrical capability.

261

An earlier black cloud, lowering in the west, had already blotted out the falling late-evening dusk. And now there was another thunderclap. So soon the darkness fell. Deep clouds, press in, and wrap the day up. Everything was shadows. What light there was is sucking at her eyes, as though through a funnel. A stiff breeze picks up. Molloy thinks she can smell the sea on the wind. The darkness feels like an eclipse without the silver ring. A queer fear steals across the tall, statuesque woman. Molloy throws down her fag, and makes her way into St. Anton's proper. Through the double doors, she strides towards the laundry-end of the everlasting corridor. (Was I seen? she asks.) From outside, everything that is not directly ahead of her seems to vanish as darkness pressed on the windows. Shadows of flimsy glass flickering out tiny familiar pictures – then nothing. There's a limit. It's the limit that you see. The first lairy pelts of rain is felt, a broadside against the skin of her face. Runs the last yards, she rushes through the double doors into the hospital. From inside, for a moment, Molloy stands her ground: There's nobody here. Where's Malone? she asks, whispering to nobody but herself. She looks across from the double doors at an ingress. The laundry? Where's Malone? she hears herself speaking, as though mulling things over. She walks slowly towards these doors, a single strap drops, but she does not think to return it to her shoulder. The bag knocks against her hip, held true by the other strap. What the hell do they want with the laundry? For God's sake, she continues, a walking commentary.

She halts her progress outside. Listens, then enters.

Malone turned, as the other walked in. They smiled. An odd grin, rigid and weird – Malone looks afraid. (Looks are deceiving, Molloy thinks.) Glancing back, that seemed a strange thing to do: the crouched one turned and then cracked a smile. At last, Malone thinks, success. Found at last. Found. A young lad, for that is what he looked like to Molloy, was cowering, silently, on the ground from where he'd been dragged by his pure blond hair. (He looked like a child, Molloy recalled thinking. I'll tell you everything that happened.) Then dropped. He fell by the wayside, dragging himself away as though out of quicksand. He is saved. The look of pain, dread abating slowly, his face red, his blue eyes looked fierce and fearful. He'd been saved. By just one word:

Malone?

That was all that she said: Malone? And then the final question mark: Malone? They suddenly turned, Molloy? Their huge back was crouched as if they retained the memory of dragging the young man ever closer to the large circular door of the washing machine. The arms are now held at their side. Malone seems to be standing to attention. Or attempting to show that their arms have no part in any of this. They smiled, not wearily, but as one who has come across their own hidden observer. The machines were hulks and stood from floor to ceiling. They were a sickly skin colour, not white, but a bilious beige. The lino was the uniform blue of the hospital, but badly scuffed in places, black streaked in others, patched too. The room was an enormous rectangular shape, but fabric-filled, and huggermugger. Huge wheeled bins lined the walls, overflowing with seemingly sorted laundry, yellow and blue sheets, assortments of clothing, shirts and trousers, pyjamas, dresses and skirts, pinnies and pants, socks and tights, bulks of indelibly stained, yet ostensibly clean, draw sheets: medieval sacking, all stacked and creased, and human-soiled in places beyond the abilities of soap and water. But just look at those walls; it was the walls which shocked. They were the colour of burnt skin, how else to describe them? An archway led into another room, further on, and there were long tunnels of silver aluminium which ran around the tops of the walls, extracting air from the enormous drying machines by day. Malone said a name, a familiar word that now sounded strange coming from their mouth. Malone's erstwhile friend, now standing there before them. Molloy? Malone said, a counterpoint to Molloy's own more definite sounding of the word, Malone? What to say? That could have been us. That could have been me. Malone looks down. Looks up. There's an odd expression of relief upon the face. (Quarry, Molloy said, I remember thinking it an unusual word in the circumstances.) Guppy has sidled up against the wall and is as still as a portrait – he stares lividly at Molloy as if her presence is disturbing him. Malone says the name again, Molloy, but paid no heed to the fact that Molloy's hand is slowly fishing for something in her bag. Malone? the other says again, her hand slowly reaching down into her shoulder bag. Malone? This hulking washing machine's fixed and made ready to roll. The door's wide open and was soon to contain a young human body; it's been set for a long wash and a fast spin. Molloy is of course unaware of the programme. (Sorry, she says, I couldn't say.) Malone did not seem at all surprised – that's what Molloy will say. At first, they made no excuses. Do you mean to put Guppy in there? Molloy says, straight to the point, nodding with her head to the vast washing machine. Guppy? In where? Malone replies, as though surprised by their proximity to the machine, and to the name: Stefan, you mean? Hardly hearing the correction, Molloy presses again: Guppy, she corrects the other's error – Guppy, she says, let's stick to Guppy.

His name is Stefan, Malone says; a faltering condition. Molloy?

Malone, what's going on here? What's got into you? The environment is alien, not a tomb, exactly, but something more akin to an abattoir without dead meat. The walls seem to run with iridescent oranges and yellows, as though lit with the sharpness of a knife, stripping the flesh, then leaving an impression of their once organic self. Malone looks confused: What, you think …? How should Malone begin? It's not … how it looks, Molls, Malone replied. He got out – Camier came to me. I was just changing Watt's dressings – he's been fine since – Murphy, she says, reluctantly, that is. Nothing to report at all … Camier came to me … The door was left open, you see? Her mind is packed with gaps and confusions – what are *they* to say; unsure of the procedure and worried about repercussions – but what are *they* to say? Edwina's her name – Edwina Malone: she's a woman by sex and by gender. (I mean, can *you* tell the difference? Molloy says so often, doing an impression.) The walk, the crouched shoulders, a habit borne on the years of teasing as a girl: I wanted to seem smaller, Malone explained. (Honestly, Molloy continues, when she sits down, you expect a pair of balls to fall out, do you know what I mean?) It was one of my first days – I'd just been introduced to Malone – she signs the notes *Edwina* with a circular dot above the 'i'. I remember laughing, someone nearby replied that they'd once looked for her moustache. (It's only a cod, Molloy always says, ameliorating the wickedness: Certainly, it's not to be taken seriously. It's just a cod. It gets us through the day. She's reasonable: I saw her out once at a do, she looked like a Sherman tank in sequins.) Everybody laughed, there were hoots in the room. Malone was quiet, within earshot, helping Williams on with his sweater – We'll go out for a breath of fresh air, love, she'd said, let's get some of the others. She'd heard every syllable. Molloy repeats her words: Malone, what's going on here? What's got into you? (It were only a lark. To get Murphy … A lark, nothing more, Malone said, neglecting to finish the earlier sentence, that's what Molloy will relay). Malone looks frantically for Guppy, as though he might corroborate the facts. That things are (*indeed*) not what they seem. (A lark, she'd said, again, repeating the words, you know. A lark.) But it is hardly a wheeze. We can't know what Guppy thought or, indeed, what was going through Malone's, as well as Molloy's, mind. (Murphy, they said again, he can't fecking get away with … Murphy …) They stop, the sentence apparently running out of steam. (Malone got aggressive, Molloy'll explain, you know what Malone's like. Full on.) Their eyes widen, their black rimmed glasses rise up from their nose. (Murphy, they'll say it flatly, oddly. Murphy. He can't fecking get away with it.) The question is repeated in this melee of total confusion. Malone, what the hell … But what she wants to say cannot be said. There is no other way of framing the question. *Away* with *what*? But there's no space and even less time. Away with what? (Nobody gets away with anything in this place, she said, and the institution has a numerous variety of deaths at its disposal.) I think I can explain; I think it's all meant as a bit of fun – there's no harm intended – nothing to worry ourselves about. Eh, Molloy? Did Camier let him out? – is it all just a cod … Molloy? They said her name, not Molls as they once would, but a more formal sound to this unhappy interaction. Molloy, the name is said, imploring her: See sense, my love, see sense. Molloy said nothing, gripping the rolling pin in her right hand. We've always rubbed along, love; we're mates, me and you. Friends. The silence removed all semblance of a sentimental light; that she simply did her work would not cut it. The upshot is a picture, your picture, and nobody else's. Well, Malone, Molloy began: He's a crafty little cur, as you well know. Molloy sped up, a staccato delivery – Nasty little swine. Malone's face is a picture, searching, quizzical – definitely confused. He saw me, Molloy explains. It was all meant to be over and done with. Tamper with Murphy's drugs. Cause a stink. A diversion, that's all it ever was. Stop all the talking – the back swiping. Malone looks dumbstruck. There's no methodical purpose in view, that's definite. (Let her move, let her try and move, the other thinks.) Malone is large and she's fitter than she looks, but that doesn't stop the stupefaction. She works hard, barely stopping from one end of a shift to the other. Who saw you, Molls? Who, love, who? Molloy nods her head in Guppy's direction. He did. Who'd d'ya think, Malone? He saw me slip the meds into my pocket. He saw; he misses nothing. The time begins to extend. They've been there for a few minutes. It seems longer. But he won't say anything, Molloy. He can't. What's the worry? Something dawns: Camier … Malone says, again, Camier? – has he something to do with this? – what did he have to say for himself?

Malone halted suddenly, looking for Guppy who had moved even further towards the wall.

Malone turned back, and they smiled, but this smile contained the measure of resignation, and survival. Malone smiled, but they did not smile for long.

Malone ran, shoulders hunched, as though going in for a scrum, then head held low as though for a try. Running for the door, that's what it seems like, to escape and to freedom. But she must pass the one who's just called her name. Molloy lifts her right arm and brings it down hard. At the first blow to their temple, they reeled back. Guppy watches, pushing his back against the skin-toned wall. Guppy has reached his limit – there's nowhere else to go. Malone did not fall, not at the first blow. The tall woman, for some reason changes hands, and brings down the wooden rolling pin to the top of Malone's head. Malone did not fall, not at once, their head was bowed, however. They are wearing a new blue sweatshirt, an insignia at the breast: the Royal National Lifeboat Institute. Their head looked kneaded by the rolling pin, a circular indentation above the left eye became evident; there was a trickle of blood, but not an outpouring. The jeans looked tight at the knees, you couldn't see their feet, but nothing mattered now. The clothes were about to be stripped from their body, leaving only the blue jeans caught up and tied around the ankles. Malone was about to begin paying, but learning to fly was out of the question and living forever was not on the cards. Nobody seemed to have noticed the large man. In fact, Malone had just clocked him before her charge for the door. It is not quite right that the only people one meets are of a kind that steal out in our dreams; there are those who steal out in our nightmares but, for a moment or two, bring some relief.

Murphy, they'd said, flatly; yes, they said, distinctly, in that flat tone they had.

He was there for a moment in the shadows. Unnoticed, he had come. He meant only to follow Guppy. Murphy, they said the singular word again. Malone was not so easy to fell. At first, the large figure appeared to take the blows to the head in their stride. Molloy stepped back, her arm hung at her side, her bag she had flung to the ground. Malone was not for falling, but coming in that second time did for them. Murphy seemed to spring into the air as Malone raised an arm, screaming for her life. An attempt, this second time, to get at Molloy was not entirely unsuccessful. Not me, Murphy, Malone cries, not me. You've got the wrong … Suddenly, somehow, Malone manages to grip the top of Molloy's hair which was piled upon her head; then yanking her down. The other arm is raised to rain down blows, but that arm was stayed. Malone suddenly rises, and the hand comes away from Molloy's fair hair. Malone is rising, it's a miracle; it's the presence of physical strength, lifting her into the air. With one last magnificent effort, Malone throws out an open hand, defending herself, but catching the man's eye. They gouge at it, but his head turns, their grip is lost. Murphy lifts Malone up by the neck, high above his own head, and he dumps her backwards into the enormous washing machine. Guppy is suddenly back on his feet, rushing towards Malone's legs half-hanging out of the machine. Without a sound, he pushes poor Malone's not insubstantial external limbs into the machine; from her polished black Doc Marten boots up – then slams the door with a banging report. Molloy can hardly believe her eyes; Murphy steps forward, then stops. Does nothing. Malone is held firmly within. Guppy knows what Guppy knows – this is yet another Guppy - the one who survives.

XIV

Many have come. The walls are whispering glass: "All have failed," she says, as though to a friend. "Many mortal men have come, all have failed. Ah, here is one – on his way."

A waxing moon casts light and shade, without and within, as if cut with a sharp knife; shimmering softly, the shadows twist and glide across the granite walls, providing them with a burnish and a silver plating. Whose hand is this, caressing his cheek with heat and ice?

*Oriane, of course, so prim and pure, sitting
so quietly on the circular wall.*

The hidden waterways can be heard coursing down from the higher castle terraces. "This hand upon my skin," he says, breathing deeply. What once was seen is now lost. The forest and the fractured coastline are fading, the immense harmonies are lost, dismantled it looks like, in the coming darkness. "But what must I do?" Oriane has placed her palm against the knight's cheek. "So fearful," he says, a hideous heat disturbing his mind. "Like boiling, burning up," he whispers, "yet frozen." His voice sounds hoarse; he is there, before her. A shiver runs through the young man, and yet he feels hot and heavy and sickly sweet. But the tapestry prince is perfectly unable to prise his eyes away: "A goddess, surely. What else can she be?" He sees for himself, so close now, the blacks of her eyes, that cloak of hair – she is darkness itself. "Can it really be?" she whispers, by way of reply: "Absent things," she continues, "we receive them as firmly as the present." He responds, quickly, his heart's beating fast. "I am here," he whispers, "just here – you see me still?" She sees, but she's called away. "I must go," she says, "before it's too late, before the duke, arrives." The loss is quickly felt. "Going," he replies, "so soon." Is that a tear, he thinks, falling down her perfect face; she is prim. "The duke will be most angry if he finds me here, and with you. The duke is so strict, so cruel, his punishments are harsh." The young woman speaks with urgency and much trepidation. "She is frightened," he thinks, mindful of what it is that ails her. "There is danger," and "I must save her," are thoughts which entwine with other thoughts: "Who?" and "How?" and "Why?" are left unsaid. The young prince is eager to do his duty; to help where he can. "This place is fraught with bad endings," she says, and he senses her urgency. He feels what he feels, but he keeps his thoughts to himself. "Fraught with bad endings?" he replies. Seeing this, in her eyes; he sees, surely, but only with her eyes. "I'll do whatever I can for you," he says, adding her name, "Oriane." Should she explain, make plain: "Do you know me?" The young man moves his head towards hers, to see more clearly, to observe her, close-up.

She wants to devour him; rip his face to shreds, if she must, so long as she gets what is owed to her:

"Kiss was. Kiss is. Kiss ever shall be." Her little forked tongue feels its way out of her hard tight lips. "Did you say something?" he asks gently. He lifts his hand as though he wants to touch her firm, cruel mouth, which looks so soft, pink, and precious to him. "I know you," he says, avoiding the awkward silence. "I know you, but do you know me?" What an innocent question, she thinks. "Anything?" she says, distracted, perhaps, somewhat frantic, it seems. "You did say anything, didn't you? Wasn't that your promise?" she asks. Is he so easily convinced? "I did say something," he says, "but I no longer recall what it was." Her hand glides across the gap of air between them. The young man halts as bade. Oriane looks around again, the ascent is trellised all the way to the top and all the way to the bottom and out to the tidal causeway. He will be made to climb to her – there is further yet to go. The path to the higher castle is precipitous and daunting. The flowers are of such abundance, softening the task, and there is a myriad assortment of fruits too, ameliorating, lulling one into a false sense of security. These patches of coloured matter are growing, somewhat incongruously, with scant interest to the season. But these plants have no interest in us, isn't that so? Oranges and lemons beside apples and pears, all dwelling at once in green waxy leaves. Shadows cast and shift and creep towards the young ones. She will not be revealed this night. There is nothing yet to know. The time is not quite right. She feels it. "Damn you," her voice screams, her attention in another place. "Curse you," and her scream, which the young man cannot hear, is greeted from afar by a yet higher scream that rises into the night; its pitch is terrifying. "The Sea-Serpent," he calls out, his hand by nature rushes to the crescent sword at his side. She hears the creature too: "I am in such danger." Her hand drops to the young man's shoulder, but has a little farther to go. "Such danger. I must leave you, while I can. But before ..."

Oriane plunges her cold hand in to the carved wooden pail.

"What are these I see, are they snakes?" he wonders. The pail is perfect, carved with the skill of ages. Precious silver snakes stretch around the structure of the wooden pail: "Such skill," he says, "who is responsible for such work?" Oriane takes a short step across to the curved wall, and plunges her hand into the perfect pail, so recently brought up from the waters of the well. For a moment, she relishes throwing the pretty prince down into the deep well, but knows she cannot; knows she must not. Through the quicksilver, she moves her fingers, as though seeking for some precious jewel. From the carved wooden pail, she fishes out something shimmering in the moon light. In her palm she clutches a silver rose, manifesting itself as if formed from the well's water. Her hand is dripping wet. "Take this, my knight, so you might know me." What can be known is therefore knowable. "Know you? But I am here, O goddess. What more is there to know?" She holds out the silver rose, and as he looked

271

down a coldness seized his heart: "But you must foreswear it," she implores him, forcing his attention from the water. "Take this," she insists, holding out the watery jewel. "You must swear that you will not be afraid. Swear it! Your allegiance. Swear." He is, naturally, eager to assuage; he is ever vigilant and fearful of losing, but fretful too of retreating into words: "I swear. I swear I will do it, my goddess," he wants to say. He feels his heart gripped by some inordinate power, seizing him: "Know you?" His great sword is drawn, and on its hilt, shaped like a cross, he begins to swear his allegiance. Quickly, as ever, distracted, he drops the sword upon the ground. The exaggerated gesture of swearing upon a sword is quickly forgotten, as he looks to put flesh upon the hissing he can hear, a now familiar sound, arising from the stony ground nearby. His sword is fallen, clattering upon the flags. He is too preoccupied with fixing his eyes on the solidity of that passing noise – the hissing stones. "What form?" he says, turning to Oriane. With its head curled about his leg, tickling him, was the large grass snake. "You are my guide," he speaks the words, slowly, "here again," but no reply is forthcoming. "O, goddess," he calls out: "goddess?" But Oriane was gone. It is night, and the night leaves only him and his guide.

"I should have liked to ask of you, O, goddess, 'What is your verdict?' But for how long?"

Then into the depths, a bright lit pool, held within the circular walls of the well. He looks down into it, a silver glass disc reflects his face back at himself. "There I am." He laughs, within the shining circle, a double arc of quicksilver, dimpling, and distorting the young man's features. "But where is she – my goddess? Gone. What is it you think of life?" he wanted to ask: Life is a stream, a wind; it is a shaft of light; part them at your peril. "Gone," he whispers as he looks back into the darkness of the water; it dimples in white lips from the moonlight. "There was someone else there," he says, "in the reflection," mirth rising in him, a momentary bout of nerves, or some other nuance – who was it, or when, or is it why? "There I am," he says, laughing into the well's waters, "it was only ever me." The sequence returns – one thing, another one, leading on, truly led, one thing following another.

Higher and higher must he climb, from terrace and the well to Oriane's castle keep. Higher and higher, further and further, drawing yet finer and finer the thread betwixt us.

Casts light and shade, still and solid in the twilight. Silvering soonest, a waxing moon, without and within, softly shimmering, twists and turns, these fractional shadows, gliding over granite walls, which must be joined to make one. Water sparkling, the scene of the seen sea far off in the distance, the shore nearing, broken and swept, a thin veil across the sand, and the distance felt in some memorial command. The argentine crescent moon makes swirling serpentine patterns, shimmering all around the young prince, lulling him to sleep without fright or dismay. The labouring day falls, leaving little more than a shallow light that hardly reaches the water's edge at all. "Is that me?" he says into the perfectly cylindrical sheet of water. The well is whisht. Deep blue luminous light fills and forms and glows in myriad hues, each moment seems somehow uniform, but no less true. This sudden world is full of dark-light, and a spot of this falls upon the knight as he slips down from the crescent wall, passing into sleep. His arm, he curls over his eyes, his body entwined in a pure white cambric shirt. A fallen statue, surely.

He moves by the light of the daybreak. And one is suddenly surprised that this precious art work is alive, shifting, breaking out of its cast. He sits up, looks around trance-like. "How long have I slept? Was I sleeping long?"

The courtyard is golden and clear-cut, the circular wall looks infinite from here, spherical to the well. Standing now, he looks down, his reflection there, looking back at him: "Don't look down," he says to the young man in the water, a sound falling away, an echoing promise lost. "Whose words were these?" Again, again, he sees himself. The shirt falls from him, his chest bare, he is delicate, slim, but his body is carved in defined extent. The chest and stomach are an armour of skin and sinew. What need had he for the metalled armour now? That encumbrance was left behind; he travelled lighter thence forward. "Ready, upward, onward," he says, laughing out loud. He turns back. "My sword," he says, returning, lifting it from its fallen grace: "Onward," he calls out, "I rise, onward bound." He throws back his hair from his face, shaking his head as though to bring back sense. The face is young, so young, without a hint of beard, his throat runs down to two nodules of bone, then spans out towards the shoulders. He pulls back the cambric shirt around him, a pure white shroud, it looks like. His attempt to recall the earlier night are in vain: "What do we know of the night?" he says, "the one just passed?" The holy well, yes, he recalls it. And the silver rose, held in his hand, felt so frozen it burnt. He looks at this magnificent jewel, closing his fingers over it, hiding it from view. He must remember the silver rose, that much he knows – and his oath: did he not foreswear the thing he is prompted to do? On the hilt of his sword, he promised his allegiance. "Didn't I drop my blade?" – or put it away from sight. Thoughts run on, and on: did I hear the hissing lawns, an oversized grass snake, restricting me, wrapping my legs in green scales? One thing, another thing, a different order. The sun is rising, rising; there are bars of red and orange and blue, and a line of strong-warm gold is running across the horizon, underlining the dense black beyond it. "The forest is at work," he says, "my time is nearing." Winds rise, the knight feels a stirring in his stomach, a substitute for that shard of dread, and one that is surprisingly most welcome. A reminder of what he might expect, perhaps. He crosses the courtyard. "Am I familiar with this place?" He walks back to the curved wall, circling the well. He looks down into the pool but it is now light, and the reflection of his face only just reaches his vision. "Am I here again," he says, "is that me?" He is looking down into the face of the young man in the round pool of water: "Don't look down," he says, intrigued by the movement of his lips, the dark holes of his eyes. The vocal sound falls away, an echo of a lost promise. "Whose words were these?" The water dimples, separating into material elements: "These queer fragments," he says, "cryptic ornaments, serpents, you know, swallowing their tails in token of eternity." He looks up, and away, and out across the silvering sea. There, to the other shore, he sees the yellow strand stretching far into nowhere and the wild woodland is fallen into sentries of bronze pillars reaching into the sky, barring the way back to his homeland. "Yes, he is there," he speaks to the soft breeze, "he is there," to the forest, the bars of trees, which stretch back for miles and miles as one single dense landscape. So deep, but fragile, and thick, somehow impenetrable, but charred: "Who is burning the woodland?" His voice is but another unheard whisper in the breeze.

He is hot and the day feels heavy, humid, and yet hollow.

The forest stands to the other side of the water like a battalion of bronze giants. He puts his hand to his cheek. "I remember you," he whispers into the soft breeze, which immediately peps him, cooling his mood. He recalls the touch but not the frozen, frigid embrace from Oriane. "He is there," he whispers from his vantage point high above the turquoise ocean, "my one and only love." Silvery fins cut across the blue as he looks up, and out to sea. "He is there," he speaks again, "somewhere," lifting his hand to his cheek, holding it there, recalling the first touch he made, feeling as though he'd die on the spot. He'd leaned his head against the ancient oak, pressing the shape of the bark into his skull as he came. "You are beautiful," he says, softly to the sea: "You are beautiful," he says, softer still to the forest, dashing away a tear to the side of his eye. "You are beautiful. But soon enough you will burn." He listens to the shrill song of the crickets, watches for blue tits and gold finches, black-backed gulls there gliding through the sky, pitch-dark choughs rise and fall. The sounds hereabouts, he is eager to heed. "They call," he says. "They call." The shape is shifting, altering the external world he sees, appearing to him. He looks up, the foreboding castle appears mountainous, and the summit seems so far away. A simple arras, creating as though from itself, the finest threads and pulls and warps and continuous replies. These are but the materials on a tapestry, nothing more – turning and twisting, being and knowing. *Before you*: shimmering waters, dimpled this moment in the sun. *Beneath you*: earth of granite and rainbow, the desolate cairns there glittering. *Beyond* ... fountains of light, descending, struck upon the hard sand ... *you now*: cathedral trees, dense, creaking, communicating, numerable and entirely nigh. The young man looks away from the castle, searching for waders far down on the sea shore. The distance is great and he can just about make out the vague shapes breaking and falling. "The sea is pure silver, but then again," he says, lifting one hand, shielding his amber eyes, then placing the silver rose in the other hand into a breast pocket. A fierce cold immediately penetrates his heart, "it is never simply one thing," he says, "but how could it ever be?" The young prince looks for the slightest movement. Not so much as a dimple is now discerned, flat and spread like hot iron, it would surely scald one, burn into the skin, if you were foolish enough to venture in for a splash, or for a dip. "There," he says, "that damnable, monstrous being." It's out there, rising from the water, contracting, rescinding, throwing itself down, then up, bubbles forming, whiteness enveloping the blue: "Is it true, the sea is boiling?" the young man says – "It's boiling. That's what it looks like, boiling ... it seems so true?"

The snake guide is there, slithering along, suddenly, out of the blue.

"Am I to follow?" Surely that is the snake guide's mission? To bring me forth to Oriane? In that case, "I shall do as I am bidden." He follows. I know you, he tries to say. Yes, it's you. We've met before. Instead, he follows. "Do I know you?" Yes, he follows. "You're very large for a grass snake," the young man, the prince, having thought plenty, eventually says. "He is handsome," the creature thinks, "those amber eyes," hissing a little as though in voice, "he is strong," passes into the creature's mind: "He will not see the morrow. The whoreson prince will burn." The grass snake puts out its daggerish tongue in some ways coquettishly, but refrains from speaking. He pays heed to the words of the knight, admiring him from his pure white cambric shirt right down to his bare feet. The young prince seems almost denuded of his past life; his form so easily understood, and most certainly enjoyed, so the snake guide thinks. "I would like to curl about him," thinks the larger-than-life snake guide, "and crush him to death."

"There is time," the snake guide thinks, "time
and all times are passing."

He opens his eyes, as though for the first time. "How have I reached these rooms," he asks of the larger-than-life grass snake. "We have walked far?" The snake simply passes on, not responding with words. "So, this is the Sparkling Castle – at last we are here?" He was following the snake, that much he recalls. Now he walks, or runs to keep up, out into the bright sunshine one moment, passing in and out of many austere rooms the next: a maze of corridors and labyrinthine avenues, some rooms hardly furnished, rooms fit for a Spartan king or queen. An awful, forbidding structure, most certainly, but as for a fortress? "This place could hardly hold off an offending force," he says to the snake guide. But for the rock upon which it rests, so high in the sky it touches the curls of cirrus. The banks of cumulus dress the high castle in its own disguise, or wraps itself around the vast walls like a string of giant pearls. "It's the rock which makes it so hostile to humans," he says to himself. The young prince is walking, or running; he tries to keep up. "How long have we been walking?" he asks. The grass snake slithers on, stopping from time to time to look back, its split dagger tongue flicks out and then in, slipping and sliding, the occasional hiss. The young man dawdles upon the rooms, his fascination pricked by the profusion of folds of light: "Who would need so many mirrors," he asks, calling out to the grass snake, "to see oneself," he says, "reflected in so much light? And chandeliers. And vases," he says, looking about in amazement, "and crystal too?" Yes, the battlements now seem unreal and made not of stone at all, but are as a painting and sometimes a tapestry, daubed in chiaroscuro or threaded together over centuries and centuries by so many skilful hands, now absent. For there is nobody in evidence as once there must have been. "But," he calls out to the snake guide, "where is Oriane?"

EPILOGUE

He whispers the name, trying it out for size, saying it again and again, reciting it in mind, again and again, until it becomes saturated or satiated, losing its meaning. Can we speak? the young prince wonders. Can you hear me? "Oriane" – yes, for there she was.

He wanders through the fields down to the ancient oak. He knows where to find me, thinks the young prince. He sees him, an image so close to true it might be taken for himself. The meadow down is numerous, all aiming for the sun, the multiple grasses linking arms, holding hands, perhaps, an endless chain of life. The head gardener's son knows each and every one, and names them as he finds them. I can see him still, better than I know myself; I see how he strives, how he lives, but no one ever sees me. He leans his head back against the bark of the tree, feeling the rigid shapes through his hair to the solid, solid bone beneath the skin. He closes his eyes. He waits. The wind picks up, the tree sounds and soughs, a warm breeze blows. The tapestry's tapping or turning, twisting, soon weaving and warping, within the depths of his head, flaring up, fast – all very fine, as the flames die down. *With the possible in us ...* Then a voice, familiar, deeper now than ever. "Prince," it says. "Prince." The young prince is full of anticipating nervousness – for what has taken place is akin to killing a god. "Master, O, Master, please." The head gardener's son rushes towards him. "Sorry, Master," he cries, lowering his head. "For what?" The prince dashes away whatever tears have fallen. "The king's dead. It's done – his head ... ." A surge of blood rushes to his cheeks. "That was hardly your fault; I should not have said ...," he stops, remembering his position: "... *what I said*," would have finished the sentence. The silence is soft, a gentle breeze sounds in the leaves, the soughing, increases, then falls back, as though a conversation has ended. He's bold, the young prince thinks – and vicious. I should name him once, but how should one name the unnameable? The feeling of it brings solace. The head gardener's son holds out his blood red hands; his face is dripping, spattered with king – the old king. The young prince takes it, holds fast, the hand is slippery, resinous, raising himself up to his feet. Face to bloodied face now, the two see something identical in the other's countenance. "His eyes," the prince thinks, "his amber eyes. Gone." The head gardener's son looks mad, that's what he thinks. There's no other way of describing it. "Gone." The other bursts into fits of laughter: "For you," the head gardener's son explains, "for what was asked. A diversion, wasn't that what you said?" The head gardener's son, his laughter diminishing, looks down, wondering whether the prince would do what he was about to do, and is only too pleased when he does. Face to face: so close he can feel his breath against his skin. "He's doing it," in essence, crosses his mind. He stands as still as a statue, looking directly into the prince's eyes. With his open hand, the prince touches the cheek of the head gardener's son. For a moment, the prince looks askance, even angry; the feeling of dismay fades fast. The other's name passes through his mind. The head gardener's son, his face so close to his own, quickly drops to his knees. Another moment passes, he presses the bark into his skull. The head gardener's face, so open, so honest, and true, is troubling to him. Another moment, he comes. The young prince wipes away the congealing liquid from his accomplice's face; feels it pulsating onto his finger-tips. The prince – now the new king – looks closely at his hand, bringing his fingers closer to his own face, he tastes the blood, touching his pink lips to the royal-red offal. "Then we are one?" the head gardener's son says, "as promised." The new king smiles, his lips so red, he licks them clean, readying himself for a kiss: "We are one," the erstwhile prince replies, "from now on ... One." After a pause, a moment of caution, he continues: "We are not gentle, no, not at all; and we were not persuaded by whims nor by the king's dreaming. 'Destroy it,' he said, but what need us now with tapestries?" the young king asks – "we are one, are we not. *One*." He is mad about the eyes, the head gardener's son thinks, mad as hell: "Say nothing, not now," he says, imploring the new king to cease this loose talk, "nothing, do you hear? We must together keep the tapestry safe. *Together*," he says, resting his arm upon the new king's shoulder, feeling the pulsing at his neck: "Here I am," the head gardener's son says, "waiting to hold you. Here ... ." He realised just then that a single edged, curved sword was passing through his body, pinning him fast to the bark of the ancient oak. "I am," the new king replies "... let me unfold you."

There, the new king's pink lips are moving, one hand clutches his chest. "Swim to me," he says, reaching for the other's hand, which remains beyond reach, "swim to me."

He is hot as though his wings were burnt by the sun's rays, feverish with fear, falling fast upon the roots of the ancient oak. He is as cold as though he were dead, his heart is surely split. He was not dead, not yet, but somehow curled up at the bottom of the sea. "My love," he says, "hold me." He is resting now, the earth feels cool, yes, but it is not the ocean floor. "Am I drowning?" he asks, looking into the eyes of his love, a face as familiar as his own. There he lay, not yet seeking darkness, not quite dazzled by the light, fighting each other for a way through wood and leaf. "Like sovereigns," he says, "remember, my love, landing all about us?" The head gardener's son is silent, tears fall, damp-spotting the new king's tunic. He notices the curved sword just there, inert and without honour, as if another's hand had done the deed. Were those really his own hands? "Rest, my only love," he says, looking upon the fast-fading blue in the new king's eyes. "Rest, you say, my love? Rest." The sound of the voice trails off, bird song rises all around them, the calls of men and women, barking as though they are dogs, anticipating a hunt.

"Ah, there, 'tis done to death, this heat of metal. I can feel you," he breathes deeply. "In me, love. Murder, murder," a moment before the repetition: "Murder. You have killed me ... my love. Me."

To come to the place where the axe falls, benignly, on fallen limbs only, on what is there, for you, us, them – for all. Well, the curving wall, the woman, the life and the living, ever landing, the only words I ever had. The life, the least of all, and what is named, as such, in words? To solemnly give myself to us, the gift of two. He is oblivious to the world, falling, falling, a struggle, as though to sit up, falling and failing. The touch, the lover, counting upon it, on two to one. To give myself to us, but there is nothing. The sea, the sea. Recall the causeway, the yellow and silver stones that rose, one by one, as the waters receded. The sea, the sea. See again the bronze trees, standing guard against a strand of yellow sand, gleaming in the sun; the heat of the sun. *Fear no more, the heat*. There it was, beyond mist, high above what was white alone. The sea indistinguishable from the sky, the sky … the sea. To ascend, in time to come, the big black rock. To fall from the Barb horse, the black-grey, neighing, enough for it not to be in contradiction with the light, dashed hard against the waves, the sea, lost and torn to shreds by the Sea Serpent. To flee, for what else was there? Too fast, wasn't that what they will say, too fast, by half? To give myself up, to us, we too. Weave, weave, weave. At the door, the duke, the bare-forked animal, the patterns, the tail, the fable told. What dropped or was ripped? The drip, sunk, the silence, the silence – divert or we're doomed – that hideous sinking feeling. "We've … we've …" What? The silence. The scene changes so quickly, and each one calls for an alternative adjustment. This one comes to the surface; sinking that one to the depths. The sound, the sea, the other side of the door – surely, yes, a father, but not – no, not. "What a surprise," you said, the evasive circularity of the wall, the murmurs are coming. I know what wall, the words, that woman's tail, the silver rose clasped in her hand, held out for a young man, transfixed by the image of a goddess. The tapestry told all to another: the head gardener's son hears and heeds, and reads each woven truth and tale –

"With the old king's death, we'll know success; with
success known now in the death of the new."

"No, not at all – kill the king? That cannot be – Impossible! Speak again." The tapestry responds:

"With the impossible in us, we know what's possible,
and with the possible in us, the impossible."

Just then, he'd heard the prince's step, drawing near. "Quick, speak again," the head gardener's son implores. The tapestry's whisht. The silver rose, the goddess, the blooded feet, the fable, and through all this time, the heat of the sun: "Fear no more," says the heart in the body, "all follow this, and come to dust." The Serpent cries, rising, the distanced screaming, the silver sea, the golden sun, the yellow sand, the heat of the sun, fear no more, the towering trees are burning bright. A dream of silence, full of light, that house of mirth, the waves breaking, the soft murmurs, these passing moments on a jet-black rock – and who are they, you ask, or what?

the unnameable – the unnameable – the unnameable
… and that is all they ever were …

FIN

GUPPY

ACKNOWLEDGEMENTS

First and foremost, I would like to thank Taylor Swift, the American singer-songwriter, for the line, "You're on your own Kid," which becomes something of a catchphrase in the text. If I may, I would also like to thank a place, Newlyn in West Cornwall: I am fortunate enough to be able to watch the sea and the trawlers and the gulls as they pass before me in this room of one's own – which brings me to Virginia Woolf. Hardly a day passes without my thoughts heading off into one or another of Woolf's wonderful phrases. I would like to show my gratitude to Jason Walter Brown but I hardly know where to start. I have read his work on microgenesis for over a decade now and I feel as though my own microgenesis persists in the pages of this work. Guppy is certainly a microgeny unto itself, as we all are. Thanks go to the University of Plymouth, UK, where I spent some fraught years engaged in doctoral research as well as simultaneously teaching their degrees at Cornwall College, now a University Centre. Min Wild and Rachel Christofides constantly reminded me of the need for numerous iterations of the work in progress – my gratitude to them both. I remember my own students with a great deal of fondness and I must thank them for listening to my lectures on critical theory and for teaching me a great deal into the bargain. I thank Kindle Direct Publishing for making this possible. Finally, I must send heartfelt thanks to my partner Jamie Hanson for the wonderful cover design of the guppy fish and for his unbelievable love and kindness throughout the years we have spent together. I would need so many lives just to scratch the surface of paying back what is owed. If you have liked what you have read, please feel free to say so but, remember, like us all, You're on Your Own, Kid! So, like Taylor, let us try to bear in mind that *no matter what happens in life, be good to people.*

Newlyn, Cornwall, United Kingdom,
23rd October 2023.

Printed in Great Britain
by Amazon

37686548R00166